THE
GOLDEN RULE

Safe Strategies of Sage Investors

JIM GIBBONS

WILEY

John Wiley & Sons, Inc.

Published by John Wiley & Sons, Inc., Hoboken, New Jersey.
Published simultaneously in Canada.

For general information on our other products and services or for technical support, please contact our Customer Care Department within the United States at (800) 762–2974, outside the United States at (317) 572–3993 or fax (317) 572–4002.

Wiley also publishes its books in a variety of electronic formats. Some content that appears in print may not be available in electronic books. For more information about Wiley products, visit our web site at www.wiley.com.

Library of Congress Cataloging-in-Publication Data:

Gibbons, Jim, 1955-
    The golden rule : safe strategies of sage investors / Jim Gibbons.
        p. cm.
    Includes index.
    ISBN 978-0-470-53875-3 (cloth)
      1. Gold.   2. Investments.   I. Title.
    HG293.G53 2010
    332.63 — dc22
                                                            2009052153

10 9 8 7 6 5 4 3 2 1

*To my wife, Mary, whose love and support has
always been crucial to my successes.*

CONTENTS

PREFACE

IT'S TIME TO
OWN GOLD

"... behold, there came wise men from the east to Jerusalem ...
they presented unto him gifts, gold, and frankincense, and myrrh."
—Mathew 2:1 and 2:11, Holy Bible, King James Version

A sage is considered a "profoundly wise person; one venerated for experience, judgment, and wisdom." Like the wise men in the Bible, if I could make one recommendation, shouting it as loud as I could, knowing that the economic survival of you and your loved ones might depend on it, it would be "Own gold!" The questions that many of you will shout back are "But how do I buy it? And from whom?" The sage men and women introduced in this book have answers. In their own words they discuss their reasons for owning gold as well as the safe investing strategies they use to purchase it. As you will see in the following pages, it's critical for you to realize that "who" you rely on for advice to purchase gold is as important as your decision to own gold.

I don't claim to be one of best gold mining stock analysts in the world, but I know several who are. And I don't claim to be one of the most knowledgeable and experienced stockbrokers in the United States dealing with small capitalized gold mining stocks and whose professional contacts are second to none. But I do describe my broker that way.

I'm also familiar with several innovative ways to physically own gold, and several of the sage men introduced here discuss perfectly legal and safe strategies to own gold outside your home country if that's what you desire. Additionally, my experience and knowledge regarding buying gold bullion and gold coins as well as numismatic coins is relatively new while several of the sage men to whom I refer you to have decades of experience in these areas. It's not just their experience that sets all these individuals apart; it's the fact that they can be trusted to offer the best advice possible—for you.

I have been reading and studying the subject of investing in gold for over 25 years and because of that I've gotten to know many leading experts on gold. With today's economic uncertainties increasing exponentially, having gold in your investment portfolio is more important than ever. It is my belief, and the primary message behind this book, that everyone should invest at least 10 percent of his or her net worth in gold as a form of wealth insurance. However, in recent years investors have been leery of holding such a seemingly risky asset that pays no dividend and earns no income. It has been a difficult investment allocation and prospective investors have had numerous questions on why, how, when, and from whom they should buy gold. This book seeks to answer those questions by introducing you to an extraordinary group of leading experts on gold who will educate you on how and when to invest in gold, from whom to buy it, and why it belongs in your portfolio—sage men all.

THE GOLDEN RULE

But, before I introduce you to these sage gold experts, it is important to understand why "who" they are is as important as the decision to buying gold.

My first real investment experiences with gold investing occurred back in the early 1980s when I worked briefly for Merrill Lynch as a stockbroker. Back then, a few of the older brokers still recommended that their customers invest at least 10 percent of their net worth in gold, sometimes referred to as "Wall Street's Golden Rule." Not only did these older, more experienced, and wise brokers know that gold often tends to rise when the stock market is falling, they knew that gold, being one of the most time-tested and safest stores of value, was the ultimate form of wealth insurance. It was a rule grounded in the fact that gold has been the ultimate store of wealth and value for 5,000 years.

By the time I began working on Wall Street, these sage brokers—who still believed in owning gold—were an anachronism about to be pushed aside by the financial wizards of the "go go 1980s and 1990s." My reading, studying, and experiences since my Wall Street days have since confirmed that what former Federal Reserve Chairman Alan Greenspan called "irrational exuberance," and what some might call Wall Street greed, not only went back centuries but was also thriving in 1984 and is still thriving today. My own work experiences with Wall Street not only helped me understand Wall Street's excesses, but also laid the initial groundwork for my belief that everyone should own gold.

In 1983 my wife, Mary, was in medical school in Philadelphia, and I was doing my best to pay our rent and make ends meet. That year I'd begun what seemed to me then to be my dream job, a stockbroker at Merrill Lynch, at the time the world's largest brokerage firm.

I had always seen myself as running my own business, but a lack of start-up capital as well as a temporarily lower tolerance for risk, pushed me in the direction of a safer corporate job. However, a broker's job at Merrill Lynch very much appealed to the entrepreneur in me as new hires were told they should treat the job as if it were their own business. We were told repeatedly that those with whom you did business and what you chose to sell them was entirely up to you. Additionally, while we were starting our respective individual businesses, the firm encouraged each of its new brokers to seek out an experienced broker, get to know him or her, and then bounce ideas and questions off him or her.

A "CUSTOMER'S MAN"

In my central city office there were 25 experienced brokers, only one of whom was a true "customer's man." This term from the early 1900s described a stockbroker who worked for his customers—not for his firm—a stockbroker who earned his income without churning his customers' accounts. A true customer's man took pride in being client-centered. Like the sage men and women profiled in this book, Martin Abrahams was such a man. Martin was a small, slightly bald-headed Jewish man who spoke with a soft voice that inspired trust. He would be the first truly sage man I came to know as I began my working life.

Martin was very thorough in his work and read constantly. Two of his favorite investment analysts were Merrill Lynch economists, Stan Salvigsen and Charlie Minter. They were putting out some incredibly well-thought-out and witty economic research on the economy at large that he encouraged me to read. Reading Salvigsen and Minter's work, I became convinced that long-term interest rates were going to decline much, much further than they already had. It was at Merrill, and because of Martin, that I grew to realize the importance of contin-ually educating oneself with quality investment research and analysis.

Several weeks into my initial three-month training, the sales manager, a young woman of 30, expressed her concerns to me about having picked Martin as my guide. It seems that Martin was not a very good salesman, not in the eyes of Merrill Lynch management. She explained that even though he was already one of the highest-paid brokers in the office, if Martin set his mind to it, he could probably double his income and outsell every broker in Philadelphia, with the emphasis on selling. In fact, she told me that if I followed Martin's example of educating my clients, doing financial planning for them, and just generally being what I knew then to be a customer's man, I might not make it as a Merrill Lynch broker because I would fail to bring in the commission dollars that were expected of new hires. Still, I took Merrill Lynch at face value when it said each of us was basically running his or her own businesses. As the sales manager and I finished our conversation, I knew full well that I wanted Martin to continue as my mentor. This would later prove to have presaged the end of my career as a Merrill Lynch broker.

MERRILL LYNCH FEDERAL SECURITIES TRUST

In the fall of 1984 with interest rates still in double digits, Merrill Lynch came out with a brand new mutual fund offering, Merrill Lynch

Federal Securities Trust (MLFST), which had been designed to compete against the high-interest-rate bank certificates of deposit (CDs) that were so appealing to yield-hungry investors and savers. Like the subprime mortgage-backed securities Wall Street brokers would hawk 25 years later, MLFST had nothing to do with meeting customer needs and everything to do with generating commission dollars for Merrill Lynch and its brokers. MLFST would become my first lesson in how important the "who" was in doing business.

Even though Merrill Lynch brokers could sell bank CDs to their customers, they didn't pay much of a commission to the broker—maybe a quarter of a percent for short-term maturities and up to 1 percent or so for longer-term maturities. A broker earned, and I use that word reluctantly, a 4 percent commission on every dollar of MLFST they sold.

The primary issue that a Merrill broker had to deal with in selling this new mutual fund was that the interest rates on bank CDs they were then selling were comparable to the rates on the U.S. treasuries and agency debt—primarily Fannie Mae and Freddie Mac—that MLFST would have in its portfolio. Basically both products would offer investors similar returns. Why would a customer invest in MLFST when he or she could earn approximately the same interest rate purchasing a CD with similar risk while paying much less of a commission for the CD?

Merrill came up with a clever idea, a gimmick in my opinion, to make it seem like its mutual fund was a better deal than just purchasing a bank CD. MLFST fund managers were going to write puts and calls on the underlying investments in MLFST to try and increase the overall yield of the fund so that it was bigger than the yield on bank CDs. However, as I mentioned earlier, Merrill Lynch's own economic forecasters, Salvigsen and Minter, thought that interest rates were going to fall. If interest rates fell and Merrill's crack fund managers made the wrong bet and wrote calls on the underlying investments in MLFST, all the high-interest-rate investments that they'd invested in would get called away by the purchasers of the calls. That would mean that all the people who'd invested in MLFST—expecting a high fixed rate of interest for three or five or even seven years—would end up earning considerably less. And that was exactly what happened.

The five-year treasury rate went from an average of 12.26 percent in 1984, to 8.48 percent in 1988, to 6.19 percent in 1992, eventually bottoming at 2.80 percent in 2008. Bank CD rates fell in tandem. But all the while MLFST fund managers wrote calls on the underlying investments in MLFST and continually had to invest in lower-yielding investments as their higher-paying investments were called away. All those little old ladies that wanted to invest their life savings in long-term bank CD's that were paying such high returns in 1984, and had instead invested their savings in MLFST, would find their MLFST investment generating less and less income each year. By 1988, yields on MLFST had fallen to less than 8 percent and *Forbes* magazine was giving the fund a C grade in its annual mutual fund survey.

But I am getting ahead of myself. In the summer of 1984, Merrill Lynch didn't just inform its brokers of this new mutual fund offering; it made the marketing effort of Merrill Lynch Federal Securities Trust one of its main priorities of the year. Every stop was pulled to make this a successful offering. Still, given my views, as well as Merrill Lynch's own economists' views, that interest rates were going down, I thought the high commission rates involved in purchasing MLFST when compared to what one could earn on a bank CD weren't warranted. In fact, I thought the fund was complete junk. But I was going to give Merrill the benefit of the doubt by checking in with my sage mentor, Martin, to see what he was thinking.

Guess what—he "wasn't touching it."

So, what does a massive Merrill Lynch marketing effort like this mean to a frontline stockbroker? For starters, MLFST proved to be the easiest product in the world to sell. At least until Wall Street started developing investment securities backed with "relatively" high yielding subprime mortgages 15 years later. Back in 1984, all a broker had to do was call up a customer or a prospect and say something to the effect of, "Why invest in a bank CD when you can earn 1 to 2 percent more by investing in MLFST? Like a bank CD, it's still basically insured by the federal government and you have the added benefit and upside potential of having Merrill's expert mutual fund managers running the show." That was the abbreviated pitch. It was hoped yield-hungry little old ladies would eat this up . . . and they did.

The brokers in our office were divided into two teams, with the team selling the most MLFST being promised a big incentive. Each day a written summary of every broker's sales of MLFST was sent around the office, on colored paper no less, so everyone could see not only how each team was doing but how each individual team member was doing. Twice a day the sales manager would go from desk to desk and ask you how much you'd sold. Once a day, Mike, the branch manager, would drop by your desk to ask the same thing. Eventually, Mike stopped asking me how much I'd sold since I wasn't going along with this plan.

I just kept reminding myself that according to Merrill Lynch it was "my business" that I was managing. Even though I was struggling to earn the commission dollars that Merrill Lynch expected of me, not one of my customers even heard about MLFST. At least not from me. Martin never bothered telling his customers either.

There were other brokers who felt as I did, but they sold it anyway, justifying themselves to me by saying, "Jim, my clients might not make a very good return, but I know they're not going to lose anything by investing in it, either. And I keep my job." What they meant by that was the customer was more than likely not going to lose any of his or her invested funds; he or she just wasn't going to get a very good return on the invested funds, either. What I realized from this whole episode, though, was how rare it was to find individuals on Wall Street who, there's that word again, would not compromise their values in the face of corporate pressure or Wall Street greed.

In 1984, Merrill brokers would sell several billion dollars' worth of Merrill Lynch Federal Securities Trust. It would turn out to be the largest securities offering in the history of Wall Street!

A week after the offering closed, Mike called me into his office and said, "We don't think you're going to make it here. You're not a team player and not Merrill Lynch material." He was right. He gave me the morning to get my things in order.

FROM MERRILL TO THE HERON INN— REJUVENATION THROUGH SWEAT EQUITY

After my experiences at Merrill Lynch, I was ready for a change and not just with my career. In 1985 we moved to the great Pacific Northwest, where Mary had been accepted into a Family Practice medical residency program at Swedish Hospital in Seattle, Washington.

Having vowed never to work for a large corporation again, and with the two of us having a combined $60,000 in educational loans and no assets, I asked Mary to take out an $18,000 "new doctor" loan at an 18 percent interest rate so that I could "build something." Hard work and thorough research during our first four months in Seattle resulted in a set of building plans for a 12-room Victorian-style country inn in La Conner, Washington, a quaint tourist town situated on the water about an hour north of Seattle.

With no building experience and $18,000, I recruited an old college friend, Bill Fairman, as a partner. Like your decision to invest in gold, the decision of "who" I would rely on for help (advice) in building the Heron Inn would prove to be as important as my decision to build the inn itself.

Bill's primary qualifications were a willingness to work for free, becoming a part owner of the completed inn in the process, and having just finished a six-month cross-country bicycling trip. In other words, he had no real plans. Like me, Bill also had no carpentry experience. Unlike Mary and me, he had no money at all. Even borrowed money. However, and more important, I had a 10-year history with Bill and knew that I could trust him. And in particular trust him to finish a project once he started it.

The plan was for me to raise more cash from the proverbial friends and family (and fools) while we physically built what would come to be called The Heron in La Conner. To conserve our meager cash, we would pay ourselves nothing while we built the inn. According to my plan, once we got most of the structure built, the banks would see what we'd done and the sweat equity we'd use to build value, and they'd then lend us the money to finish the project. In fact, the plan was so good that we even managed to convince Guy Hupy, described to Bill and me as an "ex-hippie carpenter," not only to be our third partner but the guy who would teach us how to be carpenters ourselves! You would think that having been a branch bank manager in the late 1970s, I would have known better. I laugh now, recalling the naiveté of my plan.

While my plan wasn't the greatest, Bill's and my decision to choose Guy as our general contractor would prove to be a critical component of our eventual success. Not only was Guy a true craftsman when it came to building, he would prove to be every bit as trustworthy and reliable as Bill. Once again, the "who" was crucial to our potential success.

However, 10 months into the project, having asked everyone we knew to lend us money, which only a few did, and with Mary and I having racked up over $80,000 in credit card financing to help finance the construction, we were out of funds. But, and this was a big but, we had a large structure up with a roof on, doors and windows in place, the exterior painted, and the wiring and plumbing going in. Still, the banks didn't seem to want anything to do with us, showing only minor interest in our project.

The thing was, with a large structure now half built, I and my two partners were certain that we could finish building the inn as planned.

Eventually, I would resort to dealing with loan brokers, people who made careers out of finding money for desperate people. The first loan broker I dealt with, literally picking his name out of a phone book, wanted his fee paid in advance. He seemed poised and polished, not necessarily a sage, and almost guaranteed we'd get a loan. I was familiar with the wisdom expressed in the line that "if it sounds too good to be true, it probably is," and decided to check out his story. After confirming that the company he worked for had been paying employees and actually made loans, I gave the broker an advance of $2,500. I wouldn't say it was trust so much as a calculated risk.

A week later a big story broke in all the local papers about the company being shut down by the state attorney general for fraud. (Clearly, he was no sage after all.) We'd been caught up in a Ponzi scheme of sorts. My calculated risk was a bust, and the importance of dealing with the right people was emphasized to me in ways I had only imagined up to that point in my life.

In May 2004 I received a check from the federal government for the Heron Inn's share of the settlement from the assets recovered by the government from shutting down the loan broker's company. We'd given the phony mortgage company $2,500. Seventeen years later the federal government sent us a check for "restitution for Mail Fraud." It was for $8.85.

A SAGE HARD MONEY LENDER

In spite of this inauspicious beginning working with loan brokers, we didn't have many other options. Guy and Bill were growing extremely concerned about our lack of funds, especially since the last two of the banks we were courting said they were not interested in our project. Using the telephone book once again, I eventually found myself being taken to lunch by two very professional and experienced Seattle-based loan brokers. I did not get to know them well enough to describe them as sages, but they would introduce me to one of the sagest men I've ever done business with.

Two weeks after the last bank turned us down, the loan brokers were driving a hard money lender up to La Conner to meet with us. Barry Owen, the prospective lender, would later tell me that as he was getting driven up he kept asking himself what the heck he was doing. Although the situation had been fully explained to him, all that went through his mind was that he was going to meet three young guys, two of whom had no carpentry experience, all of whom were nonetheless building a 12-room country inn, now only partially completed, that none of us had any lodging experience, and that we were out of money. He viewed it as a looming disaster with no upside.

I liked Barry. He had a deep voice and spoke with authority. He was a tall, thin man with an athletic build who dressed well. If I remember correctly, Barry had not gone to college, but 25 years as a banker and a lender had given him wisdom and experiences far beyond his years. This being my first building project, I don't think I realized how close we were to being done. But a person with experience in construction lending, like Barry, could see within a couple minutes after arriving at the construction site that with a month or so of work we'd be up and open.

In a matter of a couple of days, Barry offered us a short-term bridge loan designed to get us open and profitable so that a bank would eventually offer us longer-term financing. Being risk averse and still unsure of our eventual success, Barry was lending us just enough to finish the construction of the inn and pay off all of our creditors who said they had to get paid off. Some close family members agreed to wait and take second positions behind Barry's loan. Mary and I would also have to continue a bit longer carrying a couple of our credit card loans we'd used to help finance the construction.

Eighteen months later Barry's loan came due; we'd been open for 16 months and profitable since day one. I was stunned to find out that we still could not get traditional bank financing. I called Barry and told him that not only could we not get financing to pay off his loan, but that I also had designs on possibly expanding the inn to the lot next door. It was twice as big as the lot our 12-room country inn was built on. Barry wanted to see what I had in mind so he came up the very next day. I remember the two of us standing in front of The Heron looking at the lot next door.

Barry liked to think of himself as a realist; I suppose that came from his experiences lending to desperate people. After telling me partnerships rarely last very long, he matter-of-factly said that if I needed financing to buy Guy and Bill out he'd be interested in helping me. He told me he thought the expansion looked like it made sense and that he'd back me, or us, on that, too. One day later Barry mailed a loan commitment for a new five-year loan that would refinance the loan we had with his company and pay off all our other existing loans we still had from building The Heron.

Had Barry not retired not too long ago, I would still be recommending his services today. On occasion prior to his retirement, he would often comment on how well it spoke of Guy, Bill, and myself that our partnership lasted so long. Not only was Barry one of the finest men I've ever met, he was a man of impeccable character and one of the sagest men I've ever met.

Bill, Guy, and I were able to overcome any ill will that had arisen due to the lack of financing during the inn's construction. We remained partners for 10 years. In 1996, Guy asked to be bought out when he moved to another tourist town on Puget Sound. I still count Guy as a good friend today. My partnership with Bill would go on for four more years until he passed away from a heart attack at the age of 46. Bill, who loved life and was a fierce competitor, was one of my best friends. Two months after he died, Mary and I and Bill's wife Karol sold The Heron. We sold the inn for twice what it had cost to build.

Choosing Guy and Bill as my partners and finding a sage lender like Barry Owen were not only crucial to the success of The Heron Inn, they were critical in reinforcing my belief that the right "who" to do business with is absolutely crucial to the success of any project or goal. In contrast, my experiences with the hard money lender who basically took our money not only strengthened the importance of relying on the right "who" for advice; my using the telephone book to find that hard money lender served to emphasize the importance of having good referrals to rely on whenever possible.

Why am I telling you this story in a book about strategies for investing in gold? Simple—the "who" you learn from and do business with is the key to successfully investing in gold. To this point, I am going to introduce you to the highest-caliber investors, sage investors who will allow you to pick the right experts on gold who will not only educate you on how to invest in gold but explain to you why it belongs in your portfolio.

STUDYING AND THE ERIS SOCIETY

When I left Merrill Lynch and the corporate world to work for myself, the concept of gold as a hedge against inflation and as an insurance mechanism was fading from public view. Federal Reserve Chairman Paul Volker had tamed inflation. Although I was still interested in gold and investing after I left Merrill, building The Heron would consume every spare dollar I had and then some. However, my years at Merrill Lynch had reinforced my appreciation for quality investment research and investment books and research. So even though I had no money to invest, I was still trying to keep informed about investing as well as educating myself as to gold's role in one's personal finances.

Two books I read around this time, *Blood in the Streets* written in 1987 and *The Great Reckoning* written in 1991, both co-authored by James Dale Davidson and William Rees-Moggs, impressed me very much. The authors laid out grand investment themes that were so well presented that I started subscribing to their monthly investment newsletter, *Strategic Investments*. The publisher of this newsletter, Bill Bonner, through his company, Agora Publishing, did what publishers do and tried to entice me into subscribing to other newsletters that they published. Sometime in the mid-1990s I finally subscribed to my second investment newsletter, *International Speculator.* In some sense that second subscription would change my life . . . and my portfolio.

International Speculator was written (and still is published) by my now good friend, Doug Casey. For over 30 years, Doug has been a very successful speculator/investor who has concentrated much of his investment efforts in gold and gold mining stocks. Doug is one of the sagest men I know. I've not only read every monthly issue of *International*

Speculator for almost 15 years now, sometimes twice, over the last 5 years I've also subscribed to several other Casey Research investment newsletters.

By subscribing to Doug's letter and going out of my way to hear him speak whenever I could, my knowledge of gold and gold mining has increased greatly. As a result I've come to understand gold's strategic, long-term role in the world economy and why some amount of gold should be held as *wealth insurance* by every investor and saver.

In 2000, Doug invited me to attend my first Eris Society meeting. Eris was a small, private annual conference he began in the mountains of Colorado in 1981 and, with the help of friends, continued for over 25 years. As Doug put it, "We pay no dues and have no bylaws or voting. Rather, it belongs to those who are invited to its annual gathering." In the spirit of Eris, the Greek goddess of discord, "speakers with controversial ideas" were invited so as to "maintain a discordant, non-mainstream bent in our talks." Eris gatherings were meant to be "opportunities to meet some of the most interesting people in the world." It was here that I met many of the extraordinary sage men who have contributed to this book.

While attending six conferences from 2000 through 2005 I not only got to hear, but also—because these were small gatherings with only 100 to 150 people attending—met and conversed with these highly successful investors and leading experts on gold. Looking back, I'm not sure if the reason for the proportionately large number of successful investors attending Eris conferences was because Doug was an investor with many trusted investor friends or because sage investment advisors are naturally inquisitive folks with an inclination to attend conferences like Eris. No matter. The end result was the same— I got to know a number of world-class, sage investors.

At one of these meetings, Doug recommended I use Rick Rule as my broker. I have found Rick to be one of the most knowledgeable investors I have ever met. Not only is his track record in resource investing second to none, he's a long-time advocate of holding gold. His contribution on contrarian investing fits perfectly with the premise of owning gold because gold is considered a classic contrarian investment. Rick's been my broker for 10 years now.

After listening to a talk by Bill Bonner at an Eris conference, Rick encouraged me to begin reading Bill's free Internet newsletter

The Daily Reckoning, which I've been doing for nine years. Bill has been a long-time advocate of owning gold, recently saying that "gold outlives paper money, empires, governments . . . all of us and all of our institutions." Bill has a knack for writing witty satiric pieces that also educate and inform the reader. I chose Bill's two contributions in this book for those very reasons. Not only does Bill write about gold, he constantly writes about "who" to ask or consult for investment advice.

My friends John Pugsley and David Galland, whom I also met at Eris, are both long-time contributors and guest columnists to Bill's *Daily Reckoning.* While David's piece takes a humorous look at the reasons for holding gold, John takes a more serious look at why gold is the linchpin to both a sound money supply and a balanced economy. Additionally, I was able to listen to and meet Michael Checkan, James Turk, and many other sage investors while attending Eris.

This may come as no surprise to some, but this is how the world works. People of good character are attracted to and get to know other people of good character, and refer them on to their friends and acquaintances. "Who" matters. Just as importantly, virtually every single sage investor I met at Eris has been a long-time advocate of owning gold. The purpose of this book is to introduce a group of leading experts on gold, many of them my friends, so you can find one who meets your needs and temperament, someone you will be comfortable with in advising you how to purchase gold.

IT'S TIME TO MEET THE WHOS

The book has been divided into five parts.

I begin with an introduction, written by Jon Nadler. For many readers, Jon's contribution may well be the most memorable and important in the book because of the vivid picture it creates. It is basically a real-world case study of what gold can do for you.

In Part I, Brokers/Money Managers, you'll meet five individuals, each of whom I would describe as "A Customer's Man." Some of you may already recognize Eric Sprott and Peter Schiff from appearances on television. Adrian Day, Michael Checkan, and Rick Rule are not as well known, but they are every bit the experts on investing in gold and, like Sprott and Schiff, have founded and manage their own firms.

In Part II, Investment Newsletter Writers, you will meet seven of the best, including the leading gold experts Doug Casey, Bill Bonner, John Pugsley, and David Galland, whom I've already mentioned. In addition, you'll also meet Richard Maybury, one of America's foremost geopolitical investment analysts; Addison Wiggin, executive publisher of one of the largest and most successful subscription-based investment services; and Pamela and Mary Anne Aden, long-time investment analysts. All of these sage individuals advocate gold ownership.

In Part III, Coin and Bullion Brokers/Dealers, you'll see why virtually every leading expert on gold endorses the idea of having physical gold as part of one's investment portfolio. Although there are many ways to physically own gold, gold coins is one of the most common. The coin and bullion dealers, Van Simmons, Dana Samuelson and Bill Musgrave, and Franklin Sanders, have all been highly recommended by me and many of the other experts on gold in this book. James Turk, the founder of GoldMoney.com, will explain another innovative means to hold physical gold.

In Part IV, The Miners, you'll see why no book about gold ownership would be complete without a look at the miners who mine gold as well as its companion precious metal, silver. Robert Quartermain and Morgan Poliquin are without a doubt two of the best miners in their respective businesses. Brent Cook and Louis James both write newsletters on the mining industry and are highly regarded and referenced by many of the other gold experts contained in this book.

In Part V, Game-Changing Educators, you'll meet three experts on gold whose contributions will enhance your understanding of gold's importance to both the world economy and your future. Although Congressman Ron Paul has been writing about gold ownership and the Federal Reserve System for years, many readers' first introduction to him may have occurred in Congressman Paul's recent presidential candidacy. Paul van Eeden is without a doubt writing some of the most original analyses on gold today, while Kenneth Royce will tell you how to protect the gold you own.

Not only have the sage investors introduced in this book proved themselves to be shrewd investors capable of garnering outsized investment returns; their writings and advice have allowed me to achieve my own "Warren Buffett–like" returns. For instance, since I began using Rick Rule as my broker in 2000, and while still following Doug

Casey's advice, my wife's IRA account has appreciated by a com-pounded return of 21 percent over the last nine years that ended on December 31, 2009! To put that in perspective, the best return listed on the 2009 *Forbes* magazine mutual fund "Honor Roll" for a slightly longer period of time was 14 percent.

As exceptional as the return is on my wife's IRA, what sets these wise men and women apart from the crowd is their character. It should come as no surprise that the three character traits Warren Buffett looks for in his managers—integrity, energy, and intelligence—are all traits found in these sage men and women. More important, they are the kind of character traits that become even more valuable with experience, judgment, and wisdom.

IT'S YOUR TURN

Knowing that "who" investors rely on for advice to purchase gold is as important as the decision to own gold itself, I realized that the sage investors I'd gotten to know probably knew a few more like-minded investment advisors of sound character. Wondering who they might recommend, I decided to ask each of those I already knew the follow-ing question:

"If you were on your death bed, believing that the economy was in a very precarious place, and you were advising a loved one, telling him that he needed to own gold in some form (bullion, mining stocks, ETFs, etc.), and you wanted to give your loved one the name of one or two of people who were not only knowledgeable about gold but also individuals whose character was of the highest standing (they could be stockbrokers or money managers, coin dealers, investment newsletter writers, or even friends), whose names would you give them?"

Perhaps not so surprisingly, most replies contained the names of people who have contributed to this book. But I did uncover a few new names. Now it's your turn to learn what all these sages have to say about gold so you can decide "who" might become your expert on investing in gold.

ACKNOWLEDGMENTS

I am grateful to Debra Englander, my editor at John Wiley & Sons, for her recognition that a book like this was needed and then bringing it to publication.

A thousand thanks to Kelly O'Conner, my development editor at John Wiley & Sons, for her patient guidance in shaping the final form of this book and helping me realize the vision I had for it.

I'd like to thank my literary agent, Ethan Friedman of Level Five Media, for getting me focused and headed in the right direction from the very beginning and then providing the right encouragement throughout the writing process.

I'd like to thank Rick Rule of Global Resource Investments Ltd, Doug Casey of Casey Research, and Bill Bonner of Agora Inc. for all the education they've given me, and who I'm sure even now don't realize how much I've learned from them.

I also wish to thank all the contributors to the book, sage investors all, for generously sharing their wisdom with me and the readers of this book.

INTRODUCTION

THE TIE
THAT BINDS

Jon Nadler
Kitco Precious Metals

"The desire of gold is not for gold. It is for the means of freedom and benefit."

—Ralph Waldo Emerson,
philosopher and poet (1803–1883)

Jon Nadler has focused exclusively on precious metals and their related investment products his whole working life. After graduating from UCLA Jon established and managed several precious metals operations at major U.S.-based financial institutions including Deak-Perera, Republic National Bank, and Bank of America.

Jon's current role is that of Metals Market Analyst and Public Relations Head for Kitco, one of the world's premier retailers of precious metals. Jon's market commentaries, often on gold, are frequently quoted by the U.S., Canadian, and global financial media including the BBC, the Wall Street Journal, *Bloomberg, Reuters, and many others. Barely a day goes by in which I haven't logged onto Kitco.com to check on the markets, read Jon's latest precious metals commentary, or one of the other many commentaries that Kitco provides.*

With over 30 years working with gold and precious metals, one might wonder what inspired such passion. Have you heard the expression "a picture is worth a thousand words"? People remember it for its truth. Jon's contribution paints that kind of picture. If you remember just one contribution from this book or one lesson from these pages, it should be Jon's.

This is a story about gold. This is also a story about ordinary people and about survival. This is not a story of the gold markets, or of gold prices. This is a story of how this prized element, for which wars have been waged and in search of which continents have been discovered, has played a crucial role in the lives of a lucky few. . . .

People often ask me why I chose gold as an occupation for the past three decades. I hope to be able to best give you the answer to that question at the end of this chapter. For now, let me begin by first reaching far back in time, very, very far. The diary begins thusly:

The year is 105 CE. Roman occupation of the richest gold-bearing area in Europe is well under way. Home to the ancient Thracians in what is now modern day Romania, this is a scenic land of untold riches. The Romans exploit the province extensively, building roads, forts, bridges, and new mines.

A hamlet named Rivulus Dominarum (The River of the Young Ladies) thrives because of what lies under its neighboring hills. Enough gold is extracted from the area to be able to lay down a 1500 kilometer–long highway of pure gold—all the way to Rome.

113 CE. Emperor Trajan (Marcus Ulpius) builds the famed Basilica Ulpia and Trajan's Column with funds from the Dacian gold trove. The Roman occupation eventually ends and the Mongols overrun the land leaving it in ruin. The gold remains locked in the hills. A millennium passes.

896 CE. The Magyars, the last of the migratory tribes to establish a state in Europe, settle in the Transylvanian basin.

1003 CE. King Stephen I integrates Transylvania into the Hungarian Kingdom. All the while, the mining of the gold continues. . . .

1899 CE. Thirty-three years after the Austro-Hungarian Empire is established, the rich flow of gold from Transylvania continues. In the village of Felsobanya (Upper Mine) lives a 30-year-old man named Johann. Johann is a gold miner, like his father before him. Johann's wife is with child.

1900 CE. Johann hopes for his newborn son Johann II to become "somebody" other than a mineworker. Thus, he dutifully saves gold coins for his future. He knows firsthand how hard gold is to obtain. Life in the village is tough for Johann; life in the mines, tougher still.

Little Johann II grows up. He now dreams of a day when his father does not have to leave the house before dawn and return way after sunset, of a day when his father's clothes aren't filthy and his hair does not reek of the carbide used by miners to throw light from their helmets underground. He dreams of days like Sundays, when his father climbs the hills under which the gold lies to pick wild strawberries with him. There are too few Sundays in the year for little Johann.

1905 CE. In a village that is just kilometers away from Felsobanya, another little boy is born. His name is Nicholas.

1910 CE. Johann receives gifts of beautiful minerals from his father on most of his birthdays: pink quartz, needle-like stibnite blossoms, and lots of shiny pyrite. Fool's gold looks very real to a child, you know. He collects them all. But sometimes, Johann receives a real gold ducat, like the one that is bestowed upon him for his tenth birthday. That gift is for keeps. He knows of a certain coal iron that his father and mother keep in the attic. He has never seen its contents, but knows they must be very special. He saves his special coins in a can of Ovomaltine that he hides in the chicken coop. Called Ovaltine today, it is a brown powder to be mixed with water/milk etc. to offer decent nutrition.

1912 CE. A familiar deep boom echoes through the hills one day. The miners are dynamiting new shafts deep in the ground. But the earth keeps shaking for far longer than normal. A heavy silence descends over the village. Johann's father does not come home that night. He never does again, nor is he ever found.

1913 CE. Young Johann must go to work in the gold mines at age 14, as his mother's health is failing. Johann demands that he get paid in gold coins for both himself and for his father's widow's payments. Johann works very hard over the next two years, sometimes for 16 hours a day. Disaster strikes again, out of nowhere. A rusty old mine cart breaks loose and runs downhill. He attempts to stop it, in vain. The wheel amputates most of his right foot. Johann cannot return to work for nearly a year. It is the bleakest of times.

July 1914. The Great War erupts. Johann is spared military duty as local officials divert those like him with lesser physical abilities to dig for more gold, lead, and copper than ever before. One and one half million Austro-Hungarians perish in the conflagration. Johann works for 16 little gold ducats per month. He saves almost all of them. Now a coffee grinder and a teapot are also needed to hold the growing savings of gold. Unbeknownst to him, they will become instruments of salvation.

1919 CE. The Austro-Hungarian Empire is relegated to the history books. Hungary feels the full impact of the post-war environment. Inflation runs rampant, wages are frozen, and food shortages develop. Miners now routinely take small gold nuggets home. Otherwise, they face starvation for their families.

1921 CE. A severe case of hyperinflation takes place as the Austrian economy collapses. Prices as measured by government issued paper currency rise 14,000-fold during the inflation. In Hungary prices rise 23,000-fold. In Poland prices rise 2.5 million-fold. In Russia prices rise 4 billion-fold. And in Germany, prices rise 1 trillion-fold. Thank God for the gold. The coins in the attic save the family as some are bartered every month with local shopkeepers, farmers, and doctors. Many of Johann's friends have to take to the road after selling everything for food. Johann cuts firewood on his way home from work and sells it in town.

1923 CE. Johann's mother dies. She is laid to rest next to the empty grave of her husband. Johann soon marries an orphaned girl named Rose. They have only his mother's adobe house and the gold coins in the attic to their name. Not only his gold ducats, but those that his parents had saved and hidden in the attic, too. Soon, they will have a little girl. They will name her Roza. The gold, and her father's complete faith in it, will be her legacy.

1923 CE. The scene: the town of Sighet (Island), birthplace of famed writer and Nobel laureate Elie Wiesel. A boy named Eugene is born as the youngest of six kids. His father, Leopold, a Hungarian Jew, is a schoolteacher. His mother, Irene, has her hands full. Life in the little town is difficult after the Great War. Eugene delivers seltzer water to the neighborhood from a horse-driven cart after every school day. He grows up having to work in his spare time to help the family. Everyone pitches in.

1939 CE. Sixteen year-old Eugene is now ready to begin work in the Phoenix refinery in neighboring Nagybanya (Big Mine) as a junior chemist. He apprentices while going to school at night.

August 1939. Germany attacks Poland. The greatest conflagration the world has ever seen is unleashed. Nothing will ever be the same again, for Eugene, his family, or for the rest of the world.

December 1941. The front is still a distant event for many. The news from Sighet is that a man named Moshe escaped and came back from some kind of super-prison far away, in Chelmno, Poland, and he had stories of horror and death to relay to the townspeople. Nobody believes Moshe. After all, Hungary and Romania were part of the Axis since late 1940. Why would anyone be killing the citizens of an allied power? Nah, Moshe must be crazy. What "death camp" is he possibly imagining?

May 1943. On one of his rarely free but never worry-free Sundays, Eugene meets a young girl on a tennis court not far from his work-place. It is Roza, daughter of Eugene and Rose. They fall in love. The madness of the war around them grows larger and ever closer to home.

Their romance is cut short as Eugene is told to report to the train station to travel to a "labor jobsite" in Hungary. Eugene has to make preparations to leave. Roza meets him in secret the night before his train leaves and gives him a well-worn leather suitcase for his travels.

She tells him not to use the contents until really necessary. Eugene wonders why he would need Ovomaltine, hair color, and winter clothing that seems made for old people.

June 1943. Eugene and Roza part ways. Two days later, Eugene learns on the train that Budapest is not his final destination. The train is headed for a forced labor camp. He and two friends jump off the train during the night and make their way into Budapest on a gypsy wagon under some hay.

March 1944. The Germans occupy Hungary to prevent it from slipping into the Allied camp. Eugene and his friends dye their hair black, grow moustaches, and pose as Italian artists. Eugene "works" in a perfume shop during the day, while hiding in empty houses at night.

October 1944. The Hungarian Arrow Cross government is installed and arrests, deportations, food shortages, and Allied bombing raids are the order of the day. Eugene is in a "safe house" living in a cold attic. He bundles up in the thick garments he brought in the suitcase. He rations his brown, rancid cans of Ovomaltine. The dry powder and homemade white wine become his diet for weeks.

Curiously, the first can of chocolaty powder still weighs a lot when he is half done with it. Then he finds a carefully folded letter explaining the suitcase's contents. He stumbles upon a treasure, finding small gold coins under a false cardboard bottom in the can and more coins in the lining of the clothes given to him. Much to his dismay, he realizes had he found the letter explaining the gold coins earlier, he could have used them to get meals, medicine, and better shelter earlier.

He barters some coins in exchange for food and medicine. He learns that people are lining up in front of the Swedish embassy in Budapest where identification papers can be secured to prevent one from being shipped off to Poland.

December 1944. A man named Raoul Wallenberg is helping thousands obtain identification papers that prevent them from being deported to the death camps. An Italian businessman named Giorgio Perlasca issues forged Spanish visas after he appoints himself as Ambassador to Hungary. Huge crowds throng the embassies.

Eugene has to pay a heavy toll of gold coins to make his way in the trunk of a car to the other side of town and be able reach the long line for the invaluable papers that may grant him safe passage. He and three other people barely make the line, and it closes after them. Some deportees are literally plucked from forced march lines by Wallenberg's people and issued papers.

Eugene gets the papers. His life is likely spared. He is left with four gold coins in his winter coat. Four coins and the suitcase. He sleeps in a different building every night, for nearly half a year, in a city where only a quarter of all of the houses survive the Allied bombings. Yet, everyone prays for the American bombers to come as soon as darkness falls. . . .

May 1945. The war ends. The suffering just begins for many. Eugene jumps off another train—this one bound for the Stalinist labor camps of Russia. He makes his way back to Sighet on foot over two weeks' time. He finds strangers living in his house. His childhood street is an empty shell.

His family is nowhere to be found. Three of his sisters and his brother return to town, emaciated. They tell of deportation, of death camps, and of liberation. His parents, one sister, and her young son never return. It turns out that "crazy". Moshe was right, after all.

November 1945. Hungarians now have to live through the worst inflation in modern history. For example, before 1945, the highest denomination is the 1,000 pengő banknote. The highest denomination banknote in mid-1946 is 100,000,000,000,000,000,000 pengő. That is one sextillion pengő. Values double in hours, and minutes. Prices no longer have relevance, but gold money is still very valuable. People pull gold crowns out of their mouths and put them on the store counters. Eugene spends three of the remaining four gold coins on his survival. Now he only has one gold coin left.

August 1946. The value of the adópengő is adjusted each day, by radio announcement. When the pengő is finally replaced by the forint, the total value of all Hungarian banknotes in circulation amounts to one-thousandth of one U.S. cent.

December 1946. After securing what's left of his family, Eugene moves back to Nagybanya where he finds Roza! He returns the last remaining coin to her. He has nothing but the suitcase and the one coin left. He promises to earn it all back. Eugene opens a small cosmetics store in the town's old square.

June 1947. Eugene and Roza get married.

June 1948. The Romanian Communist government nationalizes all private property, and along with it, Eugene's store. Privately held gold becomes illegal. The stash of coins in the family's possession goes "underground" in more ways than one. They will risk everything on keeping their savings, which has helped saved their lives time and again. Who knows when it may be a time of need again?

January 1949. Eugene and Roza must take regular jobs that pay very little and try to go on with life. Working people stand in line for everything. The only money seemingly spent by the government is on military parades. They miss several chances to leave the country legally. An era of no emigration policies begins.

Every year, a few of Eugene and Roza's coins make their way into the furnace at the dental lab where Eugene's brother works. Dentists use gold but have to buy it from the government at fixed prices that are higher than the gold's market value. The clandestine proceeds are vital to supplement their meager existence.

May Day, 1954. A baby boy is born in Communist Romania. His name is Janos. The boy grows up in the relative "calm" of the Cold War after Stalin's death, but questions his parents extensively about the system in place. For instance, why his parents have to stand in line at 4 AM for cooking oil or sugar.

May 1965. At age 11 young Janos questions why he must wear military-style uniforms and learn to handle weapons in middle school. He also questions why he cannot listen to the Beatles being broadcast over Radio Free Europe. His parents explain that government cars are patrolling the neighborhood to learn who listens to anti-communist radio.

November 1968. At age 14 Janos does not question why he and his school band are not supposed to play "Back in the USSR" at a school dance and decides to go ahead and play it anyway. The local cops set out to prove that he indeed cannot. Taken into custody and beaten, his head is shaved clean and his guitar broken.

April 1972. Four years later, Janos has had enough of complying with the inane rules imposed upon him. It is time to act. He visits his grandfather, Johann, and asks for his advice. The old man tells him little more than that he sees no future for a lad like Janos in Romania. Two days later, he hands Janos a well-worn brown suitcase and tells him to use the contents when he reaches free lands. Janos signs up for a communist youth group tour of Yugoslavia and Italy.

May 1972. Janos arrives in Rome and breaks away while the group tours the Victor Emanuel monument. He is free! He reports to the UN High Commissioner for Refugees and is given shelter with a Sicilian family who owns a modest pensione in the city. Like his father before him, he finds gold coins in his suitcase.

June 1972. Janos lands a job as an interpreter, helping other refugees settle in camps in Italy. On a visit to Switzerland Janos places most of the gold into a Swiss bank storage account and sells some of it. He has good news from the United States. He has been admitted as an immigrant.

June 1973. Janos lands in New York ready to explore all opportunities and a freedom he has never known before. He has to sell another part of the gold in Switzerland to literally buy the release of his parents, Eugene and Roza, from Romania.

July 1974. The family is reunited in California and Janos starts college at UCLA. Six months later, gold once again becomes legal to own in the United States, having been made illegal by Franklin Roosevelt in 1933.

July 1979. While in graduate school, Janos starts to work at a precious metals firm founded by the boy Nicholas, born near his grandfather's town in 1905. That firm was named Deak Perera. Its founder was Nicholas Deak. Nicholas and Janos share not only ethnic and geographic roots, but a deep reverence for gold. Janos remains in the world of gold to this day.

■ ■ ■

And now, the answer to the initial question: Why did I choose to make it my career to teach people about owning gold? Answer: The story and diary entries you have just read are those of:

Johann Hering I 1867–1912 (my great-grandfather)
Johann and Rose Hering II 1898–1973 (my grandfather and grandmother)
Eugene J and Rosa Nadler 1923–2006 (my father and mother)
   and
Yours Truly, Jon "Janos" Nadler 1954–
   With Deep Gratitude to:
   The People of Baia Mare and Sighet
   The USC Shoah Foundation Institute
   The Elie Wiesel Foundation for Humanity
   The Raoul Wallenberg Committee of the USA
   My Caring Family
   and
   Nicholas L. Deak—My Mentor

PART I

BROKERS/MONEY MANAGERS

"Do not trust all men, but trust men of worth; the former course is silly, the latter a mark of prudence."

—Democritus, philosopher (460 BC–370 BC)

My broker, Rick Rule, enjoys an intellectual debate as much as I do. In that vein he and I have been exploring the issue of how much one should rely on investment advisors versus making your own investment decisions. Rick is on record as saying that no one can do a better job of managing your investments than you, and that a person will always be better off the more he or she educates him- or herself about investing. However, I've now come to the conclusion that a trusted and sage investment advisor trumps investor self-education every time.

In 1984, when I was a Merrill Lynch stockbroker advising my clients, my viewpoint was similar to Rick's. Back then I even remember commenting to my father-in-law, a surgeon, that there seemed to be a certain amount of irony in the fact that he had spent tens of thousands of hours practicing medicine and had managed to build a small investment portfolio through his long hours of work, yet was spending no time educating himself about investing so that he could keep his hard-earned savings, let alone grow them. I recommended several financial planning books for him, but like most people, he just did not have the time or inclination to read them. My message to my father-in-law was basically the same message I've often heard Rick give.

However, even if an investor were to make the effort to educate him- or herself, they will not be able to develop the industry contacts and the wealth of knowledge that a trustworthy broker or investment advisor can. Assume we have two groups of 50 investors each. One group knows virtually nothing about investing and follows every piece of advice my broker, Rick, gives them. The other 50 investors try to educate themselves about investing on a part-time basis, studying as much as they can, but selectively follow Rick's advice, using their self-taught knowledge and experiences to override his advice when they think it appropriate. My contention is that the investment results of the completely uninformed investors will be far better than the self-taught investors.

I think Rick has reluctantly come around to agreeing with my point of view but adds one very big caveat, one I am totally in agreement with. That is: Trusted advisors will be able to do a much better job for their customers when their customers are informed and able to converse knowledgeably about investment preferences and risk alternatives.

I've not asked all the money managers below if they agree with my point of view. But judging by the prolific amount of writing they do, I would have to believe they consider investor education is very important.

- **Eric Sprott:** One of Canada's most successful resource investors looks at gold's upside and explains why "gold remains the one and only go to investment."
- **Adrian Day:** After reviewing the financial crisis, deficit spending, and central bank money printing, Adrian then states that he's fond of StreetTracks Gold ETF, the exchange-traded fund that seeks to reflect the price of gold bullion. But he also reviews some gold mining stocks that he likes as well.
- **Peter Schiff:** No investment advisor was more vocal in forecasting the current financial crisis nor more emphatic about protecting your investment portfolio with gold.
- **Rick Rule:** Bear markets and rising gold prices go hand-in-hand, and Rick tells you about his favorite bear market investments. His

number one favorite being "PIPE" investing, making private investments in public equities, oftentimes in undervalued and undercapitalized gold mining companies.

- **Michael Checkan:** An expert on asset diversification who knows that "gold protects wealth" tells you how to legally purchase and store gold offshore.

The following contributions come with one caveat. In a few cases the timeliness of specific recommendations may date some of the information. However, with regard to the primary message of the book, that everyone should own gold, the message is timeless. More important, with regard to the primary purpose of the book, allowing you to get to know and understand how the sage investors introduced in this book think, the message is also timeless.

CHAPTER 1

GOLD REMAINS
THE STANDARD

Eric Sprott
Sprott Asset Management

"Give me control of a nation's money and I care not who makes
its laws."

—Mayer Amschel Bauer Rothschild,
banker (1744–1812)

*Eric Sprott is a Canadian money manager who manages over $4.5 billion
through various Sprott companies, mutual funds, and hedge funds.
Having heard Eric speak on numerous occasions and having read a
great deal of his written analysis, I can say that his numerous awards
for investment analysis and fund management over his 35-year investment career are richly deserved. While the amount of money Eric manages
as well as his long investment career may make Eric look like a Wall
Street regular to some, his unconventional and contrarian thinking, as
well his views of the important role that gold plays as wealth insurance,
clearly put him on the outside.*

Originally published in *Markets at a Glance* on October 14, 2005, as "Gold Remains the
Standard."

Eric coauthors a monthly investment strategy article, "Markets at a Glance," where he discusses his views and expectations regarding global financial markets and economies. Looking through the archives of his newsletter contained on the Sprott Resources website, www.sprott.com, one can't help but be impressed by Eric's forecasting abilities and the investment results he's realized. To cite just one example, as of October 2009, the Sprott Canadian Equity Fund had achieved a 10-year return of over 23 percent per annum.

Although the article below was written over four years ago, I included it in this book because it explains why you should invest in gold. An understanding of Eric's timeless messages—"gold is the ultimate flight-to-safety investment vehicle" and "the upside for gold is quite tremendous"—are essential to any investor.

There were a couple of interesting headlines this week singing the praises of our favorite metal. On the front page of Wednesday's *Investor's Business Daily* was the headline: "As Gold Nears an 18-Year High, Some See Signal of Inflation Rise." Similarly, in Tuesday's *Wall Street Journal* was the headline: "Stocks Fall Amid Auto-Sector Woes . . . Gold Price Shines." Indeed, during times of financial anxiety and strain, signs of which are becoming increasingly apparent to everyone, gold remains the one and only go-to investment that can protect people's otherwise heavily weighted paper portfolios. With the price of gold up $40 per ounce since the end of August, it would appear that gold is once again starting to gain traction not only in the media, but in the hearts and minds (and safety deposit boxes) of investors.

All this, of course, makes perfect sense to us. In our view, gold is the ultimate flight-to-safety investment vehicle. We won't be going into all the reasons to own gold in this article. Seventeen such reasons can be found in our "Fundamental Reasons to Own Gold," written by John Embry, which can be found on our website at www.sprott. com. Rather, we would like to dream a little and speculate on what the price of gold *could* be if a financial crisis/panic were to ensue. Although our analysis is not rocket science, it does show that the upside for gold is quite tremendous given the troubles in the financial world we see developing.

FINANCIAL CRISIS

The first question that needs to be asked is: Is a financial crisis likely? To this we would answer: Most definitively **yes**. Furthermore, it's not necessarily a crisis *per se* that is needed to send gold soaring; but rather, just the *fear* of one is sufficient. We see many reasons to be fearful in this environment. Many stock indices are now down almost 10 percent from their highs of a few weeks ago. Interest rates have been on the rise, with 10-year Treasury yields up almost 50 basis points in the past six weeks. Corporate yield spreads are widening due to the well-publicized bankruptcies in the auto and airline sectors. Energy prices are high and likely to go higher. Retail sales have been coming in weak. The real estate market is starting to crack. The consumer is spent, and sentiment numbers have been horrid. Plus, to add insult to injury, everywhere there are signs of inflation. Let's face it, the current macroeconomic environment is not conducive to rising asset prices—quite the contrary. Except for gold, one of the only asset classes to have a negative beta to the broader markets.

For those witnessing how their portfolios are performing in September and (so far in) October, suffice it to say things haven't been pretty in the paper world lately. So what's an investor to do? Many advisors and influential letter writers are now recommending a gold weighting of 5 to 10 percent in portfolios. This is something unheard of in the past 20 years, a time when financial (paper) assets held sway, and gold was trashed as a "barbarous relic" of medieval times that serves no useful purpose in a modern technologically advanced society. But the times they are a-changing! Slowly but surely, and in spite of efforts to suppress it, gold is starting to acquire mainstream appeal. A testament to this is gold's recent run up in price against **all** currencies, not just the U.S. dollar. It is no longer the case, as it has been in the past couple decades, that gold's desirability was only in the eyes of the gold bugs. But we ask: Is it even possible for *everyone* to have a 5 to 10 percent weighting in gold? Is there enough gold to go around to meet such a demand? Not by a long shot, but with one caveat: only if the price of gold goes up by multiples from here. We'll run some calculations by you later to show what we mean.

TURNING BACK THE CLOCK

But first, let's turn back the clock to 1980. For those of us old enough to recall, this was the last time there was widespread financial panic that led to a frenzied flight to gold. Back then inflation was on the rise. Interest rates were heading skyward. Geopolitical risks were aplenty, once again centered in the Middle East with Iran. The prospects for the economy were dim. There was stagflation (weak economy and rising prices). Sound familiar? Stock markets were mired in a prolonged bear cycle. Last but not least, the gold price spiked above $800 per ounce. Greed and fear were in the air.

Some may think we're cheating by using 1980 as our reference point, given that that was the all-time high for gold. True, we've had financial crises since then, namely the crash of 1987, the savings and loan crisis, LTCM, the Asian flu, and the tech/telecom bust. But none of them really led to a flight to gold, thanks to the copious amounts of liquidity generated by central banks the world over. With all the inflationary pressures that exist today, such a nefarious liquidity injection can no longer be attempted without severe consequences to global currency values. Not to mention the fact that nothing kills the real value of financial assets quicker than inflation. It is our opinion that both scenarios (central banks print to save the day, or they don't and let the financial bubbles unwind) play into gold's hands and are highly bullish for gold going forward.

So could history repeat itself à la 1980? If it does, the gold price is unlikely to stop at just $800. $800 goes nowhere near as far today as it did back then. Let's dream a little and compare some financial metrics of today versus then. Needless to say, the paper world has gotten a lot bigger since 1980. According to the Federal Reserve website, money supply as measured by M3 has risen from about $2 trillion in 1980 to $10 trillion today. That's a fivefold increase. For gold to hold its stature relative to money, it is similarly likely to increase by fivefold from what it was in the 1980 financial panic. That implies a price of $4,000 per ounce. Not bad!

Housing prices are another indicator of the mound of paper built over the years. According to the OFHEO housing price index, U.S. housing prices have tripled since 1980 (with some markets such as New York, California, and Massachusetts going up by a factor of five).

This index understates the true appreciation in housing prices because it is based on mortgages issued by Fannie Mae and Freddie Mac, which have upper limits. Be that as it may, for gold to keep pace with housing prices as measured by this index, it needs to go to $2,400 per ounce. We'll take that, too.

Now here's where things really start to get interesting. The size of global equity markets in 1980 was $1.4 trillion. Today that value is in excess of $30 trillion! Global equity markets have grown over 2,000 percent in the past 25 years. What would the price of gold need to be to have kept pace? $16,000 per ounce.

GOLD IN THE FUTURE

Finally, let's see what happens if everyone tried to have a 5 percent portfolio weighting in gold. As we already mentioned, global equity markets are about $30 trillion. The bond and fixed income markets are twice that at $60 trillion. Then we have bank assets of $40 trillion. (These numbers are from the IMF's 2004 "Global Financial Stability Report.") This equates to a total investable pool of some $130 trillion, 5 percent of which is $6.5 trillion. The gold equity market is currently a paltry $50 billion, so right off the bat we note that it's nigh impossible to have gold stocks comprise 5 percent of even the global equities portion. To do so, gold equities would need to increase in value by a factor of 30. Even we aren't that bullish!

What about gold bullion itself? Here's where it gets tricky. The value of all above-ground gold is roughly $1 trillion. However, not all of it is for sale. Much of it is tied up in the vaults of central banks or lent out and thus owed to central banks. There is also much gold (the vast majority even) that has been "consumed" in the form of jewelry and thus is also not readily for sale. But let's assume, for the sake of argument, that **all** gold ever produced is made available for sale (i.e., Fort Knox gets gutted and everybody melts wedding rings). Even under this conservative scenario (let's call it the low case), the price of gold will need to increase by 6.5 times to $3,000 per ounce in order to comprise 5 percent of all financial assets. In the high case where only the 80 million ounces that are mined in a year get put up for sale (not realistic but let's just go there), then the implied price of gold needs to be $80,000 per ounce.

It only gets better if people decide to have a 10 percent weighting in gold . . . but let's stop there! Doubtless the gold bugs are already excited as is.

This may all seem a little cheeky—we've already admitted to not being rocket scientists. But taken for what it is, the analysis does seem to show that gold could have explosive potential from here. We're not saying that gold will go to these levels and stay there (though in a hyperinflation/money printing scenario, that is certainly a possibility). What we are saying is that in a financial panic that morphs into a rush to gold, the price of the glittery metal can easily attain heretofore unseen levels.

In conclusion, gold has more upside than just about any other investment we can think of in this market at this time. Investors will turn to gold for safety in a period of financial weakness. What alternatives are there? When paper valuations are shown to be based on a flimsy house of cards, people will turn to what is sturdy, weighty, and real. We'd like to finish off with a quote from our friend James Turk:

> The gold standard may be dead . . . but gold remains the standard.

CHAPTER 2

LONG-TERM FUNDAMENTALS STILL GOOD FOR GOLD

An Interview with Adrian Day
Adrian Day Asset Management and
Adrian Day's Global Analyst

"Character is like a tree and reputation like its shadow. The shadow is what we think of it; the tree is the real thing."

—Abraham Lincoln, 16th U.S. President (1809–1865)

Rick Rule also recommended that I take a close look at Adrian Day for inclusion in this book. This will surprise many because they are direct competitors, yet both men take a global approach to investing, specialize in natural resources, are value investors, and most important, both are sages who think that gold should be part of anyone's investment portfolio.

Originally published in *The Gold Report* on September 2, 2008, as "Adrian Day: Long-Term Fundamentals Still Good for Gold." *The Gold Report* is an online report that features investment coverage of precious metals, base metals, and gems that is published by Streetwise Inc.

Adrian Day is chairman and CEO of Adrian Day Asset Management, a registered investment advisory firm that has been serving private investors and small institutions successfully since 1991. He is also editor-in-chief of Adrian Day's Global Analyst, *an email newsletter published by Investment Consultants International, Ltd.*

Although I am unfamiliar with individual performances of or in Adrian Day Asset Management, the track record at Adrian Day's Global Analyst is impressive. As of September 30, 2009, positions recommended have been held an average of 23.9 months with an average return of 82.4 percent. That's a track record that goes back to 1999! Therefore, it is no surprise that Adrian is famous for discovering many big investment winners, companies in which he invested—and urged his readers to invest—when his picks were unknown or out of favor and, just as importantly, holding them patiently, often for several years.

In an interview with Adrian that follows, you will really get a sense of how a quality investment analyst views the world. First, you'll hear about his views on the economy and the U.S. dollar and the various effects those will have on the price of gold. He then begins discussing specific recommendations on gold stocks, including junior gold mining companies and other companies that own gold royalties. Perhaps most important, Adrian discusses the "good management" at Franco Nevada Corp. and the "good people" at Allied Nevada Gold Corp. so I know that like me, the "who" is very important to Adrian.

The Gold Report: *So what's your take on where we are with the markets . . . you think we'll see a change soon?*

Adrian Day: People are still very, very concerned about the dollar and inflation, and rightly so. The core CPI numbers were up 0.7 percent in one month. That's a high number, and the precise number may be a monthly anomaly, but it's very clear that the trend in prices is up.

We are seeing a pickup in inflation, not just in the United States— and this is what's important—but all around the world. I realize, of course, that rising prices are not the same as inflation. But we are seeing rising prices in pretty much all areas of the world, and they are going up faster than the central banks themselves have targeted. With all the credit problems we've seen over the last 18 months and all the money that's been put into the system, I don't think that's going to change in the near term. So that's a bullish sign for gold. Inflation is a factor we haven't had in the gold market for quite some time.

The dollar is even more important, certainly for the next six to 12 months. And, again, in terms of the long-term fundamentals, I don't see that anything has changed. All we're seeing in the dollar is a very overdue correction to the long-term trend.

To me it's much more a correction in the strength of the euro than a correction in the weakness of the dollar. I don't think people are rushing into the dollar because they think our economy is strong and getting stronger. Rather, they are cautious on some of the foreign currencies, which have simply moved too far, too fast. It was an overdue correction, which came a lot later than I thought it would. And it would be a mistake to expect it to turn around after just a couple of weeks.

But if we look at the long-term fundamentals, the U.S. economy is still fundamentally weak, and it seems that with every passing week there's more bad news that's worse than the news before. We are a long way from the bottom in both the economic decline and the credit crisis in the United States, and there's no particular end in sight.

The dollar has to go down over the next 12 months and that's going to be positive for gold, no question. The low interest rates and the higher inflation numbers mean that at the short end we have negative rates right now. There might be a bit of a lag, but negative rates are always bullish for gold.

TGR: *September is here. The Canadians are going to be returning from summer holiday. Do you think this year is going to be similar to past cycles, where in the fall we see increases in gold purchases and the juniors, or do you think there's going to be a disconnect this time?*

AD: That's a good question and a bit imponderable. Usually, it's very strong in the fall, and we should have already bottomed. What's happened this time that's different is we've got the dollar correction and a correction in the strong Canadian dollar as well.

And that's come at the time when you would otherwise expect gold and gold stocks to be seasonally strong. Canada has housing problems and credit problems like the United States, although not to the same extent. There might be a different mood this time, and there's no evidence so far that we're seeing buying returning to the junior sector. And, remember, it's not as though the juniors were strong before the summer started, so I'm a bit concerned that we may not see that increase in the junior market in the near term.

With gold itself, the weaker dollar does actually have one huge benefit—an obvious one—which is that it makes physical buying of gold actually cheaper. The Indian market especially tends to be fairly price sensitive. When gold went over the $950 level on the way to over $1,000, there was strong evidence that the Indians started holding back purchasing. Now that gold has fallen under $850 again in the last few weeks, there's evidence that the Indians have started buying again in heavy numbers. So a stronger dollar will actually help the gold market, but it may not help the gold stocks.

TGR: *So you're saying the stronger dollar would help ETFs, coins, or actual bullion?*

AD: It would help those because of foreign buying. I don't know about gold coins, but it would certainly help the ETF, of course, which simply reflects physical gold.

TGR: *Do you own, in your portfolios, any ETFs?*

AD: The one we buy is StreetTracks Gold ETF (GLD), which is the largest and most liquid. We also own Central Fund of Canada (CEF), which is not an ETF, but a closed-end fund. Not in huge amounts, but we do buy. It depends on the client, and it also depends on the time. We are buying.

TGR: *So we've got political crises, major deficits, and central banks printing money. You would think gold would be at an all-time high. What type of event has to occur to change this? It seems like we're in a perfect storm.*

AD: It's important to give it some historical perspective. There have been a lot of graphs appearing recently showing how gold broke through its 50-day moving-average, then its 100-day moving-average, and finally its 200-day moving-average. I looked back to the middle of 2000, however, and what really stood out on that graph was that for four or five years gold moved up and down, but very close to a basic straight line, a trend line that was moving steadily upward.

And then at the end of 2005, it started moving above that trend line, until in the middle fall of 2007, when it just shot up. What is happening right now is reversion to the mean. Gold simply overshot—it wasn't necessarily completely clear to all of us in the gold market, watching it day by day, week by week, month by month.

Taking a longer-term look, it becomes abundantly clear that gold way overshot and went parabolic. Now it's simply coming back to that long-term trend line. So I'm not overly concerned about gold.

The seasonal thing has thrown all this for a loop. If this had all happened three or four months ago, I'd have been firmer in what I was saying. I don't think we can necessarily expect it to turn around suddenly after the kind of damage that has been done. I don't think a particular event's going to do it.

Going back to the long-term graph, if gold just does sometime between, say, $750 and $870 or so, whether it's three to five weeks or maybe two or three months, gold will be ready to move back up again because all the fundamentals favor gold. The bigger concern for us is the gold stocks. And you have to look at the seniors separately than the juniors.

It's a little easier to see all the reasons why the senior gold stocks as a group, with some exceptions, of course, have not really kept up with gold. The gold miners have not had such an easy time of it of late.

It's been more difficult to raise money and get permits. Permits have been delayed, mines have been expropriated. Mining is a much more difficult business than it was, and it's much more costly. So as gold moved up, so too did all of the input costs, primarily, energy, which is the number one input, and number two, the costs in local currencies: the Australian dollar, Brazilian real, Canadian dollar— all of those are very strong currencies in big gold mining countries. So the margins were not expanding the way that you would think they were.

And that's only talking about the cash cost of producing an ounce of gold out of a producing mine. There's also keeping a sustaining business going, finding a new deposit, etc.

The juniors are the more problematic because, in most cases, there simply isn't volume in these stocks. The occasional stock will do well based on some particular exciting prospect, but they are becoming increasingly few and far between.

As we all know, the irony is that sometimes companies will release relatively good news, and the stock goes down. It just reminds people that they own the thing. And then there are other companies, of course, that don't have particularly good news to put out. There just isn't any volume; the only volume I see is in stocks that are going down.

So the question really is when that is going to change and what we do about it. Certainly, if gold goes back over $950 or $900 and stays there, we'll see more interest, especially if everything else is still relatively weak. Typically, people are attracted to the gold stocks when gold is strong and other things are not so strong. But if the tech stocks are strong and the Dow is strong, people tend not to invest in junior gold stocks to the same extent. Similarly, if gold is strong, but everything else is very weak and people are worried about the overall environment and looking for liquidity, you can't expect the junior gold stocks to get that liquidity. That's fairly obvious.

The other thing that's going to happen increasingly is larger companies taking over juniors and explorers. We know they are looking; they need the reserves and many of the explorers are very inexpensive. A few takeovers in rapid succession will likely bring interest back to the sector.

The good thing is that investors can buy truly good quality juniors at remarkably cheap prices. If you can focus on companies that you know don't have to raise money and they're cheap and you're patient, you're going to do very well indeed. Look at Virginia Gold Mines [TSX: VGQ], with a $116.5 million market cap. Its market cap is more than covered by its cash and its royalty on Éléonore, which is an advanced royalty, so it doesn't depend on Goldcorp putting Éléonore into production. It's trading at less than the market cap of those two things and Virginia never has to raise another penny. I just can't see how you have a lot of fundamental risk in that. [Virginia stock has moved up since this interview, but with the increase in the price of gold, so too has the value of its royalty, so the company is still selling below its net asset value.]

Rimfire Minerals Corp. [TSX.V: RFM] would be another one. Look at Rimfire, $19 million market cap today, $9 million in cash. Again, difficult to know how a year from now that's not going to be higher . . . or at least it's not going to be significantly lower. And there's more like that. [Rimfire subsequently changed its name, following the acquisition of another exploration company, to Kiska Metals (KSK), now a larger company with more cash.]

TGR: *The company that looks exciting to me is Franco Nevada Corp. [CA: FNV], which is involved with two areas that are the future, gold and energy. What would you say about Franco Nevada?*

AD: I agree with you completely. They've got a very strong balance sheet. Equally importantly, they have access to capital. They can raise more money if they need to without heavy dilution, and, of course, you've got some of the smartest people in the business running it.

There are two basic ways to obtain royalties. One is to buy pre-existing royalties, where a company like Franco or Royal Gold might buy a royalty that already exists. But the second way of getting a royalty is to actually create a royalty from a junior that's looking for financing. And for the junior, selling a royalty can be a less dilutive way of getting financing for a project. On its last investor conference call, Franco management was discussing how this environment is going to prove good for them. A lot of companies are knocking on their door asking for them to create royalties as financing mechanisms.

Franco said they are not in any hurry and are looking for the very good deals that are going to come along over the next few months. The point I'm making is that these are really first-class value investors, and they're prepared to be patient; they're going to make very good decisions when they make them. I like Franco a lot. Its price is only 1.2 times book, which is really quite cheap for a gold company and particularly cheap for such a good quality one. We were buying it today, I should disclose.

What I'm looking for in this market are companies where one can have very high level of confidence and the absolute risk of the company is low regardless of what the potential upside might be. That confidence comes from a strong balance sheet as well as good management and a diversity of assets. Franco Nevada fits the bill to a tee.

TGR: *A company you haven't talked about before, but I know it's one that you also like, is Cartier Resources [TSX-V: ECR].*

AD: One of the reasons I haven't mentioned it is because it's so thinly traded. We bought more Cartier today. It has a $6.5 million market cap; it's very, very thin.

I like Cartier. It's got a very strong business model. It's got a strong balance sheet. It focuses not exclusively on Quebec, but on Quebec and on the eastern part of Toronto . . . so good jurisdictions, good mining camps. The main Kinojevis is a fairly long property with gold mines on either side of it and it looks as though it's a long trend. They own 100 percent of it, but they're considering partnering parts of the property. [Cartier has since subdivided Kinojevis and renamed the various segments.] Another one that's similar in many ways is Midland Exploration [TSX.V:MD], which we also own. It has a $12 million market cap, and again, on a 60-cent share, we're not talking about a lot of volume. [Midland has since moved up to the $1.35 level, so the market cap is more than twice that indicated, though still low.]

It's all in Quebec. It's diversified—not just gold, but gold-based metals and uranium. They have a gold project with Agnico-Eagle (AEM); base metals with Breakwater. They have a good balance sheet. Midland is in the position where on its current business plan it would never have to raise another penny. Its overhead's been covered by joint venture payments and it's doing the work at the moment, but it will never have to raise any more money unless it wants to, which is a very good position to be in.

TGR: *Switching gears, switching to gems, Motapa Diamonds [TSX: MTP]. This stock has been going the opposite way of the market lately. It's had a nice little move since June.*

AD: Motapa's clearly speculative. All diamonds are highly speculative because you're looking for a few big stones. Motapa also has a joint venture model on its properties throughout Africa with large companies and small. It has a project called Mothae, which is near the big diamond deposit near Lesotho. The Mothae deposit is a joint venture with Lucara Diamond Corp. [TSX-V: LUC]. Lucara is basically a Lundin company, it has nothing else in it, and there's been a lot of speculation recently that Lundin might simply take over Motapa. Certainly on a risk–reward basis and certainly if Motapa were to ever find economic diamonds, it is just remarkably cheap. As I say, the risk tends to be high in these things, but the potential is also high. [Subsequent to this interview, Lucara did indeed take over Motapa, and the shares have moved significantly higher.]

TGR: *Going to Nevada, can you talk about Allied Nevada Gold Corp. [TSX: ANV], which was a spinoff from Vista? What's the attraction there? Not having to raise money?*

AD: They certainly don't have to raise money. They've got something like $51 million right now. They did do a financing earlier in the year, which was largely to raise more money for the Hycroft Mine that they're putting into production. The idea is that Hycroft will be put into production by the end of the year and will generate enough cash flow to basically pay for some of the rest of its exploration of the deeper sulfides at Hycroft, and elsewhere. [Hycroft is now in production with a study under way on the sulfides.]

Allied has one of the largest land packages in Nevada. It was a merger of all of Vista's Nevada properties and a private land package put together by Carl Pescio. So it has good people, a strong balance sheet, and multiple properties. I think it's going to succeed, and Hycroft should be quite a good cash flow generator. So I like Allied a lot.

One more I like . . . it's almost an embarrassment of riches. It's just a question of when it is going to move. I still like Miranda Gold Corp. [TSX-V: MAD]. It's awfully cheap, very thinly traded again, but it's a $21 million market cap. It's got about $12 million in cash and several joint ventures. It follows the prospect joint venture model. It doesn't have to raise any more money, unless it has a particular purpose.

It had a string of bad luck last year with some of its joint venture partners deciding not to renew their joint ventures and a few disappointing results on some of its projects. But, you know, in the last six months, even though the market was going against it, it's tied down joint ventures on pretty much all of its properties, most of which are in Nevada, and several of them are drilling.

There are four of them that are going to be drilled for sure before the end of the year. It's difficult to see how you can go seriously wrong from here. And with various partners, a lot of properties, the odds of Miranda being successful at some point are, let's say, much higher than for most.

TGR: *Adrian, this has been great per usual. We appreciate it.*

CHAPTER 3

A GOOD
INVESTMENT
STRATEGY, BUY GOLD

Peter D. Schiff
Euro Pacific Capital

"If the American people ever allow private banks to control the issuance of their currency, first by inflation and then by deflation, the banks and corporations that will grow up around them will deprive the people of all their property until their children will wake up homeless on the continent that their fathers conquered."

—Thomas Jefferson, U.S. President (1743–1826)

Peter Schiff is one of the very few investment advisors not only to have predicted the current financial crisis, but to have done so in a very public way. I have heard him talk in person on several occasions, the most recent being at the Freedom Fest Conference held this past July where

Originally published in *Euro Pacific Economic Market Commentary* on May 30, 2008, as "Don't Be Afraid, Buy Gold," and on the Euro Pacific website as "Our Investment Strategy."

his topic was "The Collapse of the U.S. Bubble Economy and What it Means for Investors."

Peter Schiff has owned his own stock brokerage firm, Euro Pacific Capital, for over a dozen years. Over the last few years his central investing premise has been a weakening dollar and safety in gold, commodities, and foreign stocks. He is also a New York Times *best-selling author whose latest book,* Crash Proof 2.0, *clearly lays out his opinions on the world economy. It has been said that Mr. Schiff has a gift for taking today's complex financial information and presenting it in an easy-to-read manner that the average investor understands.*

In the two contributions below, Peter outlines his firm's current investment strategy as well his thoughts on buying gold. I have included the first piece because it important to understand his firm's current investment strategy, which clearly lays out the intertwined relationship between the U.S. dollar and gold. As he points out, "based on current U.S. monetary and fiscal policy, the many structural imbalances underlying the U.S. economy, the potential monetization of massive funded and unfunded federal liabilities, the purchasing power of the dollar is likely to diminish substantially over time." The corollary to the dollar decline is found in his second contribution when he says, "Gold's ascent . . . was, and is, being driven by those who prefer it as a store of value to the paper alternative offered by governments."

OUR INVESTMENT STRATEGY

In our opinion the U.S. economic ship of state is in danger of sinking. As the problems with her hull are structural, current efforts by government officials and central bankers to plug up the holes will make it difficult to keep her afloat. Though we remain hopeful that she may one day be returned to a seaworthy condition, there is nothing collectively that we can do to alter her fate, or that of the millions of Americans ignorantly dancing the night away on her decks. However, individually we can take defensive action to protect ourselves and our families by getting off the ship. In our opinion, the lifeboat of choice is a carefully selected portfolio of relatively conservative, high-dividend-paying, non-U.S. export dependent foreign equities.

Such investments provide three potential sources of protection:

1. They pay good dividends, many of which qualify for the lower dividend tax currently in effect.
2. More importantly, as these dividends are paid in currencies other than the U.S. dollar, their value will rise as the dollar falls, as will the principal value of the underlying shares.
3. They provide the potential for true capital gains, as the shares themselves may appreciate in terms of their local currencies.

As a result of these three separate and distinct sources of current income and capital gains, the U.S. dollar need not be falling for a portfolio of foreign stocks to produce positive returns. However, it is during a potential dollar crisis that such portfolios will be of the greatest value. Since no one can be certain when the inevitable dollar collapse will occur, it is better to be prepared. When it comes to getting out of the dollar, there are only two possible ways to do it: either too early or too late. At Euro Pacific we choose the former. Though the dollar will predictably experience several countertrend rallies along its downward path, we feel that it does not make sense to attempt to trade them. It would be the equivalent of leaving the safety of your lifeboat, hoping for one last dance aboard a doomed ship before it sinks. As a result of our buy and hold strategy, during those time periods when the U.S. dollar is rising in value, or when global stock markets are in decline, our portfolios will lose value. Though such declines will be partially offset by dividends, investors unwilling to assume short-term volatility as a tradeoff for absolute long-term performance should not implement this strategy.

Also, it is important not to confuse a desire not to go down with a sinking ship with patriotism. Such "patriots" who stand on the deck saluting the flag as the ship sinks will likely be of little assistance to other survivors left treading water. Only by attempting to position ourselves safely aboard seaworthy lifeboats now will we be able to participate in any future rescue efforts. Protecting our wealth today should allow us to repatriate it tomorrow, thus enabling us to help rebuild a viable American economy.

The most important step for investors to take when determining which investments qualify as being conservative is to first determine exactly what one is attempting to "conserve." If one's goal is simply to conserve the number of dollars one owns, then there are several domestic investments that will satisfy that simple criteria. However, what good is it to conserve dollars, if the dollars themselves do not conserve their purchasing power? After all, we do not want dollars for their intrinsic value; we want them for the goods and services they can buy. However, based on current U.S. monetary and fiscal policy, the many structural imbalances underlying the U.S. economy, and the potential monetization of massive funded and unfunded federal liabilities, the purchasing power of the dollar is likely to diminish substantially over time.

A truly conservative investor seeks to conserve the purchasing power of his portfolio, not merely the nominal dollar value of his holdings. At one time, when the dollar was sound and Americans produced the goods they consumed, this goal was readily accomplished with certain types of dollar-based investments. However, like the song says, "The times they are a-changing." Anyone wishing to be truly conservative must therefore be prepared to change with them.

If preserving purchasing power is the goal, we are convinced that the investments best able to achieve this goal can only be found beyond American borders. However, most stocks are not conservative, and neither are most currencies. The challenge is to choose the currencies that are most likely to conserve their purchasing power, based on objective economic and political criteria, and then to invest in conservative stocks denominated in those currencies—those that might be thought of as being for "widows and orphans" for citizens of the countries in which they are domiciled. However, "conservative stocks" are not without risk. They are merely believed to be less risky than typical stocks or those thought to be aggressive or speculative.

DON'T BE AFRAID, BUY GOLD

In 2004, former Treasury Secretary Robert Rubin predicted that if foreigners viewed U.S. budget and current account deficits as being unsustainable, confidence in our financial instruments could crack causing the dollar to fall sharply. In fact, during that same year, former Fed Chairman Paul Volcker predicted an 80 percent probability that the U.S. dollar would collapse within five years (a relatively short time horizon in the investment world). Conservative investors who take these two former government officials' warnings seriously have little choice but to seek safety abroad.

As the price of gold has taken some lumps since it crashed into the symbolically significant $1,000 per ounce mark back in March, those on Wall Street who had consistently underplayed its potential on its way up are now assuring its continued retreat. According to these gold market spectators, prices have risen solely as a result of financial panic, and now that the fear has apparently subsided, gold's gains will evaporate as well.

I have been buying gold and gold stocks for myself and my clients since 1999 and not once did I buy out of fear. In fact, from my perspective the only fear I've observed in the gold market is from those who have been too afraid to buy.

While fear may from time to time play a role in creating price spikes in gold, the underlying bull market has been driven by solid fundamentals. Those who have been too afraid to buy simply do not understand the underlying dynamics and have instead decided that the market is irrational. As a result, gold continues to climb the classic wall of worry as any dip in its otherwise upward trajectory causes the speculative investors to jump ship.

Gold's ascent from less than $300 an ounce to its current level was, and is, being driven by those who prefer it as a store of value to the paper alternatives offered by governments. As the Federal Reserve's dollar debasement policy kicks into high gear and other central banks around the world are forced to follow suit to maintain their pegs against the dollar, the rational choice for long-term investors is gold. Thus, the decision to buy is not rooted in fear but reason. On the other hand, the decision not to buy is not only rooted in fear, but in ignorance as well.

Those oblivious to gold's warnings instead place their trust in government-supplied statistics. Based simply on flimsy CPI reports, these observers believe that inflation is nowhere in evidence and that the flight to gold is therefore unwarranted. Yesterday's GDP report provides the latest illustration of this dynamic. The government was able to present an annualized first quarter growth rate of .9 percent based on an assumed annualized rate of inflation of only 2.6 percent.

In other words, inflation in the first quarter of 2008 was the lowest first quarter inflation in the last four years. How such a claim did not elicit howls of laughter is beyond me. The government previously reported that in the years 2007, 2006, and 2005, annualized first quarter inflation rates were 4.2, 3.4, and 3.9 percent respectively. Does anyone, besides Fed governors and Wall Street economists, really believe inflation so far in 2008 is 33 percent below the average rate over the past three years?

Many of those who place their faith with government figures and dismiss the movements in gold believe that inflation is not a problem so long as wages are not rising rapidly. The fact that wages are lagging other prices merely means that inflation is that much more problematic for average Americans. Ironically, what is overlooked is that wages are in fact rising, just not in America. They are rising in the nations that produce the goods that we consume, and those higher costs are indeed being passed on to Americans.

However, recent action in the bond market suggests that a few more people are getting wise to the government's con. This week, yields on long-term treasuries hit new highs for the year, with the yield on the ten-year up 90 basis points from its March low. While the Pollyannas on Wall Street attribute this move to the strengthening U.S. economy, those of us buying gold know it's more likely a long overdue increase in inflation expectations.

Got gold?

CHAPTER 4

THE BEAR MARKET IS YOUR FRIEND— FOUR WAYS TO WIN

Rick Rule
Global Resource Investments Ltd.

"As good as gold."

—Charles Dickens, writer (1812–1870),
from *A Christmas Carol*, 1843

Rick is the founder and chairman of Global Resource Investments, Ltd., a leading American retail brokerage specializing in mining, energy, water utilities, forest products, and agriculture. Rick's industry contacts and knowledge of the market form the backbone of Global Resources. He is not only one of the smartest investment advisors in the business, he may well be the hardest working. I am not the only one who thinks this way about Rick. For instance, the renowned numismatist and sage Dana Samuelson has this to say: "Rick is a

---

This is a copy of a speech given at the October 2002 *Gold Newsletter's* New Orleans Investment Conference.

genius, plain and simple. . . . and his company, Global Resource Investments, is the premier resource stock brokerage in the country."

It's Rick's attention to the risk-reward trade-off that impresses most of his clients and peers. Many of the natural resource stocks that Global specializes in are thinly capitalized with low trading volumes. In other words, they're highly speculative. Rick sees his job as managing the risk of holding these small cap stocks and then reaping the higher returns one will realize from investing in such speculative asset classes.

As stated earlier, when I was raising money for my new company, Seattle Shellfish, the only other asset my wife and I had was my wife's IRA. In 2000, Rick helped convince me that gold's time had come. To Mary's credit, she could see the logic in what we had to say and moved her account to Rick's firm. Since Rick began managing her retirement account in 2001, we've seen it appreciate by a compounded return of 21 percent per annum. There's no doubt in my mind that we will continue realizing similar returns on all our investment funds now that they are managed by Rick and his team.

Rick begins his contribution on bear markets by analyzing the success of Jim Blanchard, another contrarian and long-term gold advocate, who capitalized on the previous gold mania, which ended in 1980. He then relays some timeless bear market strategies to use in this latest upsurge in gold and ends his talk by reviewing his favorite bear market investment strategy, PIPE investing. Having been an investor in many, many of Rick's "private investments in public equities." I can attest to the effectiveness of this bear market strategy, particularly PIPEs involving undercapitalized and thinly traded junior gold companies. As you will come to understand, gold is the perfect bear market investment.

Good morning, ladies and gentlemen. It is a pleasure to be here with you in New Orleans once again. We should begin this session by thanking our host, Mr. Brien Lundin, the staff of Jefferson Financial, and the Blanchard family for continuing this great conference as a living legacy to the late Jim Blanchard.

This speech is in fact for Jim, who loved financial markets and was a true contrarian. Jim knew that bear markets were opportunities. A quick review of his career will put this speech in context.

He began his investment career as an advocate of gold during gold's wilderness years. The metal was so out of favor in this country at the time that it was illegal to own it. Jim responded by vigorously campaigning to legalize private ownership and built the world's largest coin dealer in the process. When gold came into general favor, Jim had the good sense to sell his gold company—to GE no less—I guess they thought about potential synergies between light bulbs and gold coins. At the bottom of the equities market, Jim started a mutual fund business, selling out once again as that sector returned to favor. In 1992, with silver selling for US$3.60 per ounce, Jim asked me to structure a silver investment play for him and his readers. Thanks to the fine efforts of our mutual friend Bob Quartermain, that's how Silver Standard Resources came into its current form. Jim's memory puts this speech in perspective.

If you want to increase your wealth, especially your wealth relative to competing consumers and investors, bear markets are your friends. After all, a rational descriptive word for "bear market" is sale. Shares, representing fractional ownership of businesses, or bonds, representing a secured or semi-secured priority claim to principal repayment and an interest stream, become, in the aggregate, cheaper. One increases one's wealth by purchasing investments when they are attractively priced and selling them for more than one paid. That is much simpler in bear markets. My two managed partnerships have increased in market value since inception by almost 30 percent compounded annually. The financings we made at the pricing we enjoyed would not have been possible in ebullient times.

STOCK MARKET AND OTHER MARKETS

I'd like to illustrate what should be an obvious point with an apocryphal story. Many of you who have visited my offices out in Carlsbad, California, know that we occupy a small building at one end of a retail strip mall, with a supermarket at the other end. My story involves a husband and wife who come to the center to do some shopping. This is a traditional household, not the politically correct California type, so the husband comes to our brokerage firm to shop for investments while the wife heads in the other direction, on more practical pursuits.

On this particular day, both husband and wife meet with some degree of success. While in the store, she finds a brand of canned salmon that her family is fond of for $2.00 per can, a reasonable price, and she buys a small quantity. The husband buys a micro-cap stock, coincidentally at $2.00 per share. Two weeks later the couple returns to the center and reverts to their familiar pattern. The wife visits the store and is shocked, in fact angered, to discover her family's favorite canned salmon is selling for $3.50 per can. And although she has depleted her previous purchases, she substitutes canned tuna and chicken this week.

The husband, visiting our office, is delighted to discover his stock has risen dramatically to $3.50 per share for no apparent reason. He is ecstatic and liquidates a less active stock position to double up on this fine stock. After another two weeks have past, the couple returns. The wife is very pleased to discover that the highly priced salmon was boycotted by sensible shoppers like her and is now on sale at $1.00 per can. She immediately buys two cases. The husband is disgusted to learn that his favorite micro-cap has slid to $1.00 per share and he liquidates his entire position. He needs to think about how he shops for investments.

A BEAR MARKET IS A CLEARANCE SALE

A bear market is like a gigantic clearance sale where a vast array of financial products—the good, the bad, and the ugly—go on sale. To paraphrase many ads, WHY PAY MORE? Perversely, with financial products, we think we want to pay more. The reason for this apparent lunacy is obvious when we think about it. We forget that stocks represent fractional ownership in business enterprises, deriving their value from the value of the cash stream or potential cash stream of the business. We regard shares more like lottery tickets, pieces of paper whose prices rise and fall at the whim of the market. In fact, both points of view are correct. Shares derive their value from the underlying business, while their price in the short term is created by the mood of the mob. The key to investing success is arbitraging discrepancies between share valuations and share pricing, like our salmon shopper did.

We simply want a lottery ticket going up in price, and it is price that matters to us. Price is easy to determine—look in the paper, go on the Internet, call your broker. Determining value exposes us to all we hate—indecision and WORK. Price information and decisions are emotional, while value calculations are rational. Bear markets redistribute assets from emotional participants to rational participants. Bull markets ultimately redistribute liabilities from the rational to the emotional. Which side of these trades would you prefer? It's up to you.

A gigantic clearance sale, in the form of a bear market, is upon us in my opinion, and I welcome that fact. This sale could be of long duration, meaning if we are rational, opportunities will last, while our fears may be aroused and our patience tested. So what am I putting in my shopping cart? To begin with, the most valuable financial product, one that is always on sale and always underappreciated, is education and information. This audience is to be congratulated for attending this conference. You are investing in knowledge, an asset that can neither be taxed nor stolen.

HOT TIPS

I want to give you five hot tips, right now, that could easily pay for your conference expense. They are by far the most important recommendations I will make at the conference.

1. Go online and subscribe to Bill Bonner's "Daily Reckoning" at www.dailyreckoning.com. It's both free and invaluable. In addition to receiving a wonderful daily collection of insights, the website has excellent archival information, links, and discussion groups.
2. While online visit www.berkshirehathaway.com, where you will find Warren Buffett's letters to shareholders going back to 1977. This is the collected "Magnum Opus" of the world's finest investor. FREE!
3. Also go to www.oid.com, home of *Outstanding Investor Digest*. The archival information here is free, and much of it is very valuable. It is the best site on the web for value investing.

Current subscriptions are not cheap, but invaluable. You can request a complimentary sample online.

4. Go to the conference book store or your local library and get two books: *The Intelligent Investor,* by Ben Graham—in my opinion the most valuable, easily read investment book available—and *Security Analysis,* also by Ben Graham. While not so easily read, it is the best investment book I have ever come across.

5. Give this knowledge to your friends and heirs; it is your most valuable bequest. It is nontaxable and can't be stolen.

Now on to more conventional bear market bargains.

REAL ASSET INCOME

My first bargain category is what I call "Real Asset Income Equities." This asset class consists of businesses operating simple, mundane assets that generate fairly predictable revenue streams and deliver substantial portions of the income stream through to shareholders. Typical examples would be pipelines, terminals, oil fields, developed real estate, ports, airports, and the like.

In the United States, many of these assets are structured in exchange-traded master limited partnerships. These partnerships are nontaxable at the corporate level; they pass through income and tax consequences to the investor. Dividend yields in the 7 to 10 percent level are available, and these yields are often tax deferred by depreciation, amortization, or depletion charges. An 8 percent yield, 70 percent tax deferred, in a simple business that grows at 5 percent a year is a wonderful way to avoid the ravages of a bear market or the idiocy of a bull market.

Canada offers the same general type of security, called Income Trusts. These entities are also designed as tax efficient, "pass-through" entities, where income and tax consequences flow through to the shareholder.

New Zealand also offers this kind of income security, and because of the volatility of that market, astounding bargains can be had in bear market panics.

It is important to note the tax efficiency of these investments. Conventional corporations are taxed at the corporate level and then distribute "surplus cash" by way of dividends, where the shareholders are promptly taxed yet again. These securities generally pass through the income, and tax liabilities, resulting in one layer of taxation. Because of credits for depreciation and the like, some of the distribution is treated as return of capital and is not subject to income tax. These credits are generally deducted from the investor's cost basis in the share and will ultimately be taxed at lower capital gains rates when investments are sold. By deferring the tax consequence, and converting income to capital gains, one simultaneously pays the enemy later and pays them less. In my opinion, this is both intelligent and patriotic.

CLOSELY HELD VALUE

My second bargain category is "Closely Held Value Stocks." Ben Graham and Warren Buffett began their careers and built their early wealth buying unknown, unloved, and under-owned stocks trading primarily on the pink sheets. These are typically "semi-public" companies, nonreporting issuers, with fewer than 500 shareholders. They trade sporadically at best; I often joke that one must make an appointment to make a trade. Because of the difficulty encountered in getting information, and their illiquidity, these stocks are unpopular among institutional investors and brokerage firms. This lack of popular market support can also make them dirt cheap.

How cheap? Ben Graham preferred to buy "net nets." Contrary to current thinking, these "net nets" were the antithesis to Internet stocks. These are profitable companies selling at discounts to their net working capital—or current assets minus all liabilities. Buying profitable companies at a discount to their working capital means that you get their business and any noncurrent assets for free, my favorite price.

This value stock investing is in fact my favorite "growth stock" investing style. Buying companies selling at substantial discounts to intrinsic, as opposed to potential or future, value is what I term "instantaneous growth" or "retroactive growth." All the share price has to do is reflect existent value and I enjoy a substantial profit. This is much safer than predicting prospective growth.

One of my favorite examples of this strategy is a former recommendation of mine at this conference in 1999 and again in 2000. The company, Los Angeles Athletic Club, not surprisingly owns and operates the above-named sporting facility. It also operates the California Marina in Marina Del Rey and a bunch of mini warehouse facilities. When I recommended it here, it also owned an asset that was tough to value, but I felt had value—1,800 acres in Topanga Canyon, above Malibu, California. At the time of my recommendation, the company's market cap was $60,000,000. The company subsequently sold the Topanga property for $44,000,000 and a tax credit, and that cash was rolled over into more mini warehouse facilities on a tax-free basis. The distributions have doubled, the shares have doubled, and the stock is still not unreasonably priced.

Another recommendation from that time, the mundane paint manufacturer Benjamin Moore, was subsequently bought by Warren Buffett's Berkshire Hathaway.

JUNK DEBT IS REALLY GREAT QUALITY

My third favorite bear market sale category is the junk-bond sector. While low-rated debt or unrated debt is *usually* riskier than investment-grade debt, it is invariably safer than the same issuer's equity. Remember, the bondholder must get 100 percent of principal and interest for the shareholder to have any stake in the business. While it is true that in the idiocy of U.S. bankruptcy courts, some minor modifications of this principle occur; it is still a rule to invest by. Junk debt, particularly in out-of-favor or panic-stricken sectors like pipelines, telecom, and power generation, currently can make superb speculations.

An extreme recent example was former telecom high-flyer Nortel. Despite a market cap exceeding C$8 billion and a recent US$1.2 billion equity financing, the company's short-dated, twelve-month debt fell to 52 on the market. Buyers at that rate could get a 15 percent current yield and better than 100 percent yield to maturity before equity holders got anything but bankruptcy. The bonds have since recovered to 85, where they are only a decent, rather than an excellent, buy.

This is indicative of what I believe will become an almost unbelievably lucrative sector in the bear market. Buying short-dated junk debt in enterprises that deliver steady cash flows like local telcos, utilities, and power generators, or fallen angels like cash-rich tech businesses with good equity market caps, will represent excellent speculations this cycle.

Pay attention to the short-dated debt in any out-of-favor—or better yet, panic-stricken—sector you come across. Remember junk debt is better than any equity from the same issuer.

PRIVATE PLACEMENTS

My last, and personally my favorite, category is for accredited investors only. The category is called "PIPE" investing, but doesn't involve anything like pipelines. PIPE is an acronym for "private investments in public equities," which is Wall Street speak for private placements. These are the investments that have enabled my private partnerships to increase in market value since inception by almost 30 percent compounded annually. These rates of return would be unavailable except for the bear-market conditions that have existed and continue to exist in the junior resource exploration sector. But these techniques aren't unique, either to me or to the resource sector. They will work in any out-of-favor sector that the speculator understands.

The technique involves participating in private placements in debt and/or equity in small out-of-favor public companies in need of capital. This contrasts dramatically with the so-called "pre IPO" so popular at this conference at the tail end of the last bull market. In the frothy final phase of the bull market, various hopers, schemers, dreamers, and worse sought to entice the great unwashed with the "opportunity" to invest in nescient start-up enterprises before the filing of an initial public offering, or IPO. Remember two great Wall Street truths: IPO is often an acronym for "It's Probably Overpriced," and most of these start-up "filers" end up filing for bankruptcy, not registration.

PIPE investors provide scarce expansion capital to companies that have already come public but require additional capital to grow their assets or business. PIPE speculators enjoy substantial potential advantages. They often obtain shares in proven or semi-proven enterprises at substantial discounts to the trading market. Any PIPE investor with a pulse should also negotiate for a long-dated, two-year or better warrant. These warrants are the key ingredients in my partnerships' performance because they literally double the potential upside, with no material increase in the risk. In fact, I believe that warrants have served to reduce my equity risks; they have enabled me to preserve a "call" on a speculation even as I took profits or cut losses on a share position.

Ideally, PIPE investing is analogous to finding a football team that has marched the ball 95 yards down the field but is too exhausted to run the ball into the end zone for a touchdown. The PIPE investors provide the necessary energy (cash) and receive points disproportionate to their yards gained.

I'd like to provide an example for illustrative purposes. An issuer at this conference, Vista Gold, suffered mightily through the gold bear market and was, despite management's honest and diligent efforts, out of funds. The management team adopted a safer, more rational gold-oriented strategy but needed more equity to complete the transition. My managed funds and an exhibitor here, Quest Investments, led a PIPE financing, consisting of one share and one full five-year warrant to acquire another share at US$1.50, with the entire unit priced at US$1.02. With the funds received, Vista was able to implement its new strategy, acquire two excellent new assets, and the share price soared almost tenfold before returning to realistic levels. In Quest's case, it bought 1,000,000 units for US$1,025,000, sold 300,000 shares in the market, recovering almost its entire investment, while retaining 700,000 shares currently worth US$1,950,000 and 1,000,000 warrants with an intrinsic value of US$1,250,000, and a Black-Scholes value considerably in excess of that.

Thank you all for your kind attention.

CHAPTER 5

THE TALE OF TAELS—A HARD LESSON IN HARD MONEY

Michael Checkan
Asset Strategies

"Sad to say, greed, laziness, dishonesty, stupidity, and incompetence, combined with a glib manner, are not strangers to the (stock brokerage) industry."

—Doug Casey, investor, writer, and
entrepreneur (1946–)

Michael is president of Asset Strategies International, Inc., a boutique operation working in the areas of precious metals, foreign currencies, and overseas wealth protection. ASI buys and sells precious metals (gold, silver, platinum, and palladium) in coins, bars, and certificates, plus, numismatics for delivery in various parts of the world. Prior to founding ASI with his partner Glen, Michael was senior vice president of the Deak-Perera Group (1967 to 1982); at the time the nation's oldest and largest foreign currency and precious metals investment firm. Earlier,

Michael was one of the first foreign exchange traders in the international department of one of Washington, DC's largest banks.

In March 1997, Michael and the team at Asset Strategies International began creating and developing the Perth Mint Certificate Program (PMCP), one of the most innovative and safe ways to own gold. In addition, Michael and Glen Kirsch are editors of their own newsletter, Information Line (IL), which is sent to tens of thousands of readers throughout the world.

As you will see in a contribution he wrote for this book, it was as a "moneychanger" for Deak-Perera buying gold from Vietnamese refugees where Michael saw firsthand the differences between fiat money, like the U.S. dollar, and hard money, like gold. This is one of the most moving stories I've read about the importance of owning gold, which I've included in hopes it will help you realize that "gold holds its value when nothing else will." More important, through the Perth Mint Certificate Program, which Michael introduces, he shows you one of the "safest, most secure" ways to own gold. As a means to legally hold gold overseas, the Perth Mint Certificate Program is hard to beat.

G old protects wealth. This lesson isn't new. But even I had to learn it the hard way.

Back in 1975, I was a senior officer with the world's oldest and largest dealer in precious metals and foreign currencies, Deak-Perera. I learned this lesson firsthand and it forever taught me about the importance of the "barbaric relic". . . . **gold!**

Deak-Perera was one of the few financial institutions in the United States with a combined expertise in precious metals, foreign currencies, and international banking. As a result of this knowledge, it was invited by the State Department in April 1975 to assist the South Vietnamese refugees who were pouring into the United States as Saigon fell.

Deak-Perera would soon be catapulted into the national limelight. The company became the exclusive "moneychanger" for all five of the Vietnamese refugee camps.

You may recall that, as of January 1, 1975, Americans could once again legally own gold bullion. It had been illegal to own gold since 1933, when President Roosevelt took the United States off the gold standard and ordered that all privately held gold coins and bullion be surrendered to the government.

Unaccustomed as we were to handling displaced persons, it was nonetheless clear that even the most prominent of these refugees would be arriving at the camps with little more than the clothes on their backs and whatever valuables they could carry. And who knew just how valuable some of their belongings would be?

Only one thing was certain: They wouldn't be drawing checks on their local banks. All banks in Vietnam had been taken over by the communists, along with the rest of the economy. At the time, the cruel joke was Vietnam was a true "cash-and-carry economy." If you had the cash, you got to carry off anything you wanted.

A DAY THAT CHANGED MY LIFE

May 1975 found me at Eglin Air Force Base, Florida, one of the five refugee camps. I will never forget my experience with two families in particular. The experience is burned into my mind forever.

A middle-aged Vietnamese man, trim and well-spoken, was wearing what had once been an expensively tailored suit. He obviously cared deeply for his bedraggled family. He had been a businessman in Vietnam. In fact, I was later to learn, he had been a very successful banker. But now all his family's wealth was in the small dingy canvas bag that he was hanging onto for dear life.

Even through all the adversity he and his family had recently experienced, there was still a glimmer of hope in his eyes. Despite losing his job, his home, and his country, he still wore a relieved expression whenever he gazed upon that canvas bag. It was his key to a new life in a new country, quite literally, a golden anchor.

Gently, carefully, he poured the contents of the bag onto the table in front of me. There, gleaming in the sun, was an enormous collection of golden taels. For those of you who are not familiar with taels, they are a form of gold bullion indigenous to South East Asia. Each tael was 1.2 ounces (37.5 grams) of .9999 pure gold. They looked like tiny wafers—thin sheets of gold, delicately wrapped in paper.

It was Deak-Perera's job to buy the gold taels from the refugees, and, with the proceeds, issue traveler's checks.

A LIFETIME OF SAVINGS, NOW WORTHLESS

Further back in line, there was another refugee who was less fortunate than the banker carrying the golden taels. Much like the banker, he was a successful businessman before he and his family were uprooted by war.

He approached my table with two suitcases in hand. Like his countryman with the taels, he had worked very hard, saved extremely well, and carried all his worldly wealth in those satchels.

But there was one major difference. His wealth was in the form of piasters, the currency of the Republic of Vietnam. These were paper promises of a government that no longer existed. I had to tell this man his piasters were worthless. That they would not buy anything—not even a Coke or a pack of cigarettes—in his new country.

Can you imagine toiling and saving for a lifetime for two suitcases filled with worthless paper?

Sad to say, other formerly valuable pieces of paper were now worthless as well. One was the Military Payment Certificates (MPC), issued by the U.S. military. Each one carried the likeness of a famous Hollywood movie star. Now they would not buy admission to a show.

Other items, even valuable diamonds, jade, and loose gems, were hard to exchange on the spot for a fair price. Only gold had an immediate market at a fair price.

Before that day, I always knew that precious metals were an important asset. But, after looking into the eyes of these two men and their families, I knew firsthand the value of gold and other precious metals. Gold holds its value when nothing else will.

IS THE TALE OF TAELS STILL RELEVANT TODAY?

Does gold in 2010 offer the same peace of mind and protection to Americans that it has through 5,000 years of history? Absolutely!

As an American, there are many threats to your hard-earned wealth. The most insidious is not military in nature. It is the weakening of the U.S. dollar.

For the United States, the invoices are piling up. The costs of military conflicts, out-of-control government spending, rising health care costs, and entitlement programs for more and more citizens really add up.

In the past year, these mounting costs exceeded our government's revenue by more than $1.4 trillion. Meanwhile, the Federal Reserve loaned or guaranteed another $2 trillion.

How will this debt ever be repaid? The only politically acceptable solution is to print more money and thus devalue the dollar.

GET READY FOR FIREWORKS IN THE GOLD MARKET

My friend Doug Casey likes to say that the price of gold is not only going to the moon, it's going to several planets beyond.

When this happens . . . when gold prices double from where they are now and continue rising . . . when the dollar falls into the abyss . . . which would you rather own? Which do you think will better protect your life's work?

Would you rather be holding two suitcases full of worthless U.S. paper or a canvas sack full of gold?

I'm going to choose the latter. I hope you will, too.

If you'd like to know about the safest, most secure way I've found to own gold, stick around for a few more minutes.

For more than six millennia, gold has been the safest, most reliable store of value we humans have discovered. Governments can't print more of it. They can't add zeroes to it. And there's always a market for it.

I believe that everyone should have some of the "real stuff" in his or her personal possession. And here at Asset Strategies International (ASI), we'll be glad to help you purchase whatever gold and silver coins and bullion you want. My partner and I have been specialists in that business for more than 30 years.

But in this section, I want to tell you about an exciting way to own larger amounts of precious metals. It's one I helped develop 12 years ago. And it comes with the most rock-solid guarantee you'll find anywhere.

It's called the **Perth Mint Certificate Program (PMCP).** In case you're not familiar with it, the Perth Mint is wholly owned by the government of Western Australia. It has been storing and dealing in precious metals for over a century.

The Perth Mint is the *only* depository operating today that can offer you a comprehensive storage and trading program, with the unconditional written guarantee of one of Australia's wealthiest states. In addition, all precious metals stored at the Perth Mint, including your metals lodged under this program, are insured (at the Perth Mint's cost) by Lloyd's of London.

When we designed this storage program, we wanted to make sure it was SAFE. That is, that it offered **S**ecurity, **A**ffordability, **F**lexibility, and **E**xclusivity. The **Perth Mint Certificate Program** has our highest endorsement on all counts.

Purchasing gold or other precious metals through the **Perth Mint Certificate Program** requires a small account opening investment of $10,000 or more. Sale amounts or additional purchases must be for $5,000 or more. There is no additional cost for unallocated storage; the one-time administrative fee is a very reasonable $50 per certificate.

When you are ready to dispose of some or all of your holdings, the Perth Mint will arrange to purchase them back from you at the then-current market price. Or you can take delivery of your holdings at the Mint or via insured delivery to almost any location in the world.

PART II

INVESTMENT NEWSLETTER WRITERS

"The simplest way to put together a great team is to subscribe to some great newsletters. However, you should get recommendations first, because some recommendations are not so great."

—Michael Maloney, Rich Dad's Advisor,
Guide to Investing in Gold and Silver

A big question that comes to my mind is why are investment newsletter writers becoming so popular? It may not be a recent phenomenon, but it is certainly a growing one. My personal working experience with Wall Street as well as today's economic calamities unfortunately provide an easy answer. Investors don't trust Wall Street!

While traditional Wall Street researchers and analysts can be quite good, they are often ignored by their firm's own brokers and salesmen or worse, pressured to change their opinions to conform to the latest in-house sales efforts, the most recent example being the subprime lending crisis where anyone with a brain should have been able to see what would eventually happen. Rick Rule likes to say that "subprime loans are a result of subprime thinking," the subprime thinking being that a bank would make loans to people who could not afford them and then expect to get paid back. Wall Street's role in this tragedy was to package piles of these subprime loans into individual investments in a process called securitization. Then, to top things off, Wall Street–based

53

rating services like Moody's and Standard & Poor's slapped an investment grade on many of these new financial entities.

Perhaps a tragedy that is just as great is that Wall Street has forgotten "The Golden Rule" whereby brokers recommended that their customers invest at least 10 percent of their net worth in gold! In contrast, as you will see in the following pages, every sage investment newsletter writer chronicled here has been a long-time proponent of holding gold. And while Wall Street analysts and researchers and Washington, DC, insiders say that no one could have foreseen the current economic crisis coming, every sage in this book warned his or her readers. Every one.

With Wall Street either offering bad advice or ignoring their own time-tested advice, is it any wonder that more and more of their clients are turning to nontraditional sources like these newsletter writers for guidance?

Jeffry Gittomer, the *New York Times* best-selling author, says that "trust forms the foundation for everything you do in business, and everything you do in your personal life." He does give caution by saying that "you may trust people's wisdom or knowledge, but not trust the person." Wall Street is all about the latter, what he calls "competency trust." Your typical Wall Street stockbrokers, analysts, and media pundits are all about presenting themselves as competent. In the process they've forgotten personal trust. They've forgotten the "who."

Gittomer goes on to say that "trust is a risk." I think that's true. In my opinion, it's also true you couldn't do much better than subscribing to any one of the investment newsletter writers who have made contributions to this book. Every one of them prides him- or herself on his or her values, especially trust.

- **Doug Casey:** His contribution addresses the important role gold ownership will play in getting you "through the Greater Depression confidently."
- **Bill Bonner:** Beginning with an observation by celestial beings that "humans will probably turn back to gold to protect their wealth," Bill ends with the words of former President George W. Bush, we had to "abandon free market principles to save the free market system."

- **John Pugsley:** A short piece explaining why "clever financial innovation, deceptive sales tactics, and speculative risk-taking" were components of an economic calamity that helped make junior gold mining stocks one of John's "favorite types of resource companies."
- **Richard Maybury:** Starting with the premise that "Bernanke is in charge of a fiat currency" and that "fiat currencies are frauds" and concluding with his view that "we will be very lucky if U.S. officials can get the crisis stopped before gold hits $5,000."
- **David Galland:** An entertaining piece that will educate you about many facets of gold investing including: gold, silver, gold mining shares, gold exploration companies, and what affects the price of gold.
- **Addison Wiggin:** Explains why "after decades of dormancy, gold is back" and quickly moves on to explore many, many actionable ideas for you to invest in and own gold.
- **Pamela and Mary Anne Aden:** With a quick historical look that weaves its way through past financial crises to today's "massive historical bailout" where "the dollar has lost about 95 percent of its purchasing power," it's easy to understand why the Aden sisters talk about a possible "upside target" for gold of $5,800.

CHAPTER 6

THE GREATER DEPRESSION

Doug Casey
Casey Research

"Money is the barometer of a society's virtue."

—Ayn Rand, philosopher and
novelist (1905–1982)

Doug Casey is the founder and chairman of Casey Research, a provider of subscription-based financial analysis in operation for over 25 years. As well as being a personal friend, he is also a highly respected best-selling author, publisher, and professional investor. What I admire most about him is his directness in confronting irrational thinking. He is a philosopher in many ways, a follower of both classical and Austrian economics, an ardent supporter of freedom and liberty, and a student of life. Having lived in 10 countries and visited over 175 during his 40-year investment career, his has been quite a life.

His many cross-cultural experiences as well as his thinking that "agricultural soft commodities are again very cheap" are obviously what interested him in investing in my shellfish company. As you will see in

---

Originally published in *The Casey Report*, January 5, 2009, as "The Greater Depression: Part 2."

his contribution, he believes that the only other investment worth considering would be gold, noting that "over the medium to longer term, your savings should shift exclusively to gold."

While Doug barely addresses gold in a specific way, his entire economic analysis has everything to do with the reasons why gold is one of the very few investments our sages favor. All of the many shortcomings of the U.S. economy he cites do come across as wake-up call if not a slap in the face, unfortunately, they are quite accurate. As you will see, given the massive amount of government intervention and corresponding debt now accruing within the United States, "gold is the only financial asset that's not simultaneously somebody else's liability."

In our November edition, I covered why and how the Greater Depression came upon us. This month, let's talk about what conditions will be like and about how you can get through the Greater Depression confidently, comfortably, and profitably.

I'm of the opinion that what's happening now isn't just another cyclical downturn that can be papered over by printing up some more money—although that's exactly what the U.S. and other governments are doing, and in unprecedented amounts. In fact, what the world's governments are doing is not only wrong, it's exactly the opposite of what they should be doing.

Barring the start of another world war—which is not unlikely—the physical world probably won't be changed much by the Greater Depression, but the way people relate to the world will change a great deal.

For roughly a whole generation, the U.S. government's inflation of its currency has been inviting the whole country to live beyond its means. Living beyond your means is what consumer debt is all about. Mortgage debt is where it started, and it allowed people to live in houses much bigger than they could afford. In the Greater Depression now upon us, many people won't be able to pay the mortgage. In fact, they won't even be able to pay the utilities and the taxes; maintenance will be deferred indefinitely. But that's just the tip of a very big iceberg.

Detroit is illustrative. The city is toast, no matter how many billions the government throws at it. During the last serious downturn, from 1980 to 1982, the average car on the road was seven years old.

And they were all crappy cars. Today the American fleet is not only close to brand new, but today's cars last almost forever. So they're not going to need to be replaced for a long time, meaning auto sales are going to be in the tank for a long time. Also, in the same way that many can't afford to pay their mortgages, many will be learning that they can't afford to own a car.

Total outstanding automobile loans in the country come to about $177 billion, and many of the vehicles are going to be abandoned in the lender's parking lot. To give you some sense of the thing, delinquent loans at a single credit union in Florida have increased 159 percent over the last year, to $4.3 million . . . of which roughly 60 percent is related to cars. Then, of course, there are all the loans outstanding to car dealers, some for now-depressed real estate, and some for unsold and unsalable inventory.

As late as the 1960s, most people paid cash for a car. Even in the 1970s, a loan was usually for no more than two years. Now the standard auto loan is for five years and many cars are leased, out of necessity. The average family may now have several expensive new cars in the drive-way, but typically with negative equity in every one of them. Cars have gone from being a minor financial asset to a major financial liability.

The big default snowball won't stop there; it will pick up all manner of debt as it rolls along. For instance, everybody thinks he has to go to college, generally wasting four years grazing at the claptrap smorgasbord tended by liberal-arts profs. But with the cost now running $20,000 to $40,000 per year, there are lots ($85 billion) of student loans out. They'll mostly be defaulted on when English majors find there's little market for their opinions on social engineering.

Credit card debt will likely be the last crisis. Even with $950 billion out at 18 percent, people won't default until the last minute, simply because they have no further source of funds. $2.23 trillion of state and city debt represented by muni bonds is at serious risk because these folks can't print dollars. And their receipts from income, sales, property, and every other kind of tax are going to plummet. At exactly the same time the demands from citizens skyrocket.

The $10 trillion—maybe it's really $15 trillion now—of debt that the government acknowledges it owes is actually dwarfed by another $50 trillion of net liabilities for Social Security, Medicare, and such. A large chunk of the debt that's acknowledged by the issuance of

T-bills is held by those nice foreigners who for years sent us Sonys and Mercedes in exchange for paper. That's going to stop.

If there's a way "they" can get "us" out of this mess without totally radical surgery, I simply don't see it.

WHAT HAPPENED REDUX

The problem is that for quite a while now, the United States and much of the Western world have been consuming more than they produce. It's much as though you borrowed a million dollars for consumption. You'd enjoy an artificially high standard of living . . . for a while. But when the time came to pay it back, with interest, you'd suffer a very real drop in your standard of living for a very long period.

The enjoyable part of that process is more or less what the average American has been doing for years and is now about to stop doing. But ruinous spending is even more serious in the case of government. It's a rare American who understands that government debt will eventually reach into his wallet, because in a complex economy there can be so much delay between cause and effect. So let's simplify the matter and look at a two-man economy: a peasant and his king.

Let's say the peasant produces three tons of food per year. He gives the king one for taxes (after all, kings have to eat, too), consumes one himself, and keeps the last third for seed for next year. The king would like more, but—barring a breakthrough in production technology— there simply is no more grain to be had.

Perhaps financial technology can provide an answer.

And so, after consultation with an economic soothsayer, the king offers the peasant a great deal. Lend the extra ton of seed grain to the king, who will pay it back next year, in time for planting, and with interest. The peasant buys in. But when he comes back to redeem his scrip and the king tells him that the grain was used for something that seemed like a good idea at the time, it's obvious they both have a problem. Everyone might starve next year.

This is the problem with government debt in particular. People tend to rely on it as a piece of the cosmic firmament, something with real value. But is the U.S. government essentially different from that of Zimbabwe? The answer is no.

One of the most serious problems of the next era is that it's very likely that society will believe that what passed for a free market over the last almost three decades has been discredited. Reagan, Thatcher, and many other politicians around the world delivered fairly significant tax cuts, privatizations, and some deregulation. These things, coming off a very severe recession of the early 1980s, resulted in what Herman Kahn correctly predicted would be "The Long Boom." But the boom is now over, definitively. The question is what's next.

It's interesting how the world's social mood seems to change almost in lockstep, at least at major turning points. The 1930s and 1940s were a horrible time, dominated by statism and represented by characters like Mussolini, Hitler, Stalin, Roosevelt, Peron, Mao, and Franco. The 1960s were the era of hippies. There were race riots all over the United States and student revolts all over the world—the United States, Europe, and China. The 1980s and 1990s were the era of the yuppie and his motto: "He who dies with the most toys wins." It was an era of good times and conspicuous consumption—a bit like the Roaring Twenties.

I suspect the next era will have a lot of anger. A lot of blame. Some real poverty. A good measure of violence. It's not going to be a mellow time, particularly in North America and Europe—nor in China.

But let's focus on the United States, the current epicenter.

BANKRUPTCY ON SEVERAL LEVELS

The fact is that not only the U.S. government but U.S. society itself is economically bankrupt. But, unfortunately, the situation is much more serious than economic bankruptcy.

It's very rare that anyone goes bankrupt because of one bad decision. It takes many bad decisions, a consistent pattern, and that's only possible if you have the wrong moral philosophy. America's moral philosophy has degenerated to the extent that Americans think it's okay to invade other countries that haven't attacked us. I'm not talking just about Iraq and Afghanistan, pitiful nonentities on the other side of the world. It started earlier, with even weaker prey, like Granada, Panama, Haiti, and the Dominican Republic. And, of course, Vietnam.

Moral bankruptcy started with an overt government policy of inflating the currency, which constitutes a fraud, and running up the national debt, which is an obvious swindle because it will never be repaid, as absolutely everyone knows. It started with the belief that an income tax was needed to level out incomes, which predictably did just the opposite. *Boobus americanus* thoroughly approved of all this and so much more.

So, almost always, economic bankruptcy is preceded by moral bankruptcy. And it's accompanied by intellectual bankruptcy, in this case the philosophical acceptance of economic collectivism and political statism. The exact description of the situation is fascism—which, contrary to the History Channel, has essentially nothing to do with police jackboots, bizarre racial theories, or militarism. A fascist is simply one who believes in nominal private ownership of both the means of production and consumer goods—but strong state control over both. The word derives from the Latin *fasces*, a group of rods bound together around an ax. The bound rods offer strength, the ax destructive power. It's an image that appeals to the type of people who like to control others. It wouldn't have had any appeal to the founders of America, who for a while fought under a flag that showed a rattlesnake and the warning "Don't Tread on Me."

What made America different was its foundation on a philosophy of freedom. That word has been so corrupted and leached of meaning— another sign of intellectual bankruptcy—that Bush was able to use it two dozen times in some early speeches without being laughed off the stage or targeted with rotten vegetables (or shoes). Perversely but predictably, Bush is today being represented as a free marketer, which is as much of a lie as saying the same about Hoover.

America is now economically, morally, and intellectually bankrupt. The country has wandered so far from its founding principles that it is now no different from any of the other 200 nation-states that have spread across the face of the earth like a skin disease. The United States no longer stands for anything; it's now just another piece of geography. Forget about "America"; it no longer exists. It's been replaced by "The United States"—not even "These United States," a concept that was interred by the unpleasantness of 1861–1865. As evidence, I offer you the current state of affairs.

Bankruptcy is a factual matter. Failing to declare bankruptcy when it has happened only adds to the problem. Germany and Japan were totally and absolutely bankrupt—economically, morally, and intellectually—in 1945. Following the war, should they have tried to continue with their old currencies, policies, ideas, and institutions (that is, if the Allies had allowed them to)? In a word, no. They had reached the point where the slate needed to be wiped clean, which it was. Then, within a generation, they went from being bombed-out wrecks to two of the most prosperous economies on earth.

Acknowledging bankruptcy is the first step for moving beyond it. Denying bankruptcy when it is a fact only prolongs and worsens the fact.

One obvious consequence of these layers of bankruptcy is an increasing reliance on government. It seems like a cornucopia to the average person, despite the fact that cheese distributions to the poor some years back are among the few tangible benefits it has delivered. Since the government produces nothing, anything it even *seems* to provide is at the direct expense of somebody else. This simple fact evades almost everyone, from the most ignorant voter up to the most powerful officials, like Bernanke and Paulson.

Government produces nothing but wars, pogroms, confiscations, taxes, inflation, and regulation, but people still, idiotically, look to it for salvation—even though it's the exact cause of their worst problems.

This is why I've long held that the average person is not as bright as you might hope. Once you get beyond discussing the weather, the state of the roads, TV programs, and sports, there's often no one home. And that's the average person. But by definition, 50 percent of the population is less than average. And they all vote. It's not hard to figure how they'll vote, in that an estimated 47 percent of Americans over 18 don't pay income taxes. I admit to being somewhat removed from life among these people, but it's hard to see how they can even live on so little money. Maybe they're smarter than I think. But then, people are tolerably competent at running their own lives; the problem arises when they try to run everyone else's, too. The problem arises when they become politically active.

It would appear they elected Bush, twice, during the boom, because a boom—like a bull market—makes everyone think he's a genius. The average guy initially liked Bush because he sensed he was a moron, and it was easy to feel superior to him. The problem was the average guy was right about Bush being a moron (which, incidentally, is a clinical term, not just a pejorative). But only an imbecile (another clinical term, referring to a person even less intelligent than a moron) would trust a moron to control the fate of a country. Now they all look like idiots (which is your classification if you don't quite make the grade as an imbecile).

One of the reasons OBAMA! (tip of the hat to my friend Porter Stansberry for the punctuation) won the election is that he's clearly a highly intelligent man—much smarter than McCain and, even more important, much more stable.

But OBAMA!, like almost all politicians, is a genius only at manipulating people—not a genius at dealing with material reality. It's a near certainty that, facing the Greater Depression, he's going to come up with something like the Newer Deal. That's because *Boobus americanus* desperately wants the government—which he thinks is a magical entity that can do anything and solve every problem—to Do Something. And it will. But it won't merely fail to do the right things, it is going to do the opposite of the right things.

WHAT SHOULD THE GOVERNMENT DO?

It's hard to have a conversation today, or even overhear one, without being exposed to moronic—and I now use that word in its colloquial as well as its clinical sense—opinions about what "we" should do. "We," of course, is the government. I promise you that 99 out of 100 sound like Thomas Friedman, who is at once America's most famous, most wrong-headed, most vacuous, and most pompous columnist/ busybody. Friedman, over the years, has been rarely right but never in doubt. He says what's needed is:

> . . . a massive stimulus program to improve infrastructure and create jobs, a broad-based homeowner initiative to limit foreclosures and stabilize housing prices, and therefore mortgage assets, more capital for bank balance sheets, and most importantly, a huge injection of optimism and confidence . . .

Who could possibly be against improving infrastructure and creating jobs, not to mention optimism and confidence? But why deal in half-measures? Buy everyone a new Cadillac to get Detroit back to work, a new house to stimulate that failing industry, and a $10,000 check that must be deposited at Citibank and spent at The Gap.

A plan like that certainly sounds like more fun than what I propose. But I'm afraid Americans are going to be a bit short on fun over the next little while. They used it all up over the last generation.

Here is what needs to happen if the depression is to be as brief and as therapeutic as possible.

1. **Allow collapse of bankrupt entities:** This obviously includes Fannie, Freddie, AIG, and numerous banks. They are structured uneconomically (as their bankruptcy has proven), their managements are overpaid and are proven incompetents. The bailout money that's gone into them already is simply wasted. The same for Detroit.

   But that's not nearly enough. At this point, it would be a half-measure. Perhaps only a 3-foot rope over a 12-foot gap.

   If you allow the collapse of these (and many, many more yet to come) enterprises without changing the conditions that created the problem, recovery is going to be even harder. So . . .

2. **Deregulate:** Contrary to what almost everyone thinks, the main purpose of regulation is not to protect consumers but to entrench the current order. Regulation prevents new institutions from arising quickly and cheaply. Does the Department of Agriculture really need 114,000 employees to regulate fewer than two million farms in the United States? Has the Department of Energy, whose mandate when it was created in 1977 was to ensure the availability and low cost of fuels, done anything of value with its 116,000 employees and contractors and $24 billion annual budget? How about the terminally corrupt Bureau of Indian Affairs, which has outlived whatever usefulness it might have had by 100 years. The FTC, SEC, FCC, FAA, DOT, HHS, HUD, Labor, Commerce, and scores of others serve no useful public purpose. Eliminate them and the entire economy would blossom—except for the parasitical lobbying and legal trades.

3. **Abolish the Fed:** This is the actual engine of inflation. Money is just a medium of exchange and a store of value; you don't need a central bank to have money. What would we use as money? It doesn't matter, as long as it's a commodity. But gold is the obvious choice, for reasons detailed here so often.

   The whole idea of a central bank is a swindle. The recent bailouts couldn't and wouldn't have been done without it.

4. **Cut taxes 50 percent to start:** The economy would boom. The money won't be needed with all the agencies gone. Certainly not if the next two points are followed.

5. **Default on the national debt:** I realize this is a shocker, unless you recall that the debt will never be paid anyway. And why should the next several generations have to pay for the stupidity of their parents? Governments default all the time. The only people who get hurt are those who lent money to an institution that can only repay them by stealing money from others. They should be punished. In fiscal 2008, interest on the debt is $412 billion, with interest rates at all-time lows. Rates will eventually go back to at least the 20 percent area. On a debt of, say, $15 trillion, that will add up to around $3 trillion a year—or more than total federal spending in 2007. It's inevitable. But is it sustainable? I think not.

   It's better to make a statement. Default on it.

6. **Disentangle and disengage:** The entanglements the United States needs to escape prominently include the UN and NATO. The U.S. combat troops now in over 100 foreign countries can come home. They're not "defending" anything, except for some local collaborators like Maliki and Karzai, and are just picking up bad habits and antagonizing the locals. The United States spends more money on the military than every other country in the world put together. Since the government is bankrupt, spending nearly a trillion dollars a year on the military and its sport wars significantly adds to the economy's problems.

But the chances of any of these things happening are slim to none. And Slim's out of town.

So let's look at what will actually happen.

WHAT THE GOVERNMENT WILL ACTUALLY DO

Here is what the government will actually do:

1. **Let enterprises collapse?** No way. You're already seeing the response. Every corrupt and failed institution, instead of being

allowed to turn into compost to be recycled by the economic worms into fertilizer for a new generation of businesses, is going to be propped up like a zombie. They'll continue doing the same stupid things that got the country into the current mess.

The wave of collapses is going to get much worse. Lots more banks will fail, so the FDIC will need hundreds of billions more in funding. They'll try bailing out everything, starting with the auto companies. Who knows where they'll stop? Home-builders are lining up. Can't let commercial property developers fail, because it would put that much more pressure on the banks.

I play poker. Sometimes you see a player undergo a temporary psychotic break. They'll make totally irrational, wild, stupid bets in a desperate attempt to get out even. It's called going on tilt. The U.S. government, as an enterprise, is now on tilt.

2. **Deregulate?** No, that's out of the question. Everyone is convinced it was a lack of regulation that got the country into this mess. And so, with the approval of the public, the government will set up lots of new agencies, likely starting with a new Civilian Conservation Corps. The 50,000 degraded beings who crawled out of the woodwork to work for the TSA will be the model. The 50,000 paper shufflers who were just fired from Citigroup would love to have steady jobs with, say, the IRS. I just hope one of the new organizations doesn't have a black uniform with silver flashings. Of course the largest agency of the U.S. government is now Homeland Security, so anything is possible.

3. **Abolish the Fed?** Despite having been swiftly debauched, with its assets transformed in a matter of months from almost 100 percent Treasuries to mostly defaulted mortgages, it will become more important than ever. Otherwise, the U.S. government will only be able to borrow funds from foreigners—which will become increasingly difficult, even at ever-higher interest rates. Multi-trillion-dollar deficits will become the norm, and a central bank is needed to fund them.

4. **Cut taxes?** No, taxes on the rich—or those the government decides belong in that category, people like you—are going through the roof. It's well known that Hoover, who, like Bush, is somehow painted as a free-marketer, exacerbated the

last depression by raising marginal rates from 25 to 63 percent in 1932. But with 12-figure deficits for the indefinite future, taxes will rise. Initially, it is likely to be on politically incorrect things, like tobacco, alcohol, guns, oil, coal, and luxuries . . . but that will just be for starters. I bet they'll put taxes on imports, justifying it by saying it will not only generate revenue but save U.S. jobs. Smoot-Hawley, the Hoover innovation that sealed the fate of the economy in the 1930s, could ride again.

Along with this, we'll likely see foreign exchange controls, I would guess in the form of a tax on spending and investing abroad. The rationale will be the same: It generates revenue, it keeps capital (and jobs) in the United States. But better yet, it only affects the rich (who else can afford to do things abroad?) and the unpatriotic (who else would even dream of doing anything abroad during a crisis like this?). Since the Interest Equalization Tax is still on the books—it's just at 0 percent— I suspect this one is a slam dunk.

5. **Default on the national debt?** Actually, this will happen. But only through inflation.

6. **Disengage?** No way. War is the health of the state. Like almost nothing else, it gets people to pull together, even if the boat's going to hell. The United States has a huge, bloated military machine that, if not used, will just rust away. So of course they'll use it. It's like owning a giant hammer: After a while, everything starts to look like a nail. OBAMA!'s many otherwise pacifist supporters are completely on board with his promise to shift U.S. forces from the tar pit of Iraq to the even stickier tar pit of Afghanistan. But they'll likely be disappointed by how very slowly he leaves Iraq. And how much bigger and grimmer the war in Afghanistan becomes. And how quickly the next war in the "national interest"—Saudi? Syria? Chad? Somalia? Pakistan? Fuhgedabouditstan?—could arise.

GOOD NEWS?

So the prognosis is not good. If we moved rapidly and radically toward a free-market society, we'd still have a depression—the distortions and misallocations of capital are massive and would still have to be liquidated—but although the correction would be sharp, it would also be short.

My guess is that OBAMA! won't radically change the way the government works. He'll just radically increase its size and scope. He's already surrounded himself with a crew of longtime Beltway insiders. They're not going to overthrow the private property system. Just tax and regulate it much more. But that doesn't mean this thing isn't going to be really ugly; in fact, it's going to be a nightmare. It's not just going to be bad. It's going to be worse than even I think it's going to be.

As serious as the financial problems are going to be over the years to come, adequate attention hasn't been focused on potential social problems in the United States. Don't forget that during the last depression, there was little consumer debt (people actually bought things they didn't have the money for on "lay-away" plans, if anybody remembers those). Almost everybody had some savings, as opposed to a lot of debt. People were much closer to the farm, and most actually knew how to plant a garden. Families tended to be geographically closer and more mutually supportive—a function that's been usurped by things like welfare, Medicaid, Medicare, Social Security, and such, which have given people a false sense of security. Labor was much less productive, but the average monthly "nut" was much lower, not just in absolute but in relative terms. If you lost your job, you went out to get another, at some wage, any wage. Society was vastly less regulated in those days, so it was much easier.

It's a good question what millions of people who lose their jobs now are going to do, especially if they're stuck in a suburb or exurb, surrounded by many thousands of others like themselves. Could the natives get restless? Actually, it would be a surprise if they didn't.

But there's always some good news. For one thing, I'd like to think it's unlikely the government will go for national health care, simply because even they can now see it's unaffordable. But perhaps that's just the incorrigible optimist in me getting out of control; maybe national health care is the first thing they'll do, simply because the army of unemployed voters will demand it.

It's important to remember that Roosevelt, who the urban myths say brought the country out of the last depression, had the good luck to be inaugurated dead flat at the bottom, in 1933. Even if he had been as stupid as Bush, Bernanke, Paulson, et al., things would likely have gotten better for several years from that point, strictly on a cyclical basis. He had good luck. Even though things were heading steeply downhill again by the 1938 election, his charm and rhetorical skills put him back in office.

OBAMA!, on the other hand, is coming in not at the end but at the very beginning of a downturn that is much more serious. So, unless he starts another war that's both big and popular, there's a good chance he'll be a one-term president.

So that may be some good news, depending on how bad he is and how bad the next guy may be. But the best news is that I believe it's possible to make a lot of money in the next few years. There's certainly enough that's going to be created . . .

WHAT SHOULD YOU DO?

The first thing to do in a crisis is to assess your risk. You need to dodge two hazards: investment risk and political risk.

A broad overview:

Stocks: The pundits, as well as many competent analysts, are saying that some stocks are at once-in-a-lifetime bargain levels. That may be true. A quick scan of dividend yields now shows many companies over 5 percent, a fair number around 10 percent, and some outliers at 15 percent or more.

But at major market bottoms, the *average* yield should be 6 to 8 percent. And that's after there have been lots of cuts. The DJIA yielded 13 percent at the bottom in 1933. I look at yields much more than earnings or book value, because those two things can be distorted much more by inflation and can be doctored by accounting practices. Yields (supplemented by stock buybacks) are a much better indicator of reality.

Now that stocks are off close to 50 percent, I think it's time to get interested. They're not off close to 90 percent, as was the case in 1933. And this bear market hasn't really been with us very long, either. But there's a wave of funny money coming, and lots of it is going to find its way into equities.

My view is that the economic situation is going to get much worse, and for a considerable time. But that only has an indirect effect on the direction of stock prices.

The proper approach for a speculator is only to act if you feel the odds are heavily in your favor and if you're right, you have a possibility of making a multiple on your money. You have to wait for what seem like super opportunities simply because we're all wrong from time to time. The overall market just doesn't seem, to me, to be there yet.

Stay tuned.

Real estate: In last month's edition, Andy Miller provided his insider's perspective on how far we are from the bottom. In my opinion, it won't happen until we see a lot of tax sales. On that topic, check out the number of foreclosures in process in Wayne County, Michigan. You won't believe it. But I expect to see that in many other places, especially as more people lose their jobs.

There's no hurry to buy property in Europe or North America. Especially in the United States, where there's been huge over-building that will take years to draw down. The situation is worsened by an abundance of properties of the noneconomic variety, houses that are too big and/or in places that people can't afford to get to anymore. Ghost towns will likely appear.

On the other hand, if you're sure it's a bargain and you can get a long-term, fixed-rate mortgage, you'll do fine as the mortgage gets inflated away. Just remember, a house isn't an investment; it's a long-lived consumer good.

Bonds: This is the last bubble. And likely the biggest. Since the bond market is a multiple of the stock market in size, a meltdown here will be even more traumatizing. Around today's levels, interest rates are on a one-way street up. Bonds are a triple threat to investor capital: Interest rate risk. Credit risk. Currency risk. And, of course, the arrival of high interest rates should put the final nail in the coffin for stocks and real estate.

The good news is that high rates will help complete the economy's deleveraging. And, very, very important, they will turn

Americans back into savers. That, not consumption and artificially low interest rates, is what's needed for recovery.

As a speculative opportunity or just an intelligent hedge, being short anything that's hurt by higher interest rates should be at the top of your list. Shorting long-term Treasuries now, while they're yielding about 2.5 percent, is as good a bet as shorting Internet stocks in 1999 (see the *International Speculator* edition of February 1999).

Agriculture: Soft commodities are again very cheap. You should consider buying futures contracts on them, across the board.

Energy: Those of you who receive our *Casey Energy Opportunities* know our feelings on this. But, at current levels under $40, my sense is that oil is a better buy than it was in the 20s, ten years ago. Uranium and uranium stocks are again very cheap. This is an area worthy of your attention, study, and capital now.

Gold: The only financial asset that's not simultaneously somebody else's liability. While in the short run, cash and gold are both kings, over the medium to longer term, your savings should shift exclusively into gold. Lots of physical coins close to hand, using a reputable storage program if your holdings are significant. I've always been partial to goldmoney.com for many reasons, including low costs and the ability to transfer funds anywhere. But I'm biased, since I'm a small shareholder, as is Casey Research. And I've always liked Jim Turk, who founded it and runs it.

Gold has been a good place to be but hasn't performed nearly as well as I think it should have, especially now. Is it possible the Bilderbergers, or the CFR, or the Trilateralists, or whoever are suppressing it? You'd think they'd have their hands full elsewhere just at the moment. But who knows? I don't know and don't really care. I just know I want a much bigger position in the stuff, a sentiment apparently shared by people all over the world, if you credit the reports of widespread shortages.

Even so, before this is over, gold isn't just going through the roof. It's going to the moon.

Gold stocks—I must own up to a mistake, which is clearly the case with the timing on gold shares. My guess that the next stage after the Wall of Worry would be the Mania was obviously wrong. Gold stocks went off a cliff and at breathtaking speed.

WHAT WENT WRONG?

Rick Rule and I talked about it in New Orleans recently. The over-heated character of the market was disguised by three things that only became clear in hindsight.

One, share prices never got really high, as in past bull markets, simply because the number of shares expanded so rapidly. After the devastating drought from 1996–2001, companies overfinanced. Market caps rose—but it seemed justified. So the number of new companies and the number of new shares they issued disguised what had previously been reflected in high share prices.

Two, the public never seemed to get directly involved. But, actually, they were involved, in the form of a trillion dollars in hedge funds that took money from everybody. The broad public wasn't investing individually; it was aggregated.

Three, the costs of mining have risen about as fast as gold itself. Meaning, margins went nowhere. Which made the stocks shaky.

Anyway, a costly mistake. But the good news is that the companies we monitor are solid, well managed, and full of cash. I expect a new bull market. I'm a buyer. There will definitely be an insane mania in these stocks the way things are going. Hopefully not famous last words. . . .

POLITICAL RISK?

This bears repeating to no end. And you should hear it from our friends Fitz and Simon at *Without Borders* as well. Political risk is now far higher than investment risk. Your government considers you a national resource to be exploited. If you don't get your money out of the country before the government gets your money out of you, you're an idiot, and you're going to get what you deserve. The chances of capital controls, of some description, are extremely high.

I'm spending over half the year in Argentina now, because it's very nice, very cheap, and out of harm's way. (See www.laestanciadecafayate .com for a glimpse of my preferred corner of the country.) The Argentines have been through this kind of thing before, and there's some reason to believe they're actually going to turn a corner. In any case, an intelligent foreign property diversification, somewhere, should be very high on your list.

Let me end on a positive note. The situation is hopeless, but it's not serious. It's part of the human condition. People have been contending with far worse for many thousands of years. Look at the developing chaos in the light of the Chinese symbol for "crisis," which combines the symbol for danger with the symbol for opportunity. Keep your eyes open and you should be able at least to stay out of the way of the worst that's to come. And in time, you will look back at what's going on now as an interesting, even entertaining, experience.

CHAPTER 7

BET AGAINST A FALSE PREMISE

Bill Bonner
Agora Publishing

"There can be no other criterion, no other standard than gold. Yes, gold which can be shaped into ingots, bars, coins, which has no nationality and which is eternally and universally accepted as the unalterable fiduciary value par excellence."

— Charles De Gaulle, French general
and statesman (1890–1970)

Bill Bonner is the founder and president of Agora Publishing, one of the world's most successful consumer newsletter publishing companies. He authors the free daily email newsletter, The Daily Reckoning. *He is also a best-selling author, having co-written* Financial Reckoning Day *and* Empire of Debt *with Addison Wiggin. The Daily* Reckoning *weaves information about the financial world, investing, and everyday life into an educational and entertaining format. Along with*

This chapter consists of two articles that were written by Bill Bonner for *The Daily Reckoning*. "Bet against a False Premise . . . Buy Gold" was originally published on Tuesday, January 6, 2009, while Bill was in London, England. The second article, "Said the Joker to the Thief," was originally published in *The Daily Reckoning* on Friday, January 9, 2009, while Bill was in Paris, France.

500,000 other subscribers, I often begin my day reading it, something I've been doing for almost 10 years now. Bill's personal stories and wit have made his letter the most successful in the business. It is his investment advice and economic analysis, though, that readers find so valuable.

Bill's pieces penned below support one of his most strongly held investment theories: There are times when you should own even more gold than you normally do. By Bill's reckoning, an investor really only needs to pick the right investment theme every 10 or 20 years or so to realize above-average returns. In the 1970s the theme was gold; in the 1980s and 1990s, you could have made money on almost any stock. In 2000 Bill was very open about his belief that gold should be a core part of one's portfolio. He still thinks gold has ten more years during which it will rise in value.

Each issue of The Daily Reckoning *contains two parts. The first part is usually a summary of the previous day's economic and investment activity. It's followed by an essay, sometimes by a guest, often by Bill. The two parts below are from different days, but because they fit so well together I've combined them in support of my premise that "who" investors rely on to purchase gold is as important as actually owning gold. Like the sages in* The Golden Rule, *in the first part Bill advocates holding gold as a form of wealth insurance, pointing out that "over a long, long time gold has been extremely reliable." In the second part, Bill gives an astounding account of some of the worst forecasting made in 2008, where "the thieves had been blown up by their own debt bombs, and the jokers were in control of most of America's major industries," thereby providing convincing evidence of why Wall Street can't be trusted today.*

Captain's Log: Year of our Lord 2009, 6th day.

We have landed on a strange and wonderful watery planet—the third planet in orbit around the sun, a minor star in the Milky Way galaxy. Well, they say it is a watery planet. Where we are, it is icy. But the locals say it warms up and the ice melts. We're suspicious; maybe it's just hype to attract tourists.

But what is strange about this planet is that its inhabitants all seem to play a game of make-believe, in which they all agree to believe things that every one of them knows is untrue. What is wonderful about it is that it seems so easy to make money here; there's a fool on every corner just waiting for the chance to get rid of his wealth.

Recently, humans—the race that inhabits this place—believed that their lodges and living quarters would become more and more valuable—even though it was obvious that their houses deteriorated every day as a consequence of solar radiation, wind erosion, liquor spilt on the carpets, and other natural phenomena. Then, on the back of this remarkable delusion, they built an entire world economy including extravagantly complex financial instruments that the wisest among them called "weapons of mass financial destruction."

Someone seems to have cut the power to that illusion a few months ago, so now they are taking up a new one: that if people are given more pieces of green paper they will all be richer.

Yesterday, the Dow—which measures stock prices in the United States—fell 81 points. But analysts say the technical indicators are still almost all positive; they think the United States is beginning a major rally . . . or perhaps a new bull market.

The auto industry, meanwhile, reported terrible news. Sales fell 36 percent in December; GM sold fewer vehicles than in any December in 49 years.

Oil rose $2 yesterday; amid all the gloom and doom, the oil price is moving up to nearly $50. Bond yields are rising, too, along with the dollar. And gold fell $4 yesterday—for no particular reason.

Today's press—the means by which delusions are shared and propagated—tells us that the government of this world's richest nation, called the United States of America, is planning a "stimulus package" of something on the order of $1 trillion. What's the package expected to stimulate? The idea is to get more of these pieces of paper into citizens' hands, so that they will be encouraged to act as though they were wealthier. It doesn't seem to bother anyone that the source of the misery of which so many now complain was the fact that, in the past, so many acted so much wealthier than they really were. Nor does it seem to disturb the collective fantasy that this stimulus plan is being created, more or less, by the same class of people who neither saw anything wrong with the last fantasy nor mentioned to anyone that it was going to collapse.

"Hopes pinned on rate cuts and fiscal packages," says the headline in the *Financial Times,* a leading source of financial hallucination.

It explains how the aforementioned U.S. government intends to cut taxes in order to put those aforementioned pieces of green paper into consumers' hands.

Further in the paper, another headline—"Reports of $300 billion Obama tax cuts lift mood"—tells us that the public is getting in the spirit of the new fantasy even before it is officially launched.

"Optimism about central bank and government efforts to revive the global economy helped improve investor risk appetite yesterday," continues the article.

"Fed Officials Endorse Big Stimulus to Battle US Recession," adds another source—*Bloomberg*.

What a marvelous place! Every day is magic on this planet. Every day is a new day . . . with no memory of what happened the day before . . . nor any thought to what will happen tomorrow. People are ready to believe whatever makes their day more enjoyable . . . no matter how absurd.

Anyone who bothered to think about this "bailout" plan for two seconds could see that it is a hoax and a scam. Those pieces of paper are not really wealth, they merely represent wealth. But since the U.S. government has no wealth in reserve—indeed, it is famously borrowing to make ends meet already—it can only pass out wealth to one person by taking it from someone else. It talks of "tax cuts," but we have heard nothing of spending cuts. So, what the global consequence must be is an increase in pieces of green paper—or let us say, demand for wealth—with no actual increase in wealth itself. It is just a shared illusion, in other words.

But we have to say, too, after visiting this planet for a few weeks, we have fallen in love with it. We feel so superior. Almost everyone we talk to is a dope.

Besides, where else in the universe is it so easy to make money? As you know, dear reader, the easiest way to make above-market profits is to help the fools part company with their money. What other planet has so many fools?

We paraphrase one of the smartest of the humans, George Soros, who puts it this way: "The way to make profits is to find the premise that is wrong and bet against it." As far as we can tell, almost every major premise is wrong . . . or at least the overarching premise of this new post-bubble era is as loony as the one that preceded it. Just as you can't really get rich by borrowing and speculating . . . you can't recover from a bust-up by borrowing and speculating more.

But heck, we don't make the rules down here on Planet Earth. We just try to have some fun with them.

As we were saying, making money seems so easy here, especially now. There are companies that are in the business of pulling valuable minerals out of the ground that you can buy for less than the resources they own—even at today's depressed prices. There are companies that drill and pump oil—still the major source of energy on Earth—you can buy now for only a couple times their annual profits. In Germany and Japan—two of the most productive and competitive nations on the planet—companies sell for what would normally be bargain prices, significantly less than book value. And emerging markets can now be bought at giveaway prices; considering that these economies still expect rapid rates of growth over the next 10 to 20 years, these could turn out to be fortune-builders for the next generation.

One of the easiest, surest ways to make money now is to buy high yield corporate bonds and sell low-yield U.S. Treasury bonds. When their last fantasy crashed, earthlings rushed to the apparent safety of U.S. government debt, forsaking the debt of their private enterprises. This pushed yields on the government debt to such low levels as had never been seen before, while yields on bonds rated C or worse rose over 30 percent. Of course, we have no particular opinion on what these yields should be, but it seems very likely that the "spread" between the two debt classes—now at a 100-year high—will narrow.

"If you're looking at junk bonds," adds Jim Paulsen of Wells Cap Management, "you have never had this kind of value before."

But while we are talking about the bonds, an even surer bet to us is that U.S. government debt will decline in value. There is no theory that we know of that allows Treasury bonds to go up while the supply of them increases at such a rapid rate. Next year, the feds will borrow between $1.5 and $2 trillion—as much as four times the largest previous deficit in history. That means there will be a lot more U.S. Treasury bonds offered for sale. This increased supply is bound to put downward pressure on bond prices.

And we're suspicious of those little green pieces of paper, too. When you turn in a government bond, they give you green pieces of paper. But those are the same pieces of paper that they're handing out all over town. According to the only theory we know, as supply increases—ceteris paribus—prices decrease. In this case, as they increase the number of those pieces of paper each one represents less and less wealth. The more pieces of green paper, the less each one is worth, in other words. And as we understand the earthlings' current delusion, they will intentionally increase the number of pieces of green paper until they go down in value. Yes, that is the purpose, too, not only to put more "money" in consumers' hands, but to put out so many pieces of green paper that they go down in value. Why? They want to make sure consumers won't be tempted to save them. Weird, huh? But it's just another peculiar feature of the present dementia universalis on Planet Earth; humans believe they will all be richer if people spend their money, rather than hold onto it. Of course, all of them know it isn't true; but they believe it anyway: that the more they consume their wealth, the more wealth they will have. Like we said: super weird.

But it leads us to an investment that—under the circumstances—seems like a no-brainer. The only thing that bothers us is that so many earthlings seem to favor it, too. Since humans are so prone to error, it makes us question our own judgment.

"U.S. Treasuries are my least favorite asset," says Mohamed El-Erian with Pimco. "My least favorite asset is U.S. Treasury bills . . . and I don't like the dollar either," say Tim Bond of Barclay's Capital. "Outside of a Treasury bond," adds the aforementioned Jim Paulsen, "it is a remarkably good time to buy risk assets."

Yet despite the agreement of these humans, we still think most of the species have seized onto a premise that is wrong—that dollar-based U.S. Treasury debt equals financial safety.

How do you bet against that premise? Probably the easiest way is to buy a more traditional form of money—which humans place at number 79 on their periodic table, gold. Believe it or not, over a long, long time gold has been extremely reliable. An ounce of it buys about as much bread in A.D. 2009 as it did in A.D. 9. As this present delusion blows up, humans will probably turn back to gold to protect their wealth.

As we said, the U.S. government is determined—"hell-bent," some would say—to keep consumers spending those little green pieces of paper. They have a plan to bring this about—at a cost of a trillion or so more of them. If this plan does what they hope it will do, prices will begin to rise. In fact, almost all asset classes will rise in price—especially gold. Shrewd investors will seek protection from inflation by buying gold—causing the price of the yellow metal to rise.

If the plan fails to work, on the other hand, the feds will continue emitting pieces of green paper, which will eventually call into question the value of the paper itself. Either way, probably the surest bet on the blue planet is that the price of gold will go up.

How high? Who can say? But we will be very surprised if it doesn't at least equal—on an inflation-adjusted basis—its highest price ever, set in January 1980. Then, it sold for $875. Adjust that price to today's consumer price level and you get a price over $2,400.

Daily Reckoning readers who wish to take advantage of this terrestrial phenomenon should buy gold. If you wish to increase your risk and profits, you could buy the double ETF, giving you twice the gain from each dollar gold goes up. After all, this will probably be the last bubble . . . the biggest bubble of our lifetimes. For gold bugs, it is now or never. Those who really want to go for broke should mortgage their old houses and sell their young children to raise extra cash.

This advice is free. Of course, it is worth no more than you paid for it. All we ask is that if it doesn't work out, please don't rub our noses in it. We'll feel bad enough.

SAID THE JOKER TO THE THIEF

The year of our Lord 2008 died in disgrace. It was tossed in a hasty grave . . . and mud was thrown on its face as though on a dead dictator. "Good riddance," says practically everyone. But here at *The Daily Reckoning,* we're going to miss and mourn it. It may have been the worst year in stock market history, but we can't remember when we had such a good time. We barely broke a sweat the entire year; never were there more jackasses to laugh at or more con artists to admire. So, today, we hang black crepe, spread tea roses, and bid adieu.

Among the other milestones of 2008 came word that 1 out of 100 adults in the USA was in prison; but as the year progressed, that seemed like hardly enough. Each week brought new evidence that there were still many miscreants who should be behind bars. On January 11, 2008, one of the nation's biggest mortgage lenders—Countrywide Financial—went bust. On February 17, Britain's Northern Rock was nationalized. Still, U.S. rulers missed the calamity taking place right under their noses.

"I don't think we're headed to a recession," said George W. Bush. "I don't think I've seen any scenario where the American taxpayer needs to be stepping in with more taxpayer dollars," added Henry Paulson. Then, on March 11th, the Treasury Secretary went on to explain that the fallout from subprime mortgages was "largely contained." From the report in the *Wall Street Journal*:

"Paulson, a former chief executive of Goldman Sachs Group, repeated his view that the U.S. economy is fundamentally on sound footing and would dodge a recession."

The very next day, Bear Stearns CEO Alan Schwartz told the world that his firm faced no liquidity crisis. In an exclusive interview with CNBC, he said the nasty rumors were unfounded: "We finished the year, and we reported that we had $17 billion of cash sitting at the bank's parent company as a liquidity cushion," he said. "As the year has gone on, that liquidity cushion has been virtually unchanged." That same week, SEC Chairman Christopher Cox added that his agency was comfortable with the "capital cushions" at the nation's five largest investment banks.

Four days later, the cushions seem to have mysteriously disappeared. Bear Stearns faced bankruptcy brought on by collapsing subprime prices. In a desperate measure, the firm sold itself to J.P Morgan the next day for $2 a share—a 98 percent discount from its high of $171.

But by May things were looking up again. On the 6th of the month, Cyril Moulle-Berteaux, managing partner of Traxis Partners LP, a hedge fund firm, wrote in the *Wall Street Journal*: ". . . it is very likely that April 2008 will mark the bottom of the U.S. housing market. Yes, the housing market is bottoming right now."

But by July, several things were clear: Housing had not bottomed out, the subprime problem was not contained, the banks did not have enough cash, and every official—public or private—who opened his mouth was either a joker or a thief.

On July 16th Fed Chairman Bernanke told Congress that troubled mortgage giants Fannie Mae and Freddie Mac were "in no danger of failing." The next day, ABC interviewed Fannie Mae CEO Daniel Mudd. Would Fannie Mae need a bailout? he was asked. "I think it's very unlikely," was the opinion of the top man. "And I think everybody that has described it . . . [says it's] a backstop in case things turn out different than everybody predicts."

If anyone knew what was happening in the nation's housing market, he wasn't sitting in the CEO's seat at Fannie or the Fed. By September, things were turning out different than everybody expected. On the 6th, the U.S. government nationalized both Freddie Mac and Fannie Mae, wiping out the shareholders. On the 14th, Lehman Bros. went broke. Lehman's main man, Dick Fuld, blamed the few people who actually seemed to know what was going on—those who sold the company's stock: "When I find a short-seller, I want to tear his heart out and eat it before his eyes while he's still alive." The day after, Merrill Lynch ceased to be an investment bank; it was taken over by the Bank of America. And the following day, the Fed bailed out American International Group Inc. in return for an 80 percent stake.

But by the middle of September, the financial authorities—who neither saw no evil nor heard any—were on the case. On September 18 the UK Financial Services Authority took the Dick Fuld approach; it banned short-selling financial stocks. The next day, U.S. Treasury Secretary Paulson took aim at the problem he never saw, calling on Congress to ante up $700 billion. Whence cometh the $700 billion figure? "It's not based on any particular data point, we just wanted to choose a really large number," said a Treasury Department spokeswoman.

Besides, who had time to look for data points? "If we don't do this, we may not have an economy on Monday," said Ben Bernanke to the U.S. Congress. Mr. Bernanke was as wrong about that as about everything else. Monday came. Monday went. The economy never seemed to check its agenda. But then, the U.S. House of Representatives rejected Paulson's rescue plan and stock markets all over the world crashed. The Dow Jones posted its largest point decline ever. "I believe companies that make bad decisions should be allowed to go out of business," opined George Bush.

By early October, however, the world's rescuers had their defibrillators plugged in; Congress approved the acquisition of up to $700 billion of Wall Street's toxic assets and the UK government announced 400 billion pound bank bailout. "We not only saved the world . . ." began Gordon Brown's victory speech, before he was drowned out by howls of Tories.

"I got to tell you," said Paulson on November 13th, "I think our major institutions have been stabilized. I believe that very strongly." Two weeks later, America's largest bank and its largest automaker were on the verge of bankruptcy.

By year end, the thieves had been blown up by their own debt bombs and the jokers were in control of most of America's major industries— housing, autos, banking, and finance. "The lack of specifics [in the bail-out legislation]," explained a Bloomberg report, "gives President-elect Barack Obama plenty of leeway to decide who succeeds and fails."

And as 2008 began its death rattle, America's president managed to capture the zeitgeist of the whole remarkable period with just a few flagrantly absurd bon mots: We had to "abandon free market principles to save the free market system," said he.

Au revoir, 2008 . . . sniff, sniff.

CHAPTER 8

UNDERVALUED COMPANIES AND GOLD

John Pugsley
The Stealth Investor

"Of all the contrivances for cheating the laboring classes of mankind, none has been more effective than that which deludes them with paper money."

—Daniel Webster, U.S. Senator and statesman (1782–1852)

John Pugsley has been an investor for over 35 years and has written several bestsellers on the subject, including Common Sense Economics *and* The Alpha Strategy. *Jack, as his friends call him, is also one of the founders and the current Chairman of* The Sovereign Society, *an investment newsletter that helps "individuals to protect and enhance their wealth and privacy, lower their taxes and to help improve their personal freedom and liberty." More recently, he's begun publishing* The Stealth Investor.

With his efforts spread in so many domains, it is no surprise that Jack is continuously discovering outstanding undervalued but unknown companies around the world, largely because his focus is on small micro-cap stocks that are most often totally avoided by mainstream brokers and advisors. Since the publication of the first issue of The Stealth Investor *on March 10, 2006, the S&P 500 has dropped 21.6 percent while Jack's Stealth Portfolio has risen over 70 percent as of September 2009.*

Having been a subscriber to Jack's investment newsletter for several years, I have chosen the following contribution for many reasons. For starters, Jack is aware of the many conflicts of interest and hypocrisy on Wall Street and by implication recognizes the importance of "who." Second, Jack provides a brief analysis of why paper money is exacerbating the debt problem and why gold is the solution. Finally, he gives you some framework as to his philosophy of investing in small-cap natural resource companies, particularly exploratory gold mining companies.

If you found a list of the 100 most undervalued companies in the world, the vast majority are completely off your broker's radar. Why? Two reasons.

First and foremost, federal and state securities laws often keep brokers from passing on their best ideas to clients. Companies that haven't undergone the onerous and incredibly expensive registration process with the SEC and individual state securities commissions can't be discussed or even mentioned by registered brokers, in spite of the fact that those companies' shares may be deeply undervalued and admirably suited to a client's needs.

There's another reason that brokers fail to bring deeply undervalued companies to clients . . . not enough juice to make it worth their while. Individual brokers work for a brokerage firm. The firm provides research and gives its brokers lists of stocks to push. Since brokerage firms survive on a combination of underwriting fees and sales commissions, they have no incentive to investigate companies that are too small or too narrowly traded to generate either. Hence, your broker will never hear about a global armada of outstanding, undervalued companies that you should know about.

That's where *The Stealth Investor* comes in. Thanks to the First Amendment, which exempts newsletters from censorship by the regulators, we can tell you about the outstanding natural resource companies that we specialize in and that your broker could go to jail for mentioning. Moreover, we're not seeking commissions or underwriting fees. Our research looks simply for exceptional, overlooked values.

We won't deluge you with thousands of recommendations. Our objective is to scour the world for just one outstanding, undervalued company and to bring that discovery to you every Friday.

Like all sectors of economic endeavor, in the short term the fortunes of companies in the mining, energy, agriculture, forestry, and water industries sectors wax and wane with business and credit cycles. The ups and downs of the *Stealth* portfolio (and the strategy itself) can only be understood against the background of broad economic events.

Last Sunday morning Treasury Secretary Henry Paulson announced that the government was nationalizing the nation's two largest mortgage companies, Fannie Mae and Freddie Mac. To call them "giant" is an understatement. Together, the two have purchased or guaranteed some $5 trillion in mortgages, close to half of the entire $13 trillion outstanding in U.S. real estate mortgages.

By the end of last week it was obvious that the two companies were on the verge of bankruptcy (a fate they definitely deserved). From last October's price of $67, the shares had skidded to $8 at the end of August. The situation reached crisis stage last Friday when an avalanche of sell orders hit the aftermarket. From $7, shares fell over 20 percent in a matter of hours, and then went on to plummet, finally opening on Monday morning at 73 cents. At this writing Fannie shares, all 1.07 billion of them, are priced at $0.77, having lost almost 99 percent of their market value in 11 months.

The money-masters in Washington and New York knew that if the U.S. government backed away from its implicit guarantee of these Government Sponsored Agencies (GSAs) by letting Fannie and Freddie go bankrupt, worldwide confidence would be shaken in everything implicitly or explicitly backed by the U.S. government. A flight from U.S. debt, including the dollar itself (which is nothing more than a debt of the U.S. government), could be the coup de grâce to the U.S. financial system.

As we read in the plethora of articles sweeping the financial press, the crisis is thought to have many mothers. The finger of blame is pointed at self-serving mortgage brokers that encouraged homebuyers to overstate their income and assets, thereby qualifying for loans they couldn't afford. It also is also pointed at greedy financial market innovators for inventing "securitization" (the packaging of subprime mortgages that were then sold to banks and companies like Fannie Mae). Almost everyone blames the "queen mother" of financial-market chaos, inadequate oversight by federal regulators.

IDENTIFYING THE TRUE CULPRIT

It's easy to see that clever financial innovation, deceptive sales tactics, and speculative risk-taking are components of the disaster. Almost everyone in the world truly believes that it is the function of governments to regulate the markets and prevent such disasters. What is not seen is that it is the very intervention by governments in the free exchange between individuals that leads to systemic failures. The "queen mother" of financial-market collapse is not the failure to adequately regulate, it is the regulations themselves.

Consider the ongoing mortgage crisis as an example. Nationwide real estate booms and busts didn't occur in the United States for the first 125 years of the nation's history. There were sporadic local bubbles (such as the bubble in Kansas farmland between 1881 and 1887—it popped in 1887), but such booms never became regional or national. Why not? Credit could not be expanded sufficiently to create a bubble. And why was that?

Prior to the creation of the Federal Reserve in 1913, the U.S. dollar was not a promissory note of a central bank, or of the central government. It was defined as 1/20th of an ounce of gold. State banks issued dollars in the form of banknotes, i.e., their own IOUs. A dollar bill was a depository receipt for gold. Since there were no government guarantees, depositors were responsible for the safety of their own money and naturally kept a close eye on their bankers. Banks that made risky loans with depositors' gold soon suffered bank runs and went bankrupt. Constrained by depositors' vigilance, bankers had to be prudent when loaning out their depositors' money. Since residential real estate was considered a consumption item, not an investment or speculation, the bank made sure that the individual had the ability to repay the loan. To get a mortgage for a house, a borrower typically had to put 50 percent down and pay off the mortgage in five years.

The creation of the Federal Reserve changed the game. The Fed's mandate (arranged by the bankers who wanted to be able to make more loans and the politicians who wanted to borrow) was to convince the public that they didn't have to fear bank runs, since the Fed stood ready to lend to banks that got into trouble. It became the bank of banks, and the "lender of last resort."

BIRTH OF A BUBBLE

Without the limited gold supply constraining the expansion of credit, bank lending for investment soared. Loans relative to gold on deposit were expanded dramatically, and quickly the availability of credit made speculating in stocks and real estate a national pastime. As individuals pumped borrowed money into markets, prices were driven higher and rising prices enticed more people into the credit-fueled boom. The availability of credit generated the Roaring Twenties.

The credit-induced demand created absurdly high share prices that could not be justified by fundamental or utility values. (The utility of a business is the profit it generates and the dividends it pays. The utility of a home is the shelter and comfort it provides, which can be estimated by the amount it can be rented for.) Prices rose until eventually a slowdown triggered margin calls, and in October 1929 the stock market bubble collapsed. Prices of stocks and real estate began to correct, descending toward their natural values based on their utility.

The correction that began after the 1929 crash was anathema to the bankers and politicians who profited from the vast credit bubble. As prices fell, government and bankers blamed the speculators and the free market and worked feverishly to arrest the deflation through a vast net of regulations on stock markets, banking, and private transactions. Roosevelt's New Deal created the FDIC, the SEC, and yes, in 1938, the Federal National Mortgage Association (Fannie Mae), all of which were created to prevent the free market from correcting the artificially inflated prices. So desperate were the politicians and big banks to keep the public from abandoning the new paper money that Roosevelt even outlawed gold ownership for Americans.

In a world of fiat money, the fees and interest that can be gained by financial firms by expanding loans blinds them to the long-term consequences. Human nature being what it is, the availability of an unending supply of credit naturally leads to the evolution of sophisticated and complicated structures to expand sales of everything from vacations to automobiles to residential real estate. Sellers that offer low-to-zero down payments, low interest rates, and ask for no collateral, reap profit. At least in the short term.

As people become conditioned to buying on credit, the monthly payments create a trap. Whenever growth slows, unemployment rises, and the cry goes up to lower interest rates and get the economy moving again. But this can only be done by expanding credit even further. The Federal Reserve buys IOUs from the banks, pays for them with freshly created dollars, and the bubble resumes its expansion.

A PYRAMID OF IOUs

In the past quarter century, financial-industry innovation has taken the IOU game to new levels of complexity and leverage. Consider the foundation of the money and credit system today.

You sign an IOU to make a credit-card purchase, buy a refrigerator or automobile, or a house, and exchange your promissory note for the money. You borrow for one of two reasons: You want to have and consume something that you don't yet have enough money to buy, so you decide that you can earn enough in the future to pay for it and still have it now. Or, you believe that you borrow money, invest it, and earn a higher return than your interest on the debt.

The bank takes your IOU, lending you the money of other depositors. However, it can earn even more if it first profits from the fees it charged you, then sells the loan to another entity, gets the cash back for it, and makes another loan. So, it bundles your IOU with similar IOUs from other borrowers (securitizes it), adds it own guarantee of repayment, and sells the security to someone else—perhaps an investor, perhaps another bank, perhaps another financial institution such as a Freddie Mae or Goldman Sachs. Those institutions also profit from fees and turnovers, so they repackage the newly created securities, again maybe adding their own guarantee, and sell them to mutual funds, pension funds, trusts, and other such investors. It's a long chain of IOUs backed by IOUs backed by IOUs, profitable to everyone down the line, and all wrapped in legal disclaimers and government regulations that make the risks effectively incomprehensible. When, somewhere along the chain, one of the links, one of the guarantors, gets into financial trouble and defaults, the whole system is threatened, and the Treasury or the Federal Reserve rushes to the rescue.

IN SEARCH OF THE BOTTOM

Has the takeover of Fannie Mae and Freddie Mac soothed the market enough to bring a halt to the credit crisis, the slide in real estate and stock prices, and even the recession? It's too early to tell. The odds are hard to calculate as to how close we are to a bottom. But it could be argued that prices have fallen sufficiently to bring prices back to the utility value of the underlying assets.

Whether we are at or near a bottom, however, one thing is certain. By shifting the losses of these subprime IOUs from investors and banks to the government, as is being done by the takeover of Fannie and Freddie, the default must now be covered by more government borrowing. It will be a significant addition to an already bloated deficit that the government itself has projected at $407 billion for fiscal 2008. Treasury borrowing to cover the expanding deficit will absorb lendable funds, driving interest rates up, and that will be met with popular cries for easier credit . . . so the Fed will buy up the new government IOUs, and pump more fiat dollars into the credit system. Meanwhile, government deficits will continue to rise. The increase could truly be spectacular once a new administration gets elected by promising more social spending and lower taxes.

It's the nature of a credit-based, fiat-money system to create a credit boom and drive prices beyond the utility value of the underlying assets. Collapse of a credit bubble is inevitable.

I began with the observation that *The Stealth Investor* specializes in natural resource companies and that prices in the sector wax and wane with the business cycle and credit markets. One of our favorite types of resource companies is mining exploration companies that adopt the "prospect generator" business model and look for gold. Such companies acquire or stake prospective properties, do preliminary analysis of the potential, then farm out the more costly drilling and development to larger companies. Prospect generators working on discovering gold deposits often will get a double impact, one from the discovery process and the other from the gold price.

Prices of natural resource companies were driven up significantly over the eight years leading up to late 2008, but during the past year they have seen a violent correction. It's possible that prices have corrected sufficiently that we could be near the turnaround. Whether it is in the next month or two, or eight or ten months away is not knowable, but the turn will come . . . and then the bubble will start expanding again.

CHAPTER 9

GOLD DÉJÀ VU

Richard Maybury
Early Warning Report

"Gold has worked down from Alexander's time . . . When something holds good for two thousand years I do not believe it can be so because of prejudice or mistaken theory."

—Bernard M. Baruch, American
financier (1870–1965)

Richard Maybury is widely regarded as one of the top free-market writers in America. His articles have appeared in the Wall Street Journal, USA Today, *and other major publications. He is also the publisher of the* U.S. and World Early Warning Report. *As Richard explains: "Investment trends are caused primarily by economic conditions, and economic conditions are determined, unfortunately, by that horrible scourge called politics. To forecast what our investments will do we must forecast what governments will do. Every investment analysis should begin with a look at the politics behind it."*

In the following contribution, Richard Maybury begins his analysis with the premise that "The Federal Reserve is an inherently crooked organization, and its chairman's primary duty is to deceive." The Fed's

Originally published in *Early Warning Report* in April 2008 as "The Bernanke Bomb."

deception is meant to promote a strong U.S. dollar. Actually, they are doing "whatever it takes to avoid deflation and recession." Given such a position by the Fed, a falling dollar is a foregone conclusion. What does this mean to investors? According to Maybury, "I think we will be very lucky if U.S. officials can get the crisis stopped before gold hits $5,000."

Someone should put a muzzle on Federal Reserve chairman Ben Bernanke, lock him in his office, and never let him out in public again.

Every time he is asked about the dollar, this inflationist makes some spineless comment such as, "We obviously watch the dollar very carefully."*

Watch the dollar do what?

Watch it fall.

How can these weaseling remarks strengthen confidence in the dollar? How can they possibly build the trust of Sovereign Wealth Funds and other foreign holders of dollars so that they don't rush for the exits, triggering a global financial calamity?

When Bernanke is asked about the dollar, he should sit fully upright, stern faced, then slowly rise to his feet, point into the camera lens, pound the table, and in a low, rumbling voice say, "The dollar is the finest currency ever in world history and we plan to do whatever it takes to keep it that way. We will do anything. We will raise interest rates to whatever levels are necessary. There is no risk in holding dollars. I repeat, no risk. Every holder of dollars can be fully confident his greenbacks will be as valuable 30 years from now as they are today. I have all my money in dollars, and wouldn't dream of taking the risk of switching to any other currency."

But, you might say, he'd be lying, and you'd be right. So I'll be blunt.

Bernanke is in charge of a fiat currency.

Fiat currencies are frauds.

The Federal Reserve is an inherently crooked organization, and its chairman's primary duty is to deceive. If Bernanke wants to be a boy

---

*In Senate Banking Committee testimony, February, 2008.

scout, he took the wrong job. He should either quit or grow up and face the fact that he cannot tell the truth about the dollar without launching the worst financial catastrophe in world history.

But, instead of saying he will do . . . **whatever it takes to keep the dollar strong**. . . Bernanke says the opposite; he will do whatever it takes to avoid deflation and recession.

In other words, he is implicitly promising to continue inflating the supply of dollars, thereby undermining the value of each individual dollar.

This man is poison. My advice is fire him now before it's too late.

Since August, federal agencies have provided nearly $1 trillion in direct and indirect support to U.S. financial institutions.*

On top of that, Nobel economist Joseph Stiglitz believes the cost of the war will eventually reach $3 trillion and says this money could have been used "to put Social Security on a sound footing for the next half-century."

As I pointed out in February, retired baby boomers are likely, at some point, to find the Social Security cupboard bare. In their youths, the boomers were cannon fodder for the Vietnam War, and now they've become financial cannon fodder for this war. And . . . **the cannon is being fired by Bernanke.**

Some in the mainstream press have begun to sound the alarm. On March 4th, the *New York Times* ran an article about the war titled "The $2 Trillion Nightmare."

On March 5th, the *Wall Street Journal* ran an article by economist Judy Shelton called, "It's the Dollar, Stupid." Shelton ended the article with this warning about McCain, Obama, and the Clintons: "It's time the candidates devote less time on the minutiae of configuring the next economic stimulus package, or renegotiating the North American Free Trade Agreement. They should be thinking about how they will confront the imminent global currency crisis."

Of course, this is all old news to readers of EWR. For more than six years we've been earning fat profits from gold and other investments that do well during the monetary chaos that typically accompanies wars.

---

*"Dow Rallies . . .," *Wall Street. Journal,* March 12, 2008, p. C1.

What is new is that the mainstream press is beginning to wake up and sound the same warnings. They are six years late, but they speak to millions who have now begun moving into the investments we were in before 9/11. On February 29th, in its lead front-page story, the *Wall Street Journal* quoted well-known commodity investor Jim Rogers saying, "The dollar is a terribly flawed currency and its days are numbered."

■ ■ ■

History never repeats exactly, but close enough to learn valuable lessons. As Patrick Henry said, "I have but one lamp by which my feet are lighted, and that is the lamp of experience."

During the 1979–1980 global monetary crisis, millions became afraid to hold fiat paper money, and they were fleeing into gold, silver, platinum, and other commodities.

America dodged that bullet, barely, but now history is repeating. On March 11th, the *Wall Street Journal* ran another front-page story, titled "Weak Dollar Feels New Stress." It revealed that "central banks from China to Chile," including those of the Persian Gulf, are fed up with the dollar and looking for ways to escape from it.

Note this: Inside the United States, the greater fear is of deflation and recession. Outside, it's fear is of dollar debasement. The Fed's offices are inside the United States. Foreigners afraid of dollar debasement are thousands of miles away, and they don't vote in U.S. elections. So, most of the pressure Fed officials feel is pushing them toward more inflation.

Summarizing, since the beginning of the war on terror, the federal government's financial behavior has been as responsible as that of a gang of drunken teenagers in a brewery with a credit card. And, each time Bernanke "clarifies" his attitude toward the dollar, he throws another scare into dollar holders.

If someone doesn't muzzle Bernanke, the Federal Reserve's dollar will go down in history alongside the worthless Continental and Confederate dollars as another inflationary disaster.

CHAPTER 10

THE TRIAL OF GOLD

David Galland
Casey's Daily Dispatch

"The modern mind dislikes gold because it blurts out unpleasant truths."

—Joseph Schumpeter, economist
and writer (1883–1950)

David has had a varied career, having spent time in the mining industry, as a conference director for the world's largest investment conference (National Committee for Monetary Reform), and as a financial newsletter publisher or editor for almost a half dozen publications. Currently, he is Doug Casey's partner at Casey Research and its managing director.

Casey Research currently publishes 11 publications on a variety of investment sectors. They also have two websites, CaseyResearch.com and, in a joint venture with the world's largest gold-oriented website, KitcoCasey.com. As you'll see in the piece below, Casey Research has a strong tendency to recommend investments that "are not short-term in nature, but rather look for big trends that you can invest in when they are deeply out of favor." David also serves as managing editor on most of Casey's publications as well as writing his own daily communiqué, Casey's Daily Dispatch.

Originally published in *The Room* on October 24, 2008, as "The Trial of Gold."

Casey's Daily Dispatch was reformatted this year having previously been called The Room, *which is where I originally read "The Trial of Gold." This is one of the most entertaining pieces I've read that explains why "gold's highest and best use is as money, and sometimes it can also be a terrific investment."*

They filed into the docket, faces bright and smiley despite the shackles around their arms. The leader of the gang, Mr. Gold, was pushed forward into the defendant's chair. The rest, including Ms. Silver as well as the members of the resource share clan, Biggie Goldshares, Junior Goldshares, and Ms. Silvershares, were manhandled onto the hard bench just behind. Rather than looking discomfited at the treatment or the ugly smells and sounds of the crowded courtroom, they just looked around pleasantly, as if on a church-sponsored outing to the local zoo.

Calling the court to order, the bailiff announced that all should rise for the judge. Shortly thereafter, Judge Market entered from stage left, a stern look in his eye. Approaching the dais, he arranged his robes around him and took his seat before gaveling the court to session.

The trial of Gold had begun.

"Mr. Gold, you and your cohorts have been accused of misleading investors into thinking that you would help them preserve their wealth, when exactly the opposite has been true of late. How do you plead?"

"Not guilty, Your Honor," Mr. Gold answered brightly, receiving a dour look in return.

ANDREW CUOMO CROSS-EXAMINES MR. GOLD

"Mr. Cuomo, you may question the witness," Judge Market announced impatiently.

As Mr. Gold made himself comfortable in the witness stand, Andrew "Son of" Cuomo, taking a break from his well-oiled political career, I mean, job as New York attorney general, to serve as the public prosecutor in this high-profile case, rose smoothly to his feet, patted an imaginary loose hair into place, shot his cuffs, and approached the defendant.

"Mr. Gold, behind me in this court are good folks, hard-working folks, who believed in you. Yet you have failed to perform as advertised. How can you sit there, all shiny, and claim that you have not deceived the public in this regard?"

A pleasant and, some might say, radiant smile fixed on his face, Mr. Gold responded in an even voice. "I'm just a simple metal. I've never made any claims one way or another, so I don't know where people got it into their heads that I'm anything special. But for thousands of years now, people have been chasing after me, all over the world. Beats me why."

"Your Honor, if I may." The defense attorney, Mr. Reason, rose to his feet.

"Yes?" asked Judge Market, looking grumpy.

"I know it's a bit unusual, but Mr. Gold is not exaggerating when he says he's, well, kind of simple. If it pleases the court, it might speed things along if I could ask some expert witnesses to assist in answering the prosecutor's questions. Can do?"

"Highly irregular," said the judge, glancing over at Mr. Gold where he sat, his smile and countenance oddly reassuring in the dark, smelly courtroom. "Mr. Cuomo, any objection?"

Seeing the fond looks in the eyes of many in the courtroom as they stared, fixated, at Mr. Gold . . . and after a quick consultation with his internal popularity meter and coming to the conclusion that he didn't want to appear mean-spirited, Cuomo nodded in agreement.

THE GHOST OF MURRAY ROTHBARD

"Thank you," Mr. Reason said reasonably. "Then I would like to ask the Ghost of Murray Rothbard to join Mr. Gold on the witness stand."

As the court watched, their collective mouths somewhat agape, Rothbard's ghost floated softly to the witness stand and landed on the rail next to Mr. Gold, who winked at him amicably.

"Ahh, okay, well . . ." Mr. Cuomo stammered, looking a little discomfited by the sight of Rothbard's ghost, his transparent bowtie ruffled slightly by some unfelt celestial wind. "How do you answer the charge against Mr. Gold that he has lured people to him under false pretenses?"

"I'd like to answer by quoting from an excellent book on the topic, the very best, in my opinion," said Rothbard's ghost with a wry smile. "It's called *The Mystery of Banking* and it is written by . . . me!"

> In all countries and all civilizations, two commodities have been dominant whenever they were available to compete as moneys with other commodities: *gold* and *silver*.
>
> At first, gold and silver were highly prized only for their luster and ornamental value. They were always in great demand. Second, they were always relatively scarce, and hence valuable per unit of weight. And for that reason they were portable as well. They were also divisible, and could be sliced into thin segments without losing their pro rata value. Finally, silver or gold were blended with small amounts of alloy to harden them, and since they did not corrode, they would last almost forever.
>
> Thus, because gold and silver are supremely "moneylike" commodities, they are selected by markets as money if they are available. Proponents of the gold standard do not suffer from a mysterious "gold fetish." They simply recognize that gold has always been selected by the market as money throughout history.
>
> Generally, gold and silver have both been moneys, side-by-side. Since gold has always been far scarcer and also in greater demand than silver, it has always commanded a higher price, and tends to be money in larger transactions, while silver has been used in smaller exchanges. Because of its higher price, gold has often been selected as the unit of account, although this has not always been true. The difficulties of mining gold, which makes its production limited, make its long-term value relatively more stable than silver.

Concluding with a large smile and a wave of the hand, Rothbard's ghost graciously accepted Mr. Reason's words of gratitude for taking time out of his schedule to make an appearance, then stood on the rail of the witness box and, with a flourish, took a deep bow before flying out the door to return to his ethereal seat in the heavenly branch of the Austrian School of Economics.

Mr. Cuomo played for a moment with a well-manicured cuticle before whipping around, his finger jabbing in the direction of Mr. Gold. His voice rose dramatically.

"And what, Mr. Gold, do you have to say on the topic of inflation? Can you deny that you and your friends claim to be inflation hedges? If so, then how do you answer to the fact that you are now selling for a lower nominal price than back in 1980! And, in inflation-adjusted terms, you are well behind! You, sir, are a fraud!"

Mr. Gold's smile remained unchanged, his countenance pleasant as always. "I'm sorry, but I really don't understand what you are talking about."

Mr. Reason again took to his feet. "Mr. Cuomo, if I may?"

"Oh, all right. Have at it."

TERRY COXON FOR THE DEFENSE

"The defense calls Terry Coxon of *The Casey Report*. Mr. Coxon, would you be so kind to answer Mr. Cuomo's question?"

Coxon made his way from a seat at the back of the courtroom where he had been enjoying the show and walked over to stand next to the witness box. Unable to help himself, he reached out and gave Mr. Gold a pat on the arm.

"So, Mr. Coxon," Son-of-Cuomo barked, "How do you explain that in 1980, gold touched $850? And here, 28 years later, it is trading for less than that—even though inflation has been persistent throughout the period. The claim that gold is an inflation hedge is simply false!"

Speaking slowly, to be sure that Mr. Cuomo understood, Coxon replied . . .

> What moves gold isn't the rate of inflation but the change in the rate of inflation.
>
> When people expect higher inflation, they bid up gold. When people expect lower inflation, demand for gold drops, even though "lower" may still be very high. That's why gold trended down in the 1980s, even though the inflation rate was high. The inflation rate was high, but it was declining.
>
> There is a simple reason for this relationship. Gold and the dollar are both a store of value. Gold is more reliable in the long run, and the dollar is more reliable over shorter periods. Because they do somewhat the same thing for their owners, they are competing products, but with different attributes.
>
> For example, the cost of holding dollars for their usefulness as a store of value is the gradual erosion of purchasing power—price inflation.

In a period of rising inflation, using dollars for storing value becomes relatively more expensive than using gold. So the demand for gold increases. And since the supply of gold—in ounces—is nearly fixed, the price per ounce goes up.

To sum it up, the price of gold is lower today than in 1980 because the rate of inflation now is lower—much lower—than in 1980.

Judge Market looked thoughtfully at Mr. Gold. "Mr. Cuomo, any more questions for this witness?"

"Not at this time, Your Honor," Cuomo said, flicking an imaginary piece of dust off the sleeve of his silk suit as Coxon returned to his seat and the bag of popcorn he had left there.

"But I do have a question for you!" he said, with a glare at Mr. Gold. "You sit there so calm, nonchalant, even. The public looks to you to remain a bastion of stability in challenging times. But as the financial crisis has swept over the land, you have been gyrating wildly. I accuse you of luring in investors by pretending to be calm, but in actual fact being dangerously volatile!"

Mr. Gold smiled and shrugged. Again, Mr. Reason took to his pins.

JEFF CLARK FOR THE DEFENSE

"I'd like to call Jeff Clark, editor of *Big Gold*. I believe he has some charts that might help in answering that charge. Mr. Clark."

His step enthusiastic, Clark walked briskly up to the bailiff and handed him two charts, which were, in turn, dutifully walked up to Judge Market.

"We'll call these exhibits A and B," said Judge Market, pulling on a pair of tortoiseshell specs for a closer look.

From the wings, an overhead projector was presented and Clark walked over to it, flipped it on, and laid flat a transparency. Helpfully, the bailiff lowered the lights a touch.

"I think gold has gotten a bum rap," Clark began, his face aglow from the light of the projector and, perhaps, his passion for the subject at hand.

"In fact, despite recent weakness, between January 1, 2007 and October 10, 2008, when I prepared Figure 10.1, gold is up 42.6 percent while the bellwether S&P 500 is down 36.9 percent.

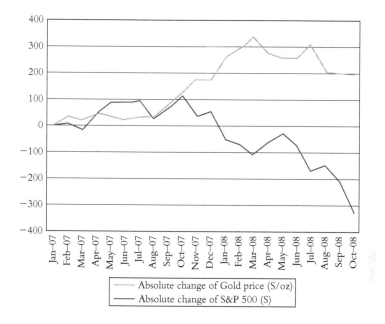

Figure 10.1 Gold versus S&P 500 (1/1/07 through 10/10/08)

"For my second chart (see Figure 10.2), I'd like to address the notion that gold is more volatile than stocks," Clark said, sliding exhibit A from the projector and replacing it with exhibit B.

Mr. Cuomo, thinking about the whupping his own portfolio of Wall Street darlings had taken of late, turned to Jeff Clark and almost spat out, "Since we're on the topic of stocks, let's talk about the big gold stocks. They were supposed to do better than the physical metals, but they have been hammered just as hard or even harder than many other stock sectors!"

In the back of the room, Biggie Goldshares examined his shoes, while Clark cleared his throat and said . . .

"No stock has escaped undamaged in the global carnage, including gold stocks. The downdrafts have been breathtaking, and it's easy to imagine that gold stocks will just keep falling. Here's what happened.

"For starters, hedge funds continued deleveraging, which can cause significant moves in market prices due to their use of margin. Withdrawals in U.S. hedge funds hit $43 billion in September alone. Meanwhile, mutual funds and "basket of commodities" ETFs continued

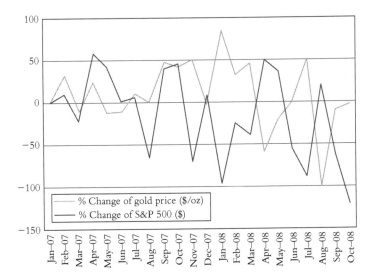

Figure 10.2   Gold Is No More Volatile than the S&P 500

selling off due to disappointed, or frightened, investors. This means the good was sold along with the bad. Add in the intensifying fear in the marketplace and few buyers were to be found.

"Second, as the sea of red numbers continued splashing across headline news, investors fled in droves. Many simply didn't want to be the last one out of what they believed was a burning building, so "Dump everything!" was the mantra. Many stocks, in a perverse use of logic, were sold because they had value. Lots of investors simply fled to cash, which is where investors reflexively go when they see a market rout.

"Last, right or wrong, gold stocks are perceived by some as riskier than your average IBM or GE. Further, few gold stocks pay dividends, and the ones that do only yield 1 to 2 percent. Some sellers might have stuck around if they were getting 8 to 10 percent.

"So, is that it for gold stocks? Look at the reasons outlined above: Where does it say investors sold because inflation is dead? Where does it say the public left because the government has promised not to print money to solve its problems? Where does it indicate gold is no longer viewed as a safe haven? Has mankind lost interest in war? Does the dollar's recent rise mean its ills have been cured? Banks are fine? The economy has a bright future?

"The bottom line: The base case for gold stocks remains intact, because at some point the public will see them as the place to go for profit. Gold will rise, and regardless of what the general market is doing at the time, gold stocks will separate and follow gold up. The best days for gold stocks still lie ahead, because a much higher gold price is assured by all the recent efforts to stave off a recession. Since gold stocks were pulled down by a general market panic and for reasons unrelated to fundamentals, our advice is to hold on. We're confident their day will come. And we'll sell when the problems that have yet to push gold to new inflation-adjusted highs have all played out. In the meantime, we need to be steady while others are fearful."

LOUIS JAMES'S OUTBURST AND TESTIMONY

From the back of the room, a hand shot up. Judge Market, already resolved that this was to be no ordinary proceedings, looked over his glasses at the owner of the hand.

"Yes? And who are you? And why are you interrupting?"

"Louis James, senior editor of the *International Speculator*," the mysterious stranger spoke up loudly for the courtroom to hear. "I would like to add a historical fact related to gold stocks in a crisis."

"Mr. Cuomo, any objection?"

In reply, Son-of-Cuomo simply shrugged and dropped into his seat.

"Go ahead, Mr. James," Judge Market said, rocking back in his chair, his eyes attentive.

Approaching the witness stand, James turned to the assemblage and proceeded.

"Homestake Mining Company (now part of mining giant Barrick Gold, NYSE: ABX) offers a worthwhile illustration of the potential of gold stocks even during depressions. As a bit of a background, for more than 100 years, the company operated the Homestake mine in South Dakota. For you television fans, you may recognize Homestake as being a centerpiece in the recent HBO series *Deadwood*.

"In any event, in 1935, right in the middle of the Great Depression, Homestake recovered enough gold to make $11.39 million in net income, a record that stood for nearly 40 years—and that was at a time when the U.S. government had set the price of gold at $35 per ounce. Homestake shares showed some volatility but weathered the great stock market crash of 1929, ending that year slightly up. From 1926 to the end of 1935, they went ten-to-one, soaring from $50 to $500.

"With fluctuations as you'd expect, they held on to those gains until taking off again during the 1970s bull market for gold. When you get home, you can learn more about it with some rather ugly but eye-opening charts available at this website: www.geocities.com/ WallStreet/Exchange/9807/Charts/SP500/HomestakeHist.gif."

Cuomo rose to his Gucci-shod feet with a wicked look on his face. "Mr. James, since you are here, maybe you could tell the jury why it is that Mr. Gold's known associate, Junior Goldshares, has done even worse, almost consistently losing money for investors over the past year. Lots and lots of money! What can you possibly say in Junior's defense?"

"Sure, happy to oblige," said the ever-obliging Mr. James, then launching into the answer. "We hold a lot of gold juniors. In hindsight, it would have been nice if we'd taken even more profits than we did in August of 2007 and gone to cash—we'd now have that capital available to back up the truck for today's screaming buys. But the economic house of cards that finally appears to be coming apart could have done so last fall. At the time, cashing in on base metal plays, which can be expected to suffer with a slowing economy, and holding on to precious metals plays, for which the opposite is true, made perfect sense.

"Today, we would certainly go to cash rather than hold on to any conventional investment that has exposure to 'toxic paper' or that can be expected to do poorly in a slowing economy.

"But gold's day in the sun is coming soon, and we still believe the stocks give us leverage on that rising star. So, as stated in the most recent edition of the *International Speculator,* we're not selling anything unless we think the company doesn't have what it takes to make it through to the other side.

"Of course, some investors might want to do some strategic tax loss selling, then look to buy back in the new year. The problem is that oftentimes once you are out of the market, you can miss the big moves while waiting for the right moment to jump back in."

"Not much consolation for investors who have already lost money to Junior Goldshares while waiting for the big returns to materialize," sniffed Cuomo, looking meaningfully at the jury.

"No, it's not," James agreed. "No one likes to take an investment loss. But I have to say something here in Junior's defense. Namely, I have to remind folks of the speculator's credo, because no one's ever made a secret out of the fact that gold shares are speculative in nature.

"And that credo goes like this: 'Speculators invest 10 percent in the hope of receiving a 100 percent return, while investors invest 100 percent in the hope of a 10 percent return.'

"In the *International Speculator,* a very apt name for the topic we cover, it has been our constant warning that investors should invest in gold shares with no more than 20 percent of their portfolio. That's for the simple reason that while these stocks can offer big rewards—life-changing rewards, in fact—investors in the sector must be willing to accept big risks. Well, today, because of panic dumping, we are seeing the worse side of gold shares.

"Even so, for illustrative purposes, let's do the math on the losses that an investor who limited her investments to just 20 percent of her portfolio would have suffered with gold shares. Assume, for example, that you lost 75 percent on the 20 percent of your portfolio that you allocated to the sector. In that case, your net loss on your overall port-folio would have been just 15 percent. Not fun, but not particularly bad, all things considered.

"Conversely, take an investor who was 100 percent invested in the S&P 500 over the period mentioned by Jeff Clark earlier. In that case, he'd now be down almost 40 percent. Actually, looking at the market action today on my iPhone, the losses would be even worse than that."

"Now, hold on!" Mr. Cuomo sputtered. "All of this is good and well, but you can't all honestly be saying that you still think gold and even gold shares are still a good investment!"

THE DEFENSE CALLS DAVID GALLAND

Mr. Reason stood again. "One more witness?"

"Oh, all right, but I want an answer to my question!" Cuomo barked, adding with a dramatic flourish, "The world wants an answer, nay, demands it!"

"Call your witness," Judge Market said, unimpressed.

"The defense calls David Galland, managing director of Casey Research."

A handsome, well-dressed man, his sublime intelligence palpable even from across the room, rose from the galley and approached the witness stand where Mr. Gold smiled happily at him.

"Okay, whoever you are, start talking," Cuomo said sharply. "You tell the jury how it is you could possibly be bullish about anything related to precious metals at this time. I mean, for gawd's sake, man, the global economy itself is collapsing. It is deflation that investors must be worried about. And yet, and yet . . . are you going to stand there and actually tell me you think investors should hold on to their precious metals investments? You are, I contend, either mad or deluded, or both at the same time!"

Unflustered by the bluster, Galland began to speak.

"Economies and investment markets are complex systems, which is to say that predicting them with any certainty is an impossibility. Thus, my comments should not be taken to reflect certainty, but rather the best interpretation I can make of the situation as we see it.

"For some years now, we have been warning that the house of cards, which has been built on a fiat monetary system, would come tumbling down.

"It was because of the excess and the distortions that this system make inevitable that Doug Casey and others in the organization looked at the tea leaves and saw a Greater Depression, but one of an inflationary nature.

"So, here we are, with the crisis upon us. There is no question that there is a massive deleveraging going on as individuals and corporations look to rebuild their stocks of ready money by dumping assets of all description. Real estate and equity markets are crashing as a result at the same time that U.S. Treasury instruments rise in value even though their yields are negative and falling. While buying into an instrument with a negative yield, at this point in time, many feel it is better to lose some money at a measured pace than take the sort of beatings being doled out in competing financial instruments.

"Of course, as U.S. Treasuries are denominated in dollars, the inflow into those instruments has helped strengthen the dollar, putting pressure on gold and silver, which are, per Terry Coxon above, viewed as a competitive form of money. You can see that correlation in Figure 10.3 that Bud Conrad, who couldn't make it today because he is preparing for a trip to New Zealand, sent over.

"The panicked reaction of investors in all sectors is understandable. The crisis we are now witnessing is not just of a once-in-a-generation scale, but once in a century. And so the scramble for safe harbors and cash is perfectly understandable. It's why Treasuries are so popular, and it's why gold has largely held its own in the broader scheme of things."

"Do you have a point to make?" Cuomo sneered from his seat.

Galland nonchalantly replied:

"I was merely setting the stage for where we are at this point in history. And by that I mean, here and now, October 24, 2008. You see, when panic and confusion are the watchwords of the day, as they now are, there are two attributes of the successful investor that become especially important. The first is to stay calm. The second is to try to look beyond the immediate.

"Many investors have, like the participants in the Charge of the Light Brigade—the anniversary of which, by the way, is tomorrow, October 25—have misread the signals and rushed straight into the

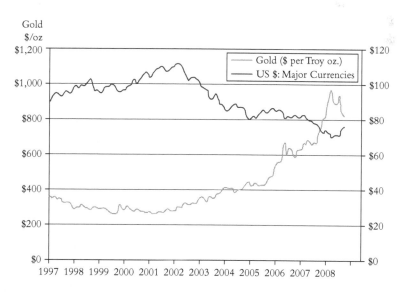

Figure 10.3 Gold and the Dollar Move in Opposite Directions

cannons of the bear market, being wiped out in the process. Or, in their rush for the rear, they have dumped everything indiscriminately, suffering unnecessarily big losses on great investments.

"Will the market continue to rig for deflation for the immediate future? Absolutely. And for the next little while, we can expect nothing other than bad economic news. Therefore, caution in all things financial is called for. Of course, if you have a good reserve of cash, then you could take positions in the inverse stock market ETFs and short positions on banks, financials, and real estate plays recommended in *The Casey Report*. But in a market as uncertain as this, such positions should be approached carefully, because of the increasing presence of governments in the markets.

"Specifically, with each passing day, the risk increases of market-distorting government interventions, including short-sale bans, trading halts, direct interventions in individual stocks, increased margins on targeted commodities, etc. That greatly increases the risk for short-sellers."

"Are we going to get back to the topic of Mr. Gold et al. at some point? I have a hair appointment at 2:00 PM," Cuomo said, looking down for his reflection on the highly polished top of the table in front of him.

"Yes. Right away," said Galland.

"You see, most of our recommended investments are not short-term in nature, but rather look for big trends that you can invest in when they are deeply out of favor. Our base case about the nature of the crisis, and especially the government's reaction to it, has not changed. In fact, if a year ago, you had asked us to estimate the amount of money the governments of the world would unleash in an attempt to head off an economic downturn, none of us, not even Doug Casey, our resident guru now wandering the highlands of Argentina, would have come remotely close to estimating the actual numbers being deployed.

"To put some meat on that point, over the last month and a little bit, the monetary base of the United States has increased by a previously unimaginable and unprecedented 20 percent.

"And our own Bud Conrad now estimates next year's U.S. government deficit at better than 10 percent of GNP, an also unprecedented number. And that doesn't even factor in the impact on the deficit from the fall-off in tax revenues that is inevitable given the likely depth of the downturn.

"And it gets worse than that, because if you step back just a bit, you'll realize that, while financial markets have been devastated, the damage to the real economy is just now getting started.

"Which is to say that the scope of the government's monetary exertions to "fix" everything are only beginning to ramp up. The Democrats, who look likely to control the whole shebang in Washington, are already calling for yet more stimulus and expensive intervention, including, this week, a call for the government to guarantee the nation's defaulting mortgages. Given that 265,968 mortgages went into foreclosure in September alone, this potential bit of largesse is unlikely to come cheap."

"Has anyone ever told you that you're long winded?" Cuomo asked.

"Yes, they have. It is a personal problem I struggle with every day.

"Be that as it may, investors today have several choices, or some combination thereof, they need to make in face of the economic crisis.

"They can choose to try and time this market over the short term, but if they do, they better use some very tight controls and pay a lot of attention, because literally anything can happen.

"They could also choose to sell everything, take the tax losses, and sit in cash until that point when the inflation we see as inevitable makes the cost of holding that cash too expensive.

"Or they can set aside enough cash to assure that their quality of life is not at risk in a collapsing economy and cautiously begin searching out the extraordinary values to be had in gold and other inflation hedges. There is no rush, but one would want to be positioned ahead of the big demand for these inflation hedges we see coming when the wall of government money begins to hit the economy next year.

"As Doug Casey recently put it, and as the ghost of Rothbard seconded above, gold's highest and best use is as money, and sometimes it can also be a terrific investment. With the caveat that the near-term deflationary pressures will continue to periodically whip up headwinds for gold and other inflation hedges, we think that Mr. Gold, Ms. Silver, and the resource share clan are screamingly good investments. Personally, I am content with my resource holdings and am holding tight."

"Mr. Cuomo, do you have any further questions or comments before I pass judgment?" Judge Market asked.

"Only that I think these gold bugs are lunatics because everyone, but everyone now thinks that we are going into a deep deflation," Mr. Cuomo said dismissively. "I rest my case."

"Yes, that is so," Galland responded. "But, sooner than most people expect, we think that everyone, but everyone will begin to believe that it is a historic level of inflation they need to most worry about. At that point, Mr. Gold and all his friends will be waiting for them."

"Mr. Reason, do you have any closing comments?"

"No, sir."

"Then would the defendants rise," the judge intoned.

"In light of the evidence presented here today, and because a sound judgment in this case involves the passage of time, I'm going to postpone judgment on this case, and release the defendants with the stipulation that they report back here in six months. At that time, we will update our arguments and Mr. Gold, you and your friends had better have made amends by that time, or else. Do you understand?"

"Not really," Mr. Gold said brightly, "but I'll be back."

■ ■ ■

Since this was written in October 2008 gold has risen from about US$750 per ounce to over $1,000, a gain of over 30 percent. Over the same time frame the S&P 500 has fallen about 14 percent. The numbers would tell a similar story if we looked back five years. Gold has risen from about $400 and is now up over 154 percent while the S&P 500 is down about 2 percent. Mr. Gold and the rest of his defendants remain free.

CHAPTER 11

BULLION AND BEYOND

Addison Wiggin
The Five-Minute Forecast

"In general, the art of government consists of taking as much
money as possible from one class of citizens to give to another."

— Voltaire, French essayist and
philosopher (1694–1778)

*Addison Wiggin is executive publisher of Agora Financial, LLC, the
renowned economic forecasting and financial research firm in Baltimore,
Maryland.*

*In his 16 years at Agora, Addison has been an avid student of, writer
about, and commentator on the financial markets and the governments
that regulate them. In the process he and Bill Bonner have co-authored
two* New York Times *Best Sellers,* Financial Reckoning Day
and Empire of Debt, *which have just been updated and published.
Additionally, Addison also conceived, co-wrote, and executive produced*
I.O.U.S.A., *the critically acclaimed documentary film and best-selling
book. He's also the creator and editorial director of Agora Financial's free
daily e-letter,* Five–Minute Forecast.

Originally published in Agora Financial in 2008 as "Bullion and Beyond: Five Stunning Ways
to Get Richer on the Epic Metals Boom Ahead!"

Addison's creative talents and editorial experience are readily apparent in one of the more comprehensive contributions in this book. Beginning by stating that "gold could easily skyrocket to over $2,000 an ounce." Then Addison shows us the reasons "why gold's impressive run is still in its infancy" and why, "just like the 'peak oil' phenomenon, we're headed for 'peak gold.'" He lists "nine different instruments" you can use when investing in gold. And then to top things off, he recommends five different strategies or action items "that will help you cash in on this unprecedented move." So, get out a piece of paper and start taking notes.

After decades of dormancy, gold is back! Since 2000, the yellow metal has soared over 184 percent—taking gold mining stocks to the stratosphere. But that's just the beginning—because this boom is just getting warmed up. We've gathered a plethora of data showing this huge leg up in the yellow metal market is no accident. It is, instead, the beginnings of what will be the biggest gold price explosion in precious metals history. In fact, gold could easily skyrocket to over $2,000 an ounce. In a moment, I'll share with you five strategies that will help you cash in on this unprecedented move. But first, let me show you why gold's impressive run is still in its infancy. . . .

A HISTORY OF VALUE

Since ancient times, gold has been a safe haven for investors worried about market volatility and political uncertainty. Even the rise of paper currencies hasn't managed to kill the idea of gold in people's minds. That's because gold is no one's liability—currencies come and go, but gold remains the same.

For that reason alone, precious metals should always have a permanent place in your portfolio. It is the ultimate hedge.

But today holding gold is more important—and can be more profitable—than it's been in years. That's because we're seeing a repeat of the same forces that pushed gold from $35 to over $800 between 1971 and 1980. I'm talking about things like a weakening dollar, easy monetary policies, and geopolitical uncertainty.

Now, if you've watched the news, you know gold has already breached the $1,000 mark. But there's every reason to suspect this is only a pause. Even after this tremendous run-up, we expect gold to head higher . . . much higher. That's because gold's "true" high is actually closer to $2,000! Let me explain. . . . When people talk about the gold price, then tend to forget one thing—the dollar's decreasing value over the years. So comparing yesterday's gold price to today's is like comparing apples to armadillos.

Adjusted for inflation, a $35 ounce of gold in 1971 would be worth $175.55 today. 1975 gold rockets to $697.02. In today's dollars, 1980 gold, the peak year at $850, *clocks in closer to $2,275.99*. So, in real terms, gold has a long way to go before it reaches its top. The question is, how likely is that?

THE TRILLION-DOLLAR SINKHOLE

Its reason is pretty simple. The Fed knows regular cash and credit injections make everyone feel rich. The theory goes, when you've got cash and low-priced credit, companies borrow and expand. Consumers borrow and spend. Families borrow and buy homes. But while that sounds good, there is a serious downside to this plan . . . debt.

Consumers are now weighed down with trillions in backbreaking outstanding credit—and every dollar needs to be paid back. The U.S. government is also running $162 billion domestic deficits. And it's about to get much worse. The first wave of baby boomers is set to retire between 2008 and 2010. Entitlement programs like Social Security and Medicare, in whatever form they exist, will start paying out larger sums of money relative to revenues.

Unfortunately, it doesn't look like there's any way to reverse this trend. It can't be from trade. The United States is currently importing over $800 billion more than it exports every year. So instead, the government has tried another tactic to make up the shortfalls—by going deeper into debt. There are trillions of U.S. dollars now held outside of the United States. Since U.S. dollars are only legal tender within the United States, whether foreigners continue holding them depends on whether they have confidence in the dollar. There is one final trick up the government's sleeve. But this "solution" isn't a solution at all. . . .

HOW CAN PUSH-BUTTON MONEY HAVE VALUE?

Before becoming Fed Chairman, Ben Bernanke famously said in a speech at the National Economists Club in Washington, in November 2002 . . .

> Like gold, U.S. dollars have value only to the extent that they are strictly limited in supply. But the U.S. government has a technology, called a printing press (or, today, its electronic equivalent), which allows it to produce as many U.S. dollars as it wishes at essentially no cost . . . We conclude that, under a paper-money system, a determined government can always generate higher spending and hence positive inflation.

In other words, if you want to juice an economy . . . turn on the printing presses and make it easy to borrow money at a low rate of interest. The Fed won't lose control, he says, until short-term rates go to zero. And maybe not even then. The problem is, money can't escape the natural law of supply and demand. *When there's too much of it floating around, each dollar is worth that much less relative to the whole.* Suddenly, you've got price inflation. Suddenly, every dollar you have in the bank is worth less. Hemingway called it the "first panacea of a mismanaged nation."

Already this disastrous stance has plummeted the purchasing power of our dollars by a mind-blowing 96 percent. Today it's worth just pennies compared to what it bought a century ago. Or even what it was worth the last time gold boomed, in the 1970s. Flooding the market with easy money like this is more like burning your furniture to keep warm! We like to think an even smarter economist, Ludwig Von Mises, got it right . . .

> There is no means of avoiding the final collapse of a boom brought about by credit expansion. The alternative is only whether the crisis should come sooner as a result of the voluntary abandonment of further credit expansion . . . or later as a final and total catastrophe of the currency system involved.

Apparently, we're not the only ones who think so . . .

LOST CONFIDENCE IN THE DOLLAR IS SPREADING

China has loaded up and almost doubled its gold reserves to protect itself from a dollar drop and to hedge some of the trillions in U.S. Treasury bonds and notes that it has purchased over the years. This 76 percent increase in holdings since 2003 still has done little to hedge its position with only a couple of percent of reserves held in gold compared to 10 to 15 percent for Western central banks. Much more buying could be on the way.

Here's how the *London Telegraph* puts it:

> China has woken up. The West is a black hole with all this money being printed. The Chinese are buying raw materials because it is a much better way to use their $1.9 trillion of reserves. They get ten times the impact, and can cover their infrastructure for 50 years.

And China is only one of many countries thinking the same thing. Why hold worthless dollars when you can hold something of finite value, like gold?

APPROACHING "PEAK GOLD"

Just like the "peak oil" phenomenon, we're headed for "peak gold." It's all about how much gold is left unprocessed underground. The more we take out, the harder it is to find more. And the harder it is to get to. For instance, miners used to pan for gold in streams. Today, just to get enough gold for a wedding band, you need to crush up to *20 tons* of rock.

And remember, gold isn't just for jewelry, coins, or bars of bullion. Gold goes into computers, cell phones, and satellites. It's used in medical lasers, industrial lasers, and in spacecrafts. It plays a major role in medical research. It's even used for treating some diseases. Tough new environmental laws and 20 years of low mining investment don't help. But it's really geology that's conspiring against the miners most. Nobody can find the big gold deposits anymore. It looks like they're all tapped out.

With gold prices up, miners are looking. More holes open up in the ground. More tons of rock go through the mills. But so far, the average quality of the gold they're finding has gone down. The low-hanging fruit of the gold mining universe—the easy deposits and rich mines—have started to disappear. Gold's already rare. But it's getting more rare by the day.

This rarity is running into increasing demand. There isn't a more fundamental argument for rising prices. And if the U.S. dollar continues to plummet, there'll be no stopping the yellow metal's upward charge. Again, it's economics at work. Gold is priced in dollars, so as the currency becomes less valuable, the metal naturally becomes more valuable. You want to accumulate gold investments now, while prices are still relatively low. And today, owning gold is easier than ever before.

NINE WAYS TO MOVE INTO GOLD

Owning gold today is a little different than it was in the past, when holding gold meant hauling bars and coins around. You don't need a house like Fort Knox to keep your gold safe. Gold has become a 21st-century investment—with enough options and oversight to ensure you're protected. There is no shortage of choices when it comes to investing in gold. Below, I've listed nine different instruments. Each one has different associated costs, benefits, and risks. In general, however, as you read down the list, you will see that safety is replaced by opportunity.

1. **Physical gold:** Bullion—whether in the form of bars, coins, or ingots—is the ultimate financial lifeboat. Throughout the ages, princes and paupers have used it as money and turned to it for security. And it has withstood every test: war, revolution, hyperinflation, and depression.

   Investing in this type of gold, however, means keeping it in your house or paying someone to store it. The first way is dangerous and means you'll have to take your gold to a market to sell it. Storing it involves fees that bite into your returns. It is also subject to widespread gaps between the bid and ask price—meaning you could find yourself paying more for your gold than the actual spot price.

If you're interested in physical gold, bullion coins may be the best way to go. They are small, so they are easy to store. They can also be quite beautiful, giving an extrinsic worth beyond its monetary worth. The coins to look at are the 1-ounce South African Kruggerands, Canadian Maple Leafs, or American Eagles.

2. **Gold certificates:** The Perth Mint Certificate Program (PMCP) is operated by the international precious metals minting and trading company Goldcorp—and offers a secure and confidential way of investing directly in gold. The company is owned by the state of Western Australia and has received a government guarantee. Plus, all precious metals controlled by the group are insured by Lloyd's of London (at the Perth Mint's cost).

   The downside is that U.S. investors need to make an initial investment of $10,000 and a minimum of $5,000 to add to the position. That's a lot of change. But there are some programs that are similar to Perth Mint Certificates that offer a lower entry price. We'll explore some in a bit.

3. **Gold shares:** A unique way to play gold directly is with gold exchange-traded funds (ETFs), which operate just like stocks and are traded on several major stock exchanges. The shares are fairly liquid and can be bought and sold intraday like stocks. When you purchase shares of an ETF, a trust is created, giving you legal title to the metal. The shares can then be redeemed or traded. This is a terrific way to hold actual bullion without the trouble of storing, transporting, or insuring the metal.

   ETFs are a relatively new way of leveraging oneself to the current bull market in gold. One of the oldest ETFs, Australia's Gold Bullion Securities, has been around since 2002. Stateside, there are only two gold ETFs available. You'll discover our favorite a little later on. . . .

4. **Gold mutual funds:** If you don't want to own physical gold and don't have the time or inclination to study individual

stocks, a mutual fund is a terrific way to go. As with any mutual fund, performance is a reflection of management as much as industry.

The Outstanding Investments portfolio has a few gold funds. Our favorite is the American Century Global Gold (BGEIX). In the past six years, the total return for the American Century Global Gold fund has averaged over 20 percent per year. If you are bullish on the long-term prospects of the price of gold, then owning a gold-based mutual fund is a good way to participate in the market movement. Additionally, one or more of the companies in the portfolio are takeover candidates because the mining sector is consolidating in the near term. It is almost always the case in a rising market that the companies with decent reserves get taken out at a premium.

Rather than try to pick which ones will prove the biggest winners, you can just own them all. Of course, the gains won't equal what you could see by pinpointing an individual potential winner.

5. **Senior gold companies:** In a bull market, senior gold stocks—large established gold mines with a history of success—are terrific investments. They offer pretty solid returns and let you sleep easy. The reason is pretty straightforward: Senior golds have the best management, technology, and reserves. But just as a $10-per-barrel increase in the price of crude doesn't have a large impact on the price of a multinational oil company, neither does a jump in gold prices manifest itself in blue chip producers the way it does in junior golds.

In a moment, you'll discover two of the best of the big ones. . . .

6. **Foreign gold companies and ADRs:** Huge fortunes were made in the 1970s and 1980s by astute investors who bought American Depositary Receipts (ADRs) of South African gold companies. An ADR is a certificate held by U.S. banks and represents a specific number of shares of a foreign stock. ADRs are traded on U.S. stock exchanges, are widely available, and

have a dollar-denominated price. And just like stocks, ADRs may pay dividends.

7. **Junior gold stocks:** These are smaller, usually less established gold and mineral companies. A few years back, they were pretty risky endeavors. Most pinned all their hopes on one or two undeveloped and sometimes unexplored properties. They were usually in debt up to their eyeballs . . . and some of them weren't even producing gold! That doesn't mean they were all necessarily bad investments— *Outstanding Investments* rode some for gains of 73 percent . . . 43 percent . . . even 108 percent. You just needed to be very selective.

   Today, with the return of higher gold prices, a lot of these little gems are attracting more interest. But it's still important to be careful and only bet on likely winners. We'll have one for you in just a bit.

8. **Gold options:** This is the line between investing and speculating. You can buy options on physical gold or gold stocks. Options can be a little bit complicated, however, and the odds are against option buyers (three out of every four options bought expire worthless).

   The big enemy when you own an option is time. You have to reach your strike price by a specific date or your option expires worthless.

   Still, options provide terrific leverage, and the most you can lose when you buy an option is the price you paid for it. Best of all, they give you an opportunity to earn home-run profits.

9. **Gold futures:** Only the most sophisticated, risk-tolerant investors play futures. For everyone else, it's better to stay away. Sure, you could make a hefty profit, but it's just as easy to lose your shirt. As far as we're concerned, you're better off staying far away from futures for now.

That covers the most well-known gold investments. But with a little digging, you can find some unique types of gold investments out there. One of our favorites is an investment that promises a good return—with all the convenience of a checking account.

THE EASIEST WAY TO OWN GOLD

A few minutes ago we told you about gold certificates offered by the Perth Mint. On the flip side, $10,000 may seem like a lot to shell out—and you might be wary of dealing with a foreign company. Luckily, our friends at EverBank offer a cheaper solution closer to home. It's called a Metals Select Account—a personal account made entirely of gold holdings. (You can also open a silver account, but silver is a story for another time.)

A Metals Select Account offers the versatility of a brokerage account with the low cost and convenience of an ETF or mutual fund. Like a brokerage account, you can take physical possession of your gold holdings. You can also buy or sell ounces from your account without worrying about broker's commission or fees. EverBank can even get you prices within 1 percent of the current gold spot price—a far cry from the 4 to 7 percent you'll pay a broker. And certain accounts also let you specify whether you want to hold bars or coins.

There are two types of Metals Select accounts. A pooled account buys you into a shared stash of gold. Of course, you can add to or sell some of your position at any time. For additional fees, you can elect to take delivery fees. The drawback is that you cannot choose what kind of gold your fund contains—it could be coins, bars, etc. But to make up for that lack of choice, the minimum investment is just $5,000, and you don't have to pay storage or maintenance fees.

For an opening balance of $7,500, you can open a Metals Select Holding Account. This kind of account gives you full control of designated gold—your choice of coins or bars, etc. You can even fill the account with IRA-eligible American Eagle coins. You'll have to pay an annual storage fee, but you'll find EverBank's prices are quite competitive.

Either way, it's one of the simplest and most cost-effective ways to add gold to your portfolio. And all you have to do is visit www.everbank .com/oi-metals to get started.

THE STOCK MARKET'S TICKET TO
EASY GOLD OWNERSHIP

If EverBank's minimum investment seems too steep, or if you'd like the ability to quickly cash in on gold's rise, you may want to consider

StreetTracks Gold Shares (NYSE: GLD). It's an exchange-traded fund, meaning it's as easy to buy and sell as any other stock. Each share represents a fixed amount of gold held in a special bank account.

From the official description:

> StreetTRACKS Gold Trust is an investment trust whose shares strive to reflect the performance of the price of gold bullion, less the trust's expenses. The trust holds gold, and is expected to issue baskets in exchange for deposits of gold and to distribute gold in connection with redemptions of baskets. The gold held by the trust will only be sold on an as-needed basis to pay trust expenses, in the event the trust terminates and liquidates its assets or as otherwise required by law or regulation.

GLD is designed to reflect the price of gold on a fractional basis of 10 percent. So with gold at $800, you'd expect the shares to sell for around $80. A $10 move in the spot price of gold would thus correspond to a $1 move in GLD. If the spot price of gold fell to $600, GLD would fall to $60. If gold rose to $1,000, GLD would move to $1,000, and so on.

The price relationship between spot gold and GLD will not always correlate perfectly, but it will be very close. If prices ever got significantly out of line, arbitrageurs would be able to lock in a risk-free profit by playing the futures against the ETF and taking delivery if necessary; Wall Street has endless rows of supercomputers dedicated to exploiting spread movements when linked relationships get temporarily out of line.

In other words, you don't have to worry too much about GLD's net asset value, discounts, or premiums. All you really care about is the price of bullion—and how many shares of GLD you own.

Also, keep in mind that owning the shares isn't exactly like owning the gold. Unlike the Perth Certificates or even EverBank's Metals Select Accounts, you cannot take possession of the gold. On the other hand, since GLD trades just like a stock, getting in and out couldn't be easier—it's just a matter of calling your broker or hitting a few keys online.

Action to take: Consider buying StreetTracks Gold Shares (NYSE: GLD).

RUN WITH THE BIG BOYS

When it comes to the "senior" gold companies, there are only a few names that instantly spring to mind: Newmont Mining, Barrick Gold, AngloGold. But we think the best of the bunch is Goldcorp. (NYSE: GG).

Goldcorp has been around since 1994, and today it is the world's lowest-cost million-ounce gold producer. It's sitting on 17.73 million proven ounces of gold spread across the globe. You can find its mines in Canada, the United States, Mexico, Brazil, Argentina, and Australia. And at last count, it was producing that gold at a cash cost of less than $140 per ounce. Let me say that again—it's getting gold out of the ground for about $140 an ounce. With gold at $800 as of this writing and rising, that means it's making $660 on every ounce it sells!

To put that into perspective, take a look at how Goldcorp's costs compare to other big names in the industry:

Company Cost per Ounce	
Goldcorp	$140
AngloGold	$357
Barrick	$377
Newmont	$388
Gold Fields	$538
Harmony	$572

As you can see, Goldcorp has a solid edge. This is pure profit to the company, from the time the whistle blows in the morning and the elevators take the workers down into the mines and pits. And Goldcorp has put that money to good use, making some smart acquisitions. In early 2005, the company bought out Wheaton River Minerals—a move that added tremendously to the company's balance sheets. In November 2006, it added Glamis Gold, which boosted the company's silver reserves. And in 2008 it acquired Gold Eagle to boast its gold reserves even more.

Obviously, Goldcorp's profit margins will become even more attractive as gold prices rise. And the company has the reserves to keep the money train running for quite some time. So even with the tremendous run-up the stock has seen, we think it has further to go yet.

Action to take: Consider buying Goldcorp (NYSE: GG).

ADD ANOTHER SENIOR

Another big gold company that should be in your portfolio is Kinross Gold (NYSE: KGC).

Kinross is the world's eighth largest primary gold producer, with the world's fifth largest gold reserves, 45 million ounces. Kinross operates nine mines in five countries: the United States, Canada, Russia, Brazil, and Chile. All of these locales are considered "friendly" to mining (yes, even Russia). Kinross has three more projects in development.

Figure 11.1 shows a breakdown of the Kinross gold reserve structure.

At the same time, Kinross trades for $231 of market capitalization per ounce of gold reserves, not including silver or copper resources,

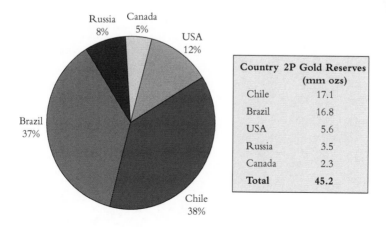

Country	2P Gold Reserves (mm ozs)
Chile	17.1
Brazil	16.8
USA	5.6
Russia	3.5
Canada	2.3
Total	**45.2**

Figure 11.1 Kinross's Reserves Are Located in Five Countries That Are Favorable to Mining

which is among the lowest premiums among major stock companies. Call it "cheap gold," considering what you would have to pay for other stocks.

As is the case with all mining companies in these times, Kinross faces pressures from the rising costs of energy, labor, freight and transportation, equipment and consumables, plus, in some cases, unfavorable exchange rates. However, the company has a continuing focus on cost control as a core part of its culture. Kinross has one of the best growth profiles in the gold industry, with the above-noted three major projects in development, which will increase its output by 60 percent over the next two years. Figure 11.2 amplifies the Kinross story.

Kinross is trading in the range of $15 per share, with a market capitalization of $10.5 billion and a forward price-earnings ratio of 21. Some 59 percent of Kinross's shares are held by institutions. Kinross's profit margin is in excess of 15 percent, although the company pays no dividend.

Kinross will be opening new mine production in the next 18 months or so, selling even more gold output into a rising market. It is also attracting some of the best professional talent in the industry to its ranks. So we expect precious metals output and profitability to increase and earnings per share growth to accelerate.

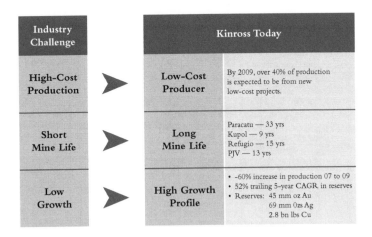

Figure 11.2   The Kinross Advantage

We believe that Kinross, along with Goldcorp, is one of the best of the larger-cap gold mining value plays around.

Action to take: Consider buying Kinross Gold Corp. (NYSE: KGC).

A ZERO-COST GOLD MINER

One of the keys to successful investing is diversity. But that doesn't just mean investing in different industries and sectors. It also means picking up different kinds of stocks *within* sectors. Goldcorp and Kinross Gold's size gives you some stability and safety in gold. For a little more risk—and a chance at bigger profits—you should also take a look at smaller companies.

Yamana Gold (NYSE: AUY)—an aggressive Canadian intermediate traded on U.S., Canadian, and London exchanges—looks a little like the Goldcorp of old, but with a twist: Its activities are focused on Latin America, and Brazil in particular.

In terms of mining focus, Brazil is excellent for a number of reasons:

- Brazil has a stable and benign political climate. This stands in contrast to other Latin American countries, not to mention less civilized areas around the world. Better still, the Brazilian government maintains a favorable stance toward mining and a friendly regulatory environment.
- Mining operations in Brazil have reliable access to power, particularly hydropower. The country is rapidly developing its transport and logistics infrastructure, which also proves a boom.
- Brazilian exchange rates and labor costs are competitive, enabling a lower long-term cost of production than many other countries. A broad labor pool, widespread availability of ethanol and subsidized diesel also help keep mining costs low.
- Brazil has a lot of "latent geological potential." In other words, there could be plenty of undiscovered gold—and copper—in them thar hills.
- As the tenth largest economy in the world, Brazil exports much besides metal, allowing it to sidestep "Dutch disease" and the problems associated with lopsided resource economies.

Yamana Gold was incorporated in 2003, specifically to pursue gold and copper opportunities in Brazil. As relative newcomers, these guys aren't wasting any time. . . . During the year ended December 31, 2008, total production from all mines totaled approximately one million gold equivalent ounces and Yamana plans to ramp up to 2.2 million by 2012. Thanks to smart financing and skillful acquisitions, Yamana is on track to reach that aggressive goal.

Yamana Gold currently has five operational mines, several development projects in Brazil and Argentina, and significant land holdings. Rapid expansion is under way, and a tidal wave of production is coming online. What do we mean by a "tidal wave"? Consider that Yamana Gold's production was a mere 100,000 ounces in 2005 . . . over 400,000 in 2006 and it's projected to mine 620,000 ounces for 2007. And 2008 totaled right around 1,000,000 ounces.

But there's an added benefit to Yamana. The company is also sitting on 2.3 billion pounds of copper—an excellent source of cash flow. Yamana Gold's CEO, Peter Marrone, argues that the company's cost of gold production is zero when proceeds from copper sales are taken into account. A gold miner with a 100 percent margin? You can't beat that with a stick.

While remaining fully exposed to the upside of gold, Yamana's management has wisely hedged its exposure to copper fluctuations. Yamana's copper prices are essentially locked in for the next two years . . . so the red metal cash flow is safe, even if the global economy keels over.

There are certainly risks to consider. You don't get astronomical upside potential without the possibility of setbacks and complications. But the potential rewards are so great, and the company's position so strong, it's hard to think of a more compelling buy than Yamana Gold right now.

Action to take: Consider buying Yamana Gold (NYSE: AUY).

THE NEXT GOLD RUSH

Governments have spent the better part of three decades trying to take gold down. But the yellow metal is too old and too ingrained in people's memories to go down without a fight. Between the United States' systematic destruction of its currency, a growing global need for financial safety and security, and the age-old forces of basic supply and demand, the stage is set for an explosive blowout. The recommendations in this report will give you a good foundation for riding these precious metals to the top.

CHAPTER 12

GOLD IS TRULY PRECIOUS

Pam and Mary Anne Aden
The Aden Forecast

"Silver and gold are not the only coin; virtue too passes current all over the world."

—Euripides, Greek Playwright, c. 480–406 BCE

"The Aden Forecast *has one of the most remarkable track records among several dozen investment publications I read regularly," stated Robert Kephart, once the "dean of financial newsletter publishers."* The Hulbert Financial Digest, *which has been tracking the advice of almost 200 investment newsletters for over 20 years, continually ranks* The Aden Forecast *as one of the top-performing investment newsletters. But Doug Casey gets to the crux of the matter when he says, "the Adens are proven right and right again."*

Pam and Mary Anne Aden have authored dozens of reports and articles and have spoken at investment seminars around the world. Since 1982, they have been publishing The Aden Forecast, *a 12-page monthly investment newsletter specializing in all major markets.*

"Gold has been the only 'international currency' and store of value accepted and known throughout the world for thousands of years . . ."

so begins the Aden sisters' contribution to this book. After reviewing "financial crises of the past," the Adens get to the essential defining characteristic of the present crisis, stating that "the debt and amounts of money spent after 1971 were almost miniscule compared to the amounts being spent today." What I Iike about this piece is how, in a very logical format, the Adens make the case that economic and banking crises will continue, concluding that "you must protect yourself and your assets from the repercussions to come" and that "the best way to do that is by owning some gold."

Throughout recorded history gold has been special. People have fought for it, talked about it, desired it, and died for it. Gold has been responsible for building empires, creating booms as well as busts, and it has brought empires down.

From the Egyptians, to the Greeks, to the Romans, to the Incas, gold has played a key role for over 5,000 years, or nearly as long as civilizations have existed. In more recent centuries, the California gold rush was instrumental in fueling the rapid growth in the American West, and the examples go on.

In spite of this, few people understand gold's historical importance and preeminence over all other forms of wealth. Not dominated by any one country, gold has been the only "international currency" and store of value accepted and known throughout the world for thousands of years.

Currencies have come and gone. In fact, there is not one paper currency that has survived, but gold has. The Founding Fathers of the United States knew this. In the Constitution they defined real money as gold and silver, and they warned against paper money.

Gold is money. It always has been and it always will be. It remains the number one measure of true wealth, and no other investment can compare. Gold is a safe haven and it thrives during times of uncertainty. It has withstood depressions, inflations, government collapses, revolutions, and wars. Gold has indeed stood the test of time.

FINANCIAL CRISES OF THE PAST

Until recently, most of us in this generation have never suffered through a financial crisis, but they are nothing new.

The past 800 years have involved a series of bubbles and busts, debt defaults, banking collapses, excessive speculation, panics, currency devaluations, recessions, deflations, and of course normal times. And ever since the first stocks traded 400 years ago, the markets have had a long history of booms and crises.

In more recent times, there was the Great Depression and the huge inflation of the 1970s. In both cases, the outcome was similar.

During the Great Depression in 1930–1935, gold instruments rose strongly. In the 1970s, it was the same story and gold's rise was dramatic. Gold rose 2,300 percent in 10 years, from $35 in 1970 to $850 in 1980. In those days, soaring inflation, the falling dollar, Watergate, and Vietnam were the dominant problems. It was primarily a U.S. phenomenon.

Last year the IMF identified 124 international banking crises since 1970. Four were in the 1970s, 39 were in the 1980s, and 74 were in the 1990s.

TODAY'S CRISIS: THE WORST YET

Still, there's no question that the current financial crisis has been the worst since the Great Depression. The entire financial system was on the brink of disaster in 2008 and an unprecedented amount of wealth was destroyed worldwide.

Massive Historical Bailout

In order to bail out the economy and get it back on track, a massive amount of money has been spent, which is being piled on to the debt that already existed, and the numbers involved are simply mind blowing. They are so huge it's hard to keep track and it's almost ridiculous to try.

At last count, if we were to take all of the debt and future obligations like Social Security and so on and pay them off at $1 million every single day, it would take around 200,000 years to eliminate the United States' existing debt and liabilities! That's right . . . we're talking about roughly the same amount of time that it took from the dawn of the first humans to walk on earth to the present.

How will this debt be paid off? It won't. Instead, the debt will be partially inflated away as the ongoing process that's been in force for many years continues, only this time it's going to be far more intense, and it'll have a wider range of repercussions.

Money and Inflation

If we go back to the beginning of the present era, debt and inflation have been rising ever since the Federal Reserve (Fed) was formed in 1913. This gave the new central bank the power to control and create U.S. dollars, and the dollar has lost about 95 percent of its purchasing power since then. Why?

The debt kept growing over the years, and as it did, consumer prices moved up too (inflation). That's because more money had to be created, along with the debt spending, which is essentially the cause of inflation. This built in inflation cheapened the U.S. dollar, making it worth less. In other words, you needed more dollars to buy the same thing you could've bought for fewer dollars a couple of years before.

This situation intensified in 1971 when President Nixon eliminated the dollar's last link to gold. By doing this he removed the last bit of fiscal discipline that existed prior to that time and the dollar became a paper currency. From that point on, the government could spend what it wanted and the Fed just created more dollars to pay for it. Debt soared and so did prices, resulting in a sharp drop in the dollar, along with surging inflation, gold, and commodity prices.

The U.S. dollar has lost about 75 percent of its value against the other major world currencies since 1971. And the dollar will continue losing its value because it's only backed by paper, by a country that has sadly become the world's largest debtor nation. (See Figure 12.1.)

More Than History in the Making

Currently, this process is intensifying again but on a much greater scale. The debt and amounts of money spent after 1971 were almost miniscule compared to the amounts being spent today. Debt has been soaring since the early 2000s, but it's really taking off now. Nothing like this has ever happened before, not even close, and nothing can compare.

At last count, the Federal Reserve and the government have either lent, guaranteed, or spent $12.8 trillion in their efforts to get the

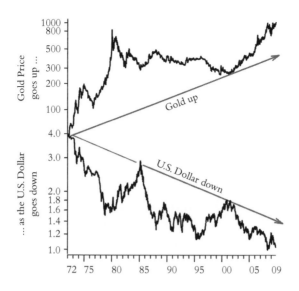

Figure 12.1 Gold Up = Dollar Down

economy back on track. We know that these numbers lose their significance after a while and it's hard to relate to them, but in an attempt to do so, consider that . . .

A couple of years ago a study was done by two respected economists estimating that the total cost of the Iraq war would eventually reach $2 trillion. At the time, people were shocked. But compared to the nearly $13 trillion for the economy, the Iraq war expenses now seem small in comparison.

Looking at it another way, the value of all the gold in existence since the time of Christ is currently worth about $4 trillion. In other words, just the costs to bail out the economy is so far going to be more than three times all of the gold that's been produced over the past 2,000 years.

This is beyond shocking, and it's difficult to know what the full extent of the repercussions will be in the years ahead. Obviously, the dollar will fall sharply and gold will soar. Beyond that, we're entering uncharted territory so no one really knows because there's never been a crisis of this magnitude in the history of mankind. Ultimately, the spending will probably make things better for now, but there's a high price to pay.

As the great Milton Friedman often noted, massive deficits and money supply will cause massive inflation. Foreign lenders will then not want to buy U.S. debt, and the Fed will have to pick up the slack. This is basically what's been taking place.

"Do What It Takes"

Again, we know that the economic and banking crisis last year was extremely serious. Action had to be taken. It had to be drastic, and it was. Obama and Bernanke were not going to sit back and let the crisis unfold on its own. They were determined to avoid another Great Depression, and their intentions were obviously good. But there's no question that the repercussions of all this will become ever more obvious in the years just ahead.

We know it's tiring to continue hearing about the ongoing record deficit spending, the soaring money supply, and the out-of-sight debt. Whether you agree with the spending or not, it will continue, and you must protect yourself and your assets from the repercussions to come.

GOLD WILL SHINE

The best way to do that is by owning some gold. Gold is once again showing that it is the safe haven and it thrives in times of global turmoil and uncertainty. That's what we're seeing now and gold is certainly behaving in traditional fashion.

It is not commonly known that gold has produced consistent gains for eight years, and 2009 will be the ninth year of consecutive gains. But this is just the beginning. Once inflation eventually kicks in, in reaction to all of the massive government spending, gold is going to soar.

Plus, it is little understood that gold moves opposite to the dollar, and that it's the ultimate currency (see Figure 12.1). It's not only been rising in dollar terms but it's also risen more than the strong currencies, and it's been stronger than the stock and bond markets.

Gold will continue to be a great investment as the dollar falls, and it will hold its value. Gold is the best inflation hedge, and there's no telling where it'll end up, at least well into the thousands of dollars in the years ahead, and maybe sooner.

Remember, gold's peak in 1980 at $850 is now the equivalent of about $2,400 in today's dollars. Gold has not even approached that level yet and the situation is far more serious now than it was then. Once the dollar falls further and inflation kicks in, it'll be another story. In the future, $1,000 gold will be truly seen as a bargain, especially considering the way the printing press has cranked up.

Using the gains in the 1970s as an example to forecast where gold could end up, . . . $5,800 would be the equivalent upside target. As wild as this may seem, remember that $5,800 in the future will not be worth the same as it is today. So far, gold has only gained about 300 percent since 2001.

Whatever the outcome, it's not going to happen from one day to the next, but this underlying foundation is pushing gold's bull market higher, and it's not going away any time soon. That's why investors are moving to gold, and it's why we've been recommending buying and staying with gold. It's your best, and probably only, solid bet looking out to the years ahead.

Currently, the general mainstream investor is not invested in gold. It's still early, even considering the almost nine-year rise, but as gold heads higher, it will attract attention. This upcoming bull market rise will have plenty of new demand from investors like these, who normally don't look at gold. These investors know things aren't right, they realize the dollar is vulnerable, but they're not sure what to do about it, or how to protect their assets. This will eventually change, especially considering the Chinese wild card.

WHEN CHINA TALKS, IT PAYS TO LISTEN

Regardless of how you feel about China, you have to admit that it is money savvy. In less than half a generation the government has transformed China from a poor rural country into one of the world's richest and most powerful. This is simply amazing, so it pays to watch what China is doing.

Currently, China is concerned because it has too many dollars and U.S. bonds. It is the United States' largest creditor. China is also concerned that the Western monetary stimulus is going to trigger global inflation, along with weak bond markets and a falling dollar, so it's taking action.

China is cutting back on its U.S. bond purchases, and it is buying gold in significant amounts. China has increased its gold reserves by an impressive 76 percent in the past six years. This is obviously to hedge against rising inflation and a weak dollar.

China is now considering increasing its gold reserves by seven fold to spread its foreign exchange risk. This is a growing tendency among other countries as well, and it will cause a further jump in gold demand.

Also important, there are about 50 percent, or three billion, more people in today's global economy who weren't around in the 1970s. Aside from China, where citizens are being encouraged to buy gold, there's also India and the former Soviet countries. In the 1970s, these countries were either very poor or closed, or both, but that's not the case anymore.

In essence, much more money is now chasing a limited amount of gold. Assuming there are 135,000 tons of gold in existence today at $1,000 an ounce, the total dollar value of all gold above ground is a mere $4.32 trillion dollars.

With global demand growing and the government planning to spend over $12 trillion dollars to revive the economy, combined with stimulus programs around the world, you can see why gold is an excellent investment in spite of its already eight-year-old bull market rise.

Overall, gold will likely be stronger this time around because of the unusual crisis we are experiencing. Gold is the ultimate safe haven, and as long as economic imbalances and uncertainty prevails, gold will be the place to park your money.

PART III

COIN AND BULLION BROKERS/DEALERS

"In the long run, gold will retain its value. Since that's all we ask of it, we are always satisfied. . . . Gold is not a speculation for us; it is a means of saving money."

—Bill Bonner, publisher, investment author, satirist (1948–)

Gold's role as wealth insurance and a store of value, particularly in times of calamity and tragedy, is thousands of years old. More often than not, the people who financially survive these devastating events are aided by the fact they had the foresight to have some gold on hand. More recent examples include the Jewish Diaspora of WWII, the Vietnamese boat people of the 1970s, and many of the Hong Kong Chinese who were prepared for the takeover by communist China in the late 1990s.

It's during the worst of times that gold has proved its importance as a means of wealth protection. Whether today's economic stresses of failing banks, growing unemployment, and the prospects of a world-wide depression now being discussed prove to be such a time for some individuals in some countries remains to be seen. However, at the very least Wall Street's inability to deal with the crisis, or properly prepare its clients for it, let alone own up to its involvement in its causes, should give pause to every investor and saver.

Gold's history as money predates modern times by centuries, with precious metals, including gold and silver, being used in trade centuries before the first known hard money currency of the ancient Greek states over 2,500 years ago. Again I turn to my friend, Doug Casey, who has pointed out to me and others on many occasions that it was Aristotle in the fourth century BCE who described the properties necessary for sound money. As Doug paraphrases Aristotle, "it had to be durable, not like wheat; divisible, not like diamonds; convenient, not like lead; constant, not like real estate; and best of all, as jewelry, it has intrinsic value." Both Aristotle and Doug believe that over thousands of years, whenever gold was available to humans, it has become the money of choice. With the advent of paper money and fractional reserve banking and a debt-based monetary system, Doug has since added an important sixth property that makes gold such sound money: "Gold cannot be created by government."

It was Greece's Alexander the Great who, in and around 330 BCE would conquer and then unify the known ancient world, using silver, a reliable gold substitute, as the backbone of a sound monetary system. His hard currency system, as well as lowered barriers to trade, resulted in widening commerce and a thriving empire. After his death in 323 BCE, the Roman Republic would eventually adopt a hard money currency that would lead to Roman rule for 1,000 years. More recently, the British Empire from the seventeenth to the twentieth centuries had a currency backed by gold. And until President Nixon unilaterally canceled the direct convertibility of the United States dollar to gold in 1971, the United States had been on a gold standard. In fact, Bill Bonner, of Agora Publishing, is fond of pointing out that "it took about an ounce to buy a toga during the Roman era. It takes about an ounce to buy a nice suit now." Think about that. The same ounce of gold held its value for 2,000 years!

Given gold's popularity as money, it should come as no surprise that there are several innovative ways in which one can purchase physical gold, including modern gold bullion coins, gold bars, and numismatic or rare gold coins. The contributors in this section are some of the most respected coin and bullion dealers in the business. They have practical advice on what and how to buy as well as the legal challenges in purchasing gold in an era when gold is no longer legal tender.

- **Van Simmons:** Beginning with a short economic review that notes that "the world is awash in money," Van then asks, "What is going on in the rare coin market?" Why this question? Because "generally, the rare coin market tends to follow the (gold) bullion markets."
- **Dana Samuelson and Bill Musgrave:** Also noting that "the gold and rare coin markets have been heating up," Samuelson and Musgrave point out that coin dealers do business in an "unregulated industry" and, addressing a key point of this book, emphasizing "it's important to know 'who' you're dealing with." More important, their piece features four rare coin canards or "classic examples of marketing schemes now afoot in the marketplace."
- **James Turk:** Explains an innovative way to own gold by "taking the world's oldest money, gold, and using twenty-first-century technology to enable its circulation as a currency in global commerce." James summarizes his contribution with the bold statement that "GoldMoney is creating a currency that is more efficient—it is better—than the currencies that exist today."
- **Franklin Sanders:** Because gold truly is money, this is a great story about what happens when someone working in the rare coin or gold bullion markets crosses the line in the eyes of the state and federal government by pointing out that "the monetary emperor is naked! Federal Reserve notes aren't really money!"

CHAPTER 13

RARE COINS AND GOLD BULLION

Van Simmons
David Hall Rare Coins

"Deep down in our heart, we know that we have given our children a legacy of bankruptcy. We have defrauded our country to get ourselves elected."

—John Danforth, U.S. Senator (1936–)

Perhaps noted sage investor Adrian Day spoke for many of those who know Van Simmons when he said, "I have known Van for over a decade, referred many clients to him, and traded coins with him myself. He is thoroughly knowledgeable and ethical, and always a pleasure to deal with." Having now met and done business with Van myself—my youngest son got his first silver dollar from him—I agree.

In 1986, Van and David Hall launched Professional Coin Grading Service (PCGS), the largest coin grading service in the world. PCGS determines the condition and authenticity of each coin it grades to provide consumers with a rating on which to judge the coin and then encapsulates the coins in sealed see-through plastic holders. PCGS expert

Originally published in *The Velvet Tray* on November 1, 2007, as "Van's Two Cents Worth."

coin graders have now graded over 18 million coins with a total value of over $18 billion. They are considered the industry standard in third-party certification of coins.

While Van's article is not primarily about gold, as his contribution makes note, the rare coin market and gold bullion markets often move in tandem. Knowing how important economics is to the gold bullion market, it only makes sense that Van would begin his piece by reviewing the world today, China, as well as the Fed, and the U.S. dollar. But then he delves into the rare coin market, telling you what his favorite coins are in a rising gold bullion market.

"In times of trouble millions flee to gold, silver, and platinum. When gold breaks through its previous high of $850, this will draw attention to the metals, and I believe certified numismatics will ride on their coat tails. Numismatics (collector coins) are the rarest form of the metals, and I think that for every $10,000 you earn in gold, silver, and platinum bullion coins, you'll earn $50,000 in certified numismatics. They'll be like the dotcoms of the 1990s, totally insane."

—Richard Maybury, *U.S. and World Early Warning Report*, September 2007

THE WORLD TODAY

I will get back to the above quote later on in this letter, but first let's look at what is going on in world today. To begin with, MONEY is what is happening, and there is a lot of it. The world is awash in money. The central banks of the world have turned on the cash spigots.

There is a website called "Shadow Government Statistics," written by John Williams. When Greenspan stopped exposing what the M3 or the broad money supply figure was last year, a few smart guys have figured ways to monitor what it would be today. Mr. Williams has the money supply figures now growing at a staggering rate of 15 percent!

The Economist magazine recently wrote that the year-over-year dollar index of all items is up 16.7 percent. It also lists food up 31.6 percent year-over-year. Is there any way in the world we can take our government figures of 1 percent at face value? It's sad, but most of the people in our country believe the government figures.

This is higher than when President Jimmy Carter was in office.

It should be obvious to anyone in the money business that Bernanke is not going to let the economy fall. He is now showing he will fight any recession with every dollar he can create.

Most people I read feel he will continue to lower rates. This will continue to crater the value of the U.S. dollar. This is being done partly to help the falling real estate market, and partly to help our exports, which will create more jobs. We will also be less reliant on imports, which should produce more jobs over here.

CHINA

One of the more serious sides to this is that Chinese exports will begin to suffer. My guess is China will do everything it can to weaken its currency to compete. This puts China in a position it has never been in before. Competing for exports must be like learning a new foreign language to them.

Don't get me wrong, China will continue to be the major force in the world's market. Its world is expanding at an unbelievably fast rate. I read the other day that China is now using 60 percent of the cement and steel produced in the world. It is building the equivalent of the entire city of Houston, Texas, every 30 days. It has 75 percent of the operational cranes in the world. Do you realize that more Chinese people speak the English language than all the other countries in the world combined, including the United States?

Anyway, every day I read whatever comes across my desk on the economy, and I try to figure out what it all means based on past history and current psychological patterns of humans. I mean, we all change from time to time.

As I said earlier, fewer imports and higher exports will help sustain our economy's growth. Most of the business people I talk to every day do not have any intention of cutting back at this time. Most of their businesses are doing great as credit is available to most basic businesses.

THE FED AND THE U.S. DOLLAR

For the past several years many businesses have been running with a very thin inventory. Now with prices rising, most of the people I talk to do not fear building up their inventories as they once did.

So I guess the question is, what does this have to do with the rare coin market? Well the big picture is, since the Fed is creating so much money while at the same time lowering interest rates, the money is going to be worth less.

Many in the world are looking for tangibles or things of value to place money into. Unless our government can create a way to increase the faith in the U.S. dollar, I don't see this trend changing anytime soon.

The U.S. dollar has been beaten up quite a bit recently. I have been writing for several years now that you would someday begin hearing about the weakness on the nightly news, and now you are. It is going to have to take a break from its recent decline at some point in time. Our weakening dollar is going to hurt other countries' exports, so they will have no choice but to compete and weaken their own currencies against the dollar.

As most of you know, I think the U.S. dollar at some point will go to zero. But not this week. It has been and will continue to be a slow death over decades. Our politicians will continue to steal our hard-earned dollars from us every chance they get.

It really is a sick situation. Our government officials tax us to death while we work hard and try to save the small amount left over after they take their cut. Then they have the gall to create all the money they need out of thin air, thereby making the money we have been able to save worth less.

Taxes seem to me to be a way for them to keep us at their mercy, afraid of any retribution. I know I am afraid not to pay my taxes.

So if they can create all the money (literally out of thin air), why don't they create enough to pay all their bills? I mean why pick on us through taxation? We're just trying to get by and make it day by day. The tax system seems to be a large issue of nothing more than control by our government over its "working class" citizens.

THE RARE COIN MARKET

So what is going on in the rare coin market?

To begin with, it is busy, very busy. The bullion markets have created quite a bit of interest in rare coins, yet the prices really haven't followed the price of bullion in its recent upward rise. This is a great thing as the rare coin market is giving us a longer window of opportunity to get involved and place some bets.

Generally, the rare coin market tends to follow the bullion markets, which in turn follow the currency or inflation markets. In other words, if you create money out of thin air, the value of your currency goes down, thereby creating inflation, which in turn creates a craving for gold or real money.

It would make my life easier if the rare coin market mirrored the price of bullion, but it doesn't. Sometimes there will be a large supply of coins on the market that will last for years before we see any significant rise in prices. Although when the supply diminishes and the demand increases, rare coins offer a much more unique opportunity because in most cases you can't just pick up the phone and order anything you want to.

This is very similar to the situation we saw in late 2005 through the first quarter of 2006. Prices soared about 30 percent in just a few months as the supply of coins was very thin. Many of you remember having to wait up to 60 days for me to supply coins for very "tradable" sets like the eight-piece gold type set.

The more common coins like Saint Gaudens were somewhat available, yet they too went up by 30 to 50 percent.

So now we are in a situation where the supply is slightly available, but much less than it was six months ago, and the demand is increasing. Prices on gold coins in the grade MS65 and higher are firm and rising, with slight fluctuations due to the price of gold bullion.

Some of the best values are $2.50 Liberties, Type One and Type Three gold dollars, $5 Liberties, and MS66 Saint Gaudens.

The rare date and higher grade (MS66 and MS67) gold coins really haven't participated with any price moves over the last three to four years like we have seen in MS65 graded gold coins.

These coins seem to be very inexpensive at current levels. These are usually the coins in past markets that have the most demand and command the highest prices. Once again, there are certain areas of this coin market that have been leaving plenty of time for us to get involved.

The proof gold coins are still one of my all-time favorites. They are expensive, starting in the $12,000 range and going up to six figures, but still very cheap. They have been moving up slightly in price, but in a hot coin market these coins usually go into hyperspace in demand and price.

For those of you who check my website on a daily basis, you are aware that I usually get one to two proof gold coins a month. Of course, there are times when I will go 30 to 90 days without having any.

That being said, I do see them from time to time for sale, but in most cases they are either lower grades or priced so high I am unable to stretch enough to buy them.

For all you big hitters in the world, this is an area you can equate with great paintings, large flawless diamonds, or a home on a point overlooking the ocean without neighbors being able to see you or hear you scream at your kids.

The modern coin arena is very hot in the rare dates and dead in common dates. This also will change over time. Some of the more common coins are so inexpensive they are becoming a joke.

If you want to take a long-term bet, say seven to ten years from now (and maybe much sooner), take a look at the common dates in Buffalo nickels, Mercury dimes, or Walking Liberty half dollars. Most of these are selling at 10 to 20 cents on the dollar of their past highs.

Morgan dollars are in a very similar situation as the common dates are a joke. You can buy MS65 Morgan dollars for around $150. These would wholesale for $850 to $1,000 in 1986. We have seen the price of silver bullion increase by 300 percent in the last four years, yet the Morgans have moved up in price by only about 30 percent. Again, we are in a situation where this market is giving us plenty of time to get involved. But it can and will change, and it can change quickly.

The rarer date Morgans are also very good deals. This is one of the most collected areas of the rare coin market. I love the coins in the $1,000 to $5,000 range, and of course the very rare dates.

The Silver Commemorative market is very quiet. Since most of the attention is being paid to gold coins, it also leaves this area very cheap. As I have said in the past, when the market gets hot and you can't buy proof gold or rare date gold, the coin dealers and collectors of the world need to buy something, and silver commems are the perfect arena. This is a very popular set, and most of the coins are available. In a hot market you can kiss the rarer coins goodbye as they become impossible to find. There are 50 different types in this set, and you can buy them one at a time starting in the $150 range.

One interesting note on these is that the U.S. Mint has been making new commemoratives every year now, with a mailing list passing the 60,000,000 mark. We are now seeing collectors of the more modern commemoratives calling to buy the older coins. We should see the demand increase by multiples over the coming years.

These are coins I put away almost every month myself. They are also great coins to buy for your kids or grandkids. They are very popular, and each coin represents a different time in our history.

The nineteenth-century-type coins are doing well with very few nice coins available. Prices are starting to move up, but they are still very inexpensive compared to their rarity and popularity. I love the coins that are out of favor, such as the Shield nickels, Liberty nickels, and Three Cent nickels as these coins are very cheap at current prices. I also think all the coins in this area are great buys at current price levels.

I guess that is my summation for the coin market for the last 60 days. I haven't been able to write this letter every month and I apologize, but I have been busy, and the supply of coins is thin. The other thing is that there is just too much to say. I think about writing this letter every day, but there are so many things to write about I just can't fit it in. I could write everyday if I had the time. The world is changing so fast day by day it takes my breath away.

FAMILY LESSONS

Last month I took a week off and went to a cabin I have in the Midwest with my two sons (ages 13 and almost 18). We raked and burned leaves, hunted for four days, and had a great time. The most interesting thing we did was build a 10-foot-by-10-foot treehouse. I am not a builder, but my sons convinced me that we could do it, and we did. I am not trying to be sappy or anything, but I have to tell you that this was one of the absolute best weeks of my life. Both of my boys had a great time, and spending 12 hours a day arm-in-arm with them was a great learning experience for each of us.

A funny thing happened at a small diner we had lunch at one day. There were two older farmers at the counter next to us complaining about the article in the local paper on how the dollar has been dropping in value. My youngest son pipes in and says, "That's only because our politicians are stealing from us by creating worthless paper. Anyone should have known it was going to drop in value." I laughed so hard I almost fell off my stool. It was a great trip.

There is a great book you may want to get your sons or grandsons called *The Dangerous Book for Boys* by Conn Iggulden. This book lists things all boys should know, how to tie different knots, use Morse code, etc., and of course how to build a treehouse, with instructions. I heard they came out with a similar book for girls also.

CONCLUSION

So back to the economy before I sign off. I recently read a study that shows the U.S. dollar index since 2001 has lost 37 percent of its value to date. If you figure in a little (and I mean little by government statistics) inflation, and the loss of purchasing power, for Americans it is quickly becoming quite devastating. Remember this loss of purchasing power occurred while home prices were rising and the Dow was making new highs. My feeling is that most people aren't going to be very happy with the purchasing power of the dollar in the coming next few years.

I now ask you to please reread the first paragraph, which is a quote by Richard Maybury, a man who has been one of the best at forecasting the economy. He is a little too extreme for most people to read, but he has a great track record.

I feel he is right on the money on his prediction for rare coins. I have seen major moves in the rare coin market myself several times in the last 30 years.

Please don't hesitate to call if you see anything inside that rings your bell or if you have any interest in building positions in any of the areas I have mentioned. Until next year, I hope you all have a wonderful holiday season!

CHAPTER 14

RARE COIN CANARDS

Dana Samuelson and Dr. Bill Musgrave
American Gold Exchange

"An almost hysterical antagonism toward the gold standard is one issue which united statists of all persuasions. They seem to sense . . . that gold and economic freedom are inseparable. . . ."

—Alan Greenspan, economist, 13th Chairman of Federal Reserve (1926–)

Dana Samuelson has been a professional numismatist since 1980 and has personally traded more than $400 million in rare coins and precious metals. For nearly a decade, he was a personal protégé of James U. Blanchard III, one of the true giants of the industry and the individual most responsible for re-legalizing the private ownership of gold in the U.S. (Executive Order 6102 signed on April 5, 1933 by U.S. President Franklin D. Roosevelt "forbidding the Hoarding of Gold Coin, Gold Bullion, and Gold Certificates" by U.S. citizens was repealed by President Gerald Ford in December 1971.) Bill Musgrave, a Phi Beta Kappa graduate of the University of North Carolina at

Originally published as a Special Report in July 2004 on the American Gold Exchange website.

Chapel Hill, holds a doctorate in English from the University of California, Berkeley, and has been a coin collector since the age of 10.

Together Dana and Bill focus on the value in rare coins and hard assets. Dana Samuelson founded American Gold Exchange, a leading national precious metals and rare coin company that specializes in dealer-to-dealer trading and direct sales to the public, in 1998. Bill Musgrave is the vice president.

Although I own gold coins—both modern bullion coins and rare gold coins—there are many, many people who have never bought physical gold because of the associated risks. The primary purpose of Dana and Bill's contribution "is to alert you to some of the most common numismatic canards, or falsehoods, now circulating in the market" surrounding the purchase of physical gold. Should you encounter such marketing schemes or canards, their "advice is to hang up and call someone you trust!" With such practical advice and such an emphasis on how important the "who" is, their contribution is a must read for anyone contemplating or involved in the gold bullion and rare coin market.

A s the gold and rare coin markets have been heating up, legions of new investors and collectors have been entering our marketplace. That's wonderful news! When purchased intelligently from a reliable dealer, rare coins can be a superb investment and collecting them a supremely enjoyable pastime. Unfortunately, we're hearing reports about some shoddy practices on the rise among some dealers. Many of these practices seem sensible enough on the surface but they're designed to take advantage of uninformed investors. The purpose of this article is to alert you to some of the most common numismatic canards, or falsehoods, now circulating in the market. Once you know what to look for, these misleading tactics are easily avoided.

Like coins themselves, all coin dealers are not created equally. Although many dealers are extremely scrupulous, others place their own profits above the interests of their customers, bending the truth to the detriment of the entire industry. Because coin dealers are all independent operators doing business in an unregulated industry, it's important to know who you're dealing with. In reality, some of these so-called dealers aren't genuine rare coin dealers at all, but merely marketing companies that happen to be selling precious metals and rare coins.

Their goal is simply to move as much product as possible by whatever means necessary, and often at inflated prices. Unfortunately, they give the rest of us a bad name.

Here are several classic examples of marketing schemes now afoot in the marketplace. If you run into one or more of these canards, your "dealer" is, most likely, simply trying to separate you from your hard-earned cash. Our advice is to hang up and call someone you can trust!

CANARD 1: BUILDING A SET ENHANCES YOUR INVESTMENT

Some dealers will try to talk you into building a "set," or a mini-collection organized around some unifying theme. Among the more commonly pushed sets are the "eight coin U.S. gold type set" and the "$20 Liberty gold coin type set." The unifying theme of sets might seem quite reasonable, but in most cases the real goal is simply to sell you more coins.

The hook used by dealers pushing sets is the claim that a complete a set will increase the value of all coins in the set. In most cases, this claim is an absolute canard. The only sets that truly enhance the market value of the coins that comprise them tend to be very expensive, time consuming, and difficult to build. Typically, these sets would make any seasoned collector's mouth water because of the quality and scarcity of the included coins. The added value of a set like this represents the immense time, effort, and expertise—not to mention investment—required to locate and assemble the individual coins.

For example, we've been building a very special proof set for one customer for more than seven years now. We add to it when-ever the right coin comes into the market, which is seldom, and we've passed up hundreds of coins over the years because they didn't measure up. When completed, this will be one of those "knock me over with a feather" sets that experienced collectors will drool over. Why? Because all of the coins are very rare, from the same year, from same mint, and all are superb proofs with the same "look." In other words, this set will be unique and compelling, and when offered on the market, serious collectors will be happy to pay a pre-mium for it. But sets like this are rare. Sets that are relatively common and easy to build or replace, however, offer no real enhanced market value at all.

The classic set pushed by marketeering dealers is the "Eight Coin U.S. Gold Set," featuring one each of the following coins:

- $2.50 Liberty
- $2.50 Indian
- $5.00 Liberty
- $5.00 Indian
- $10.00 Liberty
- $10.00 Indian
- $20.00 Liberty
- $20.00 Saint Gaudens

You'll be told that a complete set of this kind can be resold for more than the individual coins. But unless the Liberty or Indian coins are all the same date, grade, mint mark, and grading service, this set is simply a small, random collection of eight gold coins representing the major denominations, and it's worth no more than the sum of its parts. If you're a new hobbyist, and if your dealer has sold you some nice coins, this would be fun little collection to build. But as an investment, the simple fact that you have one of each denomination does nothing whatsoever to increase the value of the coins. If your dealer tells you otherwise, you're being misled.

CANARD 2: HIGH-GRADE, CERTIFIED GOLD EAGLES ARE WORTH MORE

Some dealers (and one huge dealer who certainly knows better) are building their profits by selling high-grade, certified modern issue gold eagle and platinum eagle bullion coins at exorbitant prices. They claim these coins are scarce and worth a premium because of their certified high quality. Another canard!

Because of today's excellent minting technology, virtually every coin produced by the U.S. Mint, whether for circulation or as bullion, is almost perfect. Nonetheless, some dealers are now sending gold eagles and platinum eagles to grading services like PCGS and

NGC, having them "slabbed" in plastic holders with a certified grade, and marketing them at ridiculous markups. These dealers claim that certified gold and platinum eagles are rare and therefore worth the high prices. It's true, they are relatively rare—but only because so few (so far) have been submitted to the certification services! These dealers are simply trying to create a premium market for what are, in reality, common bullion coins.

The sleight-of-hand in this classic canard might fool some of the people some of the time, but the reality is this: If the entire mintage of gold or platinum eagles were to be submitted to the grading services, perhaps 90 percent would be certified as MS68 or higher, the grades for which these dealers are charging so much. Basically, all modern bullion coins are just about perfect; and because they're minted every year in virtually unlimited quantities, none of them are scarce enough to justify any significant premium. The extra money you pay for one of these certified bullion coins goes directly out of your pocket and into the dealer's. Later, when you try to sell it to anyone other than the dealer who sold it to you, you'll be very disappointed.

We believe the market for certified eagles coins will eventually collapse on itself due to oversaturation, much like the market in modern world gold and silver issues, so much the rage in the mid-1980s, collapsed on itself in 1989. Just think about it: If prices for certified eagles move substantially higher, a tidal wave of coins will be sent to PCGS and NGC for grading; the certified populations will simply explode; and the prices will plummet because of the abundant new supplies. Don't be fooled! An eagle is an eagle, except when it's encased in plastic—then it's a canard!

CANARD 3: ALL GRADING SERVICES ARE THE SAME

Have you heard this one yet? "Psst! Hey buddy! I've got coin certified in MS65, and it's half the price of other coins certified in the same grade! But you gotta buy it right away before I sell it to someone else!"

It's the same old scam in a different holder. If something seems too good to be true, it probably is! Sure, the coin might be real. And sure, it's certified—but by whom? That's the question.

Only two grading services are fully supported by U.S. rare coin dealers: PCGS (Professional Coin Grading Service) and NGC (Numismatic Guarantee Corporation). When it's time for dealers to pull out their checkbooks to buy your coins, only these two services make the grade. (To find out more about them visit www.amergold .com/library/coin_certification.shtml.)

Other grading services (which, for legal reasons, shall remain nameless) are also in the market to "authenticate and grade" classic U.S. coins. But coins graded by most other grading services simply do **not** carry the same market value and trust as coins from PCGS and NGC. Remember the cardinal rule: Only buy PCGS and NGC certified coins! It's that simple.

CANARD 4: SHIPWRECK COINS ARE A GOOD INVESTMENT

In recent years, new technology has enabled the recovery of some incredible shipwrecks laden with gold and silver coins from the 1850s and 1860s. When they come to market, the coins recovered from ships like the *S.S. Central America* and the *S.S. Republic* create immense excitement. But later, when the hoopla dies down and they've been absorbed into the market, shipwreck coins generally turn into immense disappointments for the investors who paid the exorbitant prices commanded at the time of their initial sale.

Often coins recovered from shipwrecks are marketed in ways that artificially inflate their initial value, usually by exaggerating the hype and romance surrounding wrecks while carefully controlling the distribution and pricing of the coins themselves. One recent example is the *S.S. Central America* shipwreck, which contained virtually the entire mintage of 1857-S $20 Liberty gold coins. The coins survived in remarkable condition and were sold into the market by a tight cartel of dealers at high initial prices. The shipwreck story was exciting and the advertising campaign was immense. However, far too many coins were released into the market to support their dispersal prices.

Recognizing at the time of their initial offering that the *S.S Central America* $20 Liberty 1857-S coins were likely to be poor investments, we published an extensive report, *Hoard Coins Past & Future,* predicting that these coins would probably drop by about 50 percent in value before they found natural market equilibrium. Within 18 months they fell by about 45 percent in real dollar terms. Investors who spent $14,000 on a coin saw it drop to under $10,000, while other gold coins gained in value.

If you're a history buff, a nautical hobbyist, or a collector of numismatic oddities, go ahead and buy a newly released shipwreck coin—but just one! If you're looking for a numismatic investment that's likely to appreciate in value, however, we strongly recommend that you wait until the initial buzz has worn off and the excessive premiums have evaporated. In general, if you're tempted to invest in shipwreck coins, always remember that it's far more prudent to purchase the last 100 coins of the dispersal than the first 100. Give the market time to absorb the new population of coins and determine their true value. Don't buy on hype!

AGE CORE PRINCIPLES

At the American Gold Exchange we have three core principles by which we live:

1. We treat our clients' money like it is our own.
2. We only offer what we believe to be good value in the marketplace.
3. We stand behind our products.

Unlike some dealers, who push their program coins and run, we'll be here for the long haul. Whatever coins we sell today, we hope to buy back in the future when you liquidate your hard assets. We go to exceptional lengths to be certain that all of our coins are accurately graded, problem free, and fairly priced. And we always give the best advice we possibly can. You can invest with confidence with AGE!

CHAPTER 15

THE INTERNET GOLD AND CURRENCY PROVIDER

James Turk
GoldMoney

"Paper money eventually returns to its intrinsic value—zero."

—Voltaire, French essayist and
philosopher (1694–1778)

There are a number of ways one can own gold, and one of the most innovative has been developed by James Turk, the founder of GoldMoney. com. GoldMoney is a new electronic currency that can be used in ecommerce and enables you to buy gold and silver that is fully insured and stored securely in specialized bullion vaults in Zurich and London.

Mr. Turk also writes the Freemarket Gold and Money Report, *an investment newsletter that analyzes gold, gold stocks, and gold's relationship to the world's paper currencies (www.fmgr.com). He has also written several books, his most recent being* The Coming Collapse of

Originally published in *Freemarket Gold and Money Report* on January 8, 2001, as "Gold in the New Economy."

the Dollar, *published in 2004. He often appears as a featured guest on radio and television and frequently appears at investment conferences on gold, money, and banking.*

In James's contribution below, he explains how you can use GoldMoney to purchase gold and silver. Given the risky nature of holding physical gold at one's home, as well as continuous government limitations placed on citizens who own gold (including the government of the United States in 1933), he makes a strong case why everyone should be using GoldMoney.com. More important, the independent, third-party audits on the gold that GoldMoney holds in vaults around the world on behalf of its customers goes a long way in eliminating much uncertainty of the "who" from the decision to purchase and own gold. Finally, the piece fully explains why "gold is money, but any currency of a bank (or a central bank) is only a money substitute."

On December 3rd (2000), the *Sunday Telegraph,* which is one of London's leading newspapers, published an article about my new Internet venture, GoldMoney.com. The article read in part:

The oldest medium of exchange moves online. . . [*in January 2001*] with the launch of GoldMoney.com, an Internet currency provider that will allow users to pay for products anywhere.

GoldMoney, based in the Isle of Man, says it has developed an e-commerce payment system that enables global buyers and sellers to make and accept instantaneous payments in weights of gold called GoldGrams. A GoldGram represents a gram of gold [*31.1034 grams = one troy ounce*] held in vaults with the system working on the principle that users transfer gold from buyer to seller without it leaving the vault.

The current price of a GoldGram can be checked on the web site in various currencies. The gold price has been falling, but the company points out that while a GoldGram would have fallen in value against the yen, it would have risen in value against the euro over the past year.

The system, aimed at corporations and cross-border traders, is designed to eliminate payment risk as there is no possibility of default on payment and it uses high strength encryption software, downloaded by account holders. Payments are processed in real time with funds transferred instantly. It also offers low transaction fees . . . [that are] much less than bank fees for wiring currency.

James Turk, founder of GoldMoney, said: "We are taking the world's oldest money, gold, and using 21st century technology to enable its circulation as a currency in global commerce." He aims to make it the common currency of global commerce.

The story behind GoldMoney is an interesting one over 20 years in the making. Along the way, I secured two U.S. patents on a unique process that enables gold to circulate electronically as currency.

HERSTATT RISK

I conceived the idea behind the patents and GoldMoney in February 1979 as a solution to Herstatt risk. I was the assistant manager of the Chase Manhattan Bank in Bangkok, Thailand, when the Herstatt Bank failed in June 1974, so I witnessed first-hand the devastating impact on international commerce from this collapse. It seemed absurd that the failure of one medium-sized bank in what was then West Germany could have such a crippling effect, but it did bring many banks around the world to their knees, severely impairing the global economy. So in my spare time I set about learning more about the nature of currency in order to seek a solution to Herstatt risk.

Over the 26 years since Herstatt failed, the big banks have spent hundreds of millions trying to solve Herstatt risk, but given the nature of their currency, that task is impossible. They can reduce/minimize Herstatt risk, but they cannot eliminate it. This recognition eventually led to my solution in February 1979, and that solution is embodied in GoldMoney.

Simply put, currency today is a liability on the balance sheet of banks. Cash currency is a liability of central banks; deposit currency— the money in checking and savings accounts—is a liability of commercial banks. These central/commercial bank liabilities circulate as currency only because they are backed by assets with value. If these assets become value impaired, the liabilities backed by the assets become impaired as well, creating Herstatt risk and other currency distress. And these problems can only be solved if assets, as opposed to liabilities, circulate as currency. This point can be explained with a simple example.

A gold coin passed from the hand of the buyer of some good or service to the hand of the seller is an asset circulating as currency. The gold coin is not issued by a bank, nor is it backed by any asset—IT IS the asset. Compare this example with a Gold Certificate circulating as cash currency. The Gold Certificate is a liability of a bank, backed by the assets of that bank. To use two historical definitions not often seen today, gold is *money*, but any currency that is a liability of a bank is only a *money substitute*. It perforce is not *money*.

MONEY SUBSTITUTES

While gold over the centuries has proven to be good money, it has also been an inconvenient and inefficient currency, which explains why money substitutes—like paper currency and bank deposits— were created. It was more efficient to leave the gold in a bank and accept that bank's note for use in commerce. But what worked well in the eighteenth and nineteenth centuries began to break down in the twentieth, largely because the monetary process was increasingly usurped by government for political objectives. As a result, money substitutes became increasingly unsound, causing governments to attack their competition, namely, money/gold. But this policy of government is, I believe, doomed to fail.

Even back in 1979 it seemed to me that when viewed within the sweep of history, money substitutes—the currency of today's nation states—would in time face increasing competition from new sources, particularly in cross-border commerce because these transactions are beyond the scope of any one country. That new competition in my view would be "electronic" asset currency, which was the essence of my idea. But though I was only 32 at the time, I never thought this idea could be put to use in my lifetime. The technology just didn't exist back then. PCs were a hobby, not the necessity they've become; no one ever heard of the Internet; and transatlantic telephone calls cost a small fortune, if you were actually fortunate enough to make the connection.

PERSONAL COMPUTERS AND PATENTS

In September 1979, I bought my first personal computer, an Apple II, and while I recognized the potential of the PC, even then I did not think that the technology would move forward fast enough to make GoldMoney a practical reality. But by the late 1980s, I began to sense that the technology was developing quickly enough so that maybe my earlier assessment was incorrect, and that GoldMoney might soon be possible/practical.

Because I recognized in the late 1980s that I was still early in my thinking, I set about researching how best to protect this new currency solution to solve Herstatt risk. By 1990 I was studying patent law to see whether I could secure the idea, with a view to turning it into a business when the technology was ready. In 1992 I hired a patent attorney and filed the first application in February 1993. Even back then the Internet was still more a vision than a reality, but it seemed that we were getting close to the technology I required.

The first patent was finally awarded four and a half years later in September 1997. By this time my son, Geoffrey, joined me to develop this business opportunity. We jointly filed the second patent application, which was awarded in November 1999. A third patent application we again filed jointly is still pending.

My patent attorney says that the four and a half years it took for my first patent to be awarded was the longest time he ever saw an application pending. In the end, though, the patent was granted because it advanced the "prior art." In other words, I created a new form of currency that was better than existing currency. The proof of this statement is that it eliminates Herstatt risk.

GRESHAM'S LAW AND GOLDMONEY

Nobel Laureate Robert Mundell, in a paper about Gresham's law www.columbia.edu/~ram15/grash.html, makes an interesting and I think accurate observation about the history of currency:

> Among the precious metals, gold drove out others . . . because it was more efficient from the standpoint of effecting transactions at the least

cost. The dollar became the dominant international money in a world of paper currencies . . . because, among the alternatives, it best satisfied the characteristics of an international money.

Note the use of his qualifier, "among the alternatives." The world today is much different from when the dollar became international money at the Bretton Woods Conference in 1944. And most important, we today have alternatives, made possible in part by technology. Moreover, we have the incentive to search for these alternatives because the dollar today is not the pillar of monetary stability that it was in 1944. In short, the dollar today is no longer "as good as gold," the popular phrase at the time that characterized the dollar's unchallenged position.

I think we are moving full circle back to gold, but gold will circulate as currency in a way that overcomes the impediments that stopped it from circulating as currency in the past. GoldMoney aims to deliver a currency that is more efficient than any currencies now existing.

With GoldMoney, owners of GoldGrams (one gram of gold, and the unit of account of GoldMoney) always own their metal. GoldMoney never takes possession of it. The metal is placed in vaults around the world (we use the term *Storage Sites*) and is always held in the name of the customer, until it is spent. At the moment the GoldGrams are spent, the ownership of those GoldGrams changes. The weight of gold remains in the Storage Site, but the ownership changes the instant the GoldGrams are spent. It's the electronic equivalent of a gold coin passing from one hand to another, but the gold always remains in the vault. A couple of points of explanation will be useful here.

1. GoldMoney is not a fractional reserve system. The total quantity of GoldGrams in circulation is always exactly equal to the weight of gold in the different Storage Sites.
2. One GoldGram is composed of 1,000 mils for precision in transactions. At $311 per ounce, one GoldGram exchanges for $10, and one mil exchanges for 1¢. At the current price of $268 per ounce, one GoldGram exchanges for $8.62.
3. Access to GoldMoney is provided anywhere in the world through a standard web browser, with 24/7 availability and access to your money.

4. All payments are made in real time, so there is no float, clearing, etc. Therefore, GoldMoney avoids the problems these processes create, ranging from the niggling, such as lost wire transfers, to the catastrophic, like Herstatt risk.

The above explanations are not meant to be all encompassing, but rather, they highlight some basic attributes of GoldMoney. I think it also shows that GoldMoney is well thought out, which shouldn't be too surprising because I've been thinking about it and working on it for 21 years now.

CONCLUSION

I think that with GoldGrams we are creating the currency of the twenty-first century. That may sound presumptuous, but it seems logical to me. After all, all we are doing is taking the world's oldest money, and enabling it to circulate as currency in a way that overcomes those impediments that stopped gold from circulating as currency in the past. Even though many of gold's fundamental attributes as money have been forgotten, they have not disappeared. GoldMoney will see whether those attributes remain important, and if they do, then the market will prove whether GoldMoney will be commercially successful.

Finally, the Internet today—when it comes to money and currency—is very much like the automobile 'industry' at the beginning of the twentieth century. When the car was first invented, it was a horse-carriage (a "buckboard") without the horse, a guy sitting up top, trying to drive this new contraption with a stick. Those early inventors/entrepreneurs did not realize the invention of the automobile was so profound that they no longer had to think of transportation as what it was conceived to be up until that moment in time. New ideas about power, weight, and comfort evolved slowly, so it took a few years before an automobile that we could recognize as "modern" emerged with fenders, doors, glass, and a roof.

Attempts to circulate plastic credit/debit cards on the Internet today are not unlike those first automobiles, which looked better suited to being pulled by a horse than having any similarity to what we now consider to be a car. Just like those early automobile inventors/

entrepreneurs, those who have "created" the early versions of Internet "currency" are merely transpositions of what currency is conceived to be today—mainly plastic. These early Internet currency promoters have not generally recognized that the invention of the Internet is so profound, we are not restricted to thinking narrowly about what currency will be or should be on the Internet in the future. Currency will evolve in e-commerce like those first automobiles evolved, with trial and error. And given gold's historical role as money, I expect that GoldMoney will become an important currency on the Internet. It is our objective to make GoldMoney the common currency of global commerce. Of course, only time will tell whether we will be successful, but that result is the beauty of an unfettered market and the outcome of competition.

I hope this information is of interest. In the meantime, you may want to visit www.goldmoney.com and record your email address to receive updates on our progress as we approach the launch date.

In summary, GoldMoney is creating a currency that is more efficient—it is better—than the currencies that exist today. I am therefore hopeful that GoldMoney will benefit its users, thereby making GoldGrams essential in the new economy of global ecommerce.

CHAPTER 16

GOLD, FIAT CURRENCY, AND INTEGRITY

Franklin Sanders
The Moneychanger

"We define character as the sum of those qualities of moral excellence that stimulates a person to do the right thing, which is manifested through right and proper actions despite internal or external pressures to the contrary."

—United States Air Force Academy

In 1980 Franklin Sanders opened his own company brokering physical gold and silver. Since then, Mr. Sanders has also published and edited a monthly newsletter, The Moneychanger, *"to help Christian people prosper in an age of monetary and moral chaos." In medieval Europe a moneychanger was necessary to facilitate the trade of the many different coins then being issued by various cities and towns, most of which were not backed by gold or other precious metals.*

Originally published in *Chronicles: A Magazine of American Culture,* a publication of The Rockford Institute in Rockford, Illinois, in February 1997, as "Most Dangerous Man in the Mid South." It has been reprinted with permission.

Working for grassroots monetary reform, in 1984 Franklin opened a gold and silver bank (warehouse exchange). "This angered the federal government and IRS. . . ." That is putting it mildly. Franklin's contribution is a precursor of "unchallenged state power" and what it could lead to.

In the contribution below, Franklin tells the story of how he began his business believing that "exchanges of gold and silver money for paper money weren't subject to sales tax, since they were exchanges for money." That position, and his more controversial "gold and silver bank" that he opened in 1984, would eventually lead to his arrest and imprisonment. As Franklin words it, "we landed in the Catch 22 maelstrom of official suspicion." Eventually, Dr. Edwin Vieira, Jr., constitutional attorney and America's foremost expert on monetary law, would argue Franklin's case to no avail. Why fight such a battle? As we're all learning in our present financial crisis, "the fiat money system is both the strength and weakness of America's tyrants."

Almost 30 years ago, just a few weeks before I got married, on a drugstore bookstand I found a strange book: *Capitalism, the Unknown Ideal.* It was a collection of essays about a philosophy of freedom. Two dealt with the American monetary system. The author explained that nothing—no gold or silver—backed our currency. He argued that sooner or later, this fiat money system would lead to disaster and that only money backed by real value—gold—could last.

That author was Alan Greenspan.

Since then our careers—Alan's and mine—have taken very different paths.

In 1967, Alan Greenspan was already a fairly well known economic consultant. In the 1970s, President Ford appointed him to his Council of Economic Advisors. In 1987, Alan Greenspan was appointed Chairman of the Federal Reserve Board of Governors.

Funny, he doesn't talk much about gold anymore.

In 1967, I was a college senior. Susan and I were married on December 16, and when I graduated in 1968 the draft board gave me 30 days to frolic before conscription. I arrived at Fort Polk, Louisiana, one hot October night, caught the Army bus out to the post, and sat down behind the driver, facing across the bus. I opened my copy of Aristotle's *Works* and began reading.

I noticed I was the only man on board with hair. The fellow sitting across from me asked, "Whatcha reading?" Wordlessly, I flipped up the book so he could read the title on the spine. "Boy," he said without any reflection. "Have you come to the wrong place."

In 1969 I retired from the Army to attend graduate school in German at Tulane University. The next year I received a full scholarship to the Free University in West Berlin, where I saw first hand what unchallenged state power could do. The West was pulsing with life and light, the East dead and empty. In the Museum of the Wall at Checkpoint Charlie I read the last radio message from the Free Hungarians in 1956: "Tell Europe we are dying for them."

After Susan and I came home late in 1973, I worked in several businesses, learning first hand what it means to "make your way in the world." I kept studying economics and monetary systems, on my own and in graduate classes.

FIRST BUSINESS, ARKANSAS TRIALS

In 1980 I opened my own business in West Memphis, Arkansas, across the Mississippi from Memphis, selling physical gold and silver. First thing I did was write to the Arkansas attorney general to explain that I thought exchanges of gold and silver money for paper money weren't subject to the sales tax, since they were exchanges of money for money. What was his official position?

He never bothered to answer my certified letter. Or the second. Or the third.

When he finally responded, it was only to say he wouldn't answer. I wrote to the Commissioner of Revenue, and told him what I was doing. Nobody ever bothered to answer that certified letter either, so I reported all my sales as "exempt." Every month.

A year later, in 1981, a Revenue officer showed up to audit my books. I told her what I did wasn't taxable, and that every trade contract contained a confidentiality guarantee to my customer. She could see them if she would indemnify me in case some customer sued for breach of contract. Alas, she didn't want to cooperate, so she just multiplied all my "exempt" sales by the sales tax percentage, added penalties and interest, and sent me a bill for about $30,000.

Thus began my merry pilgrimage through the courts. I had landed smack in the middle of Legal Never-Neverland: monetary law. Of course, Article I, Section 10 of the U.S. Constitution says, "No State shall make any Thing but Gold and Silver Coin a tender in payment of debt." Of course the definition of "money" at the head of the Arkansas tax title says, "The term 'money' or 'monies' shall be had to mean and include gold and silver coin." Of course, the U.S. Code at Title 12, Section 152 says that "lawful money" means gold and silver coin of the United States.

Of course, of course, of course . . . it goes on and on. State and federal constitutions, state and federal statutes, state and federal court decisions, U.S. Supreme Court decisions, all speak with one voice: Gold and silver coin are money, bank notes are not money. But whether I raised the issue in a Revenue Department administrative court, chancery court, or federal district court, I ran into the same terrified reaction. "The monetary emperor is naked! Federal Reserve notes aren't really money! Quick, rule against this clown and drag him out of here!"

I appealed the agent's assessment and lost at the administrative level. Then at the administrative court, too. I appealed to chancery court. Had a trial. Lost there, too. By then it was December 1983, and I received a letter from the Arkansas Revenue Department demanding I fork over $120,000!

MOVE TO TENNESSEE, VISIT FROM THE IRS

A few days later two deputies came to collect their "judgment." Through several well-nigh miraculous providences, they got nothing. That night, I decamped from Arkansas. I was so amazed at God's protection through this event that I wrote a friend a long letter about it. Remember that letter.

I moved my business to Tennessee, doing exactly the same thing, exchanging gold and silver money for Federal Reserve notes. By this time I had realized that although every American had a constitutional and legal right to gold and silver money; the problem was, you couldn't use them in everyday business. We had the right to sound money, but no means. We needed an interface between the paper system and gold and silver.

So in May 1984 I opened a gold and silver bank. It attracted depositors like wildfire, but somebody didn't like my idea. On June 18, 1985, two IRS Criminal Investigation Division (CID) agents popped in to announce that I was under criminal investigation. ["Surprise! We just dropped by to pull out your fingernails with pliers!"].

In the next three years the IRS treated me to the full-court press. They got my bank records, and on U.S. attorney's stationery wrote all my customers, demanding that they send records from their dealings with me to the IRS CID agent and threatening the recalcitrant with subpoenas. These letters remarkably chilled my customers' enthusiasm. It got harder and harder to make a living.

On September 18, 1986, five agents from the Tennessee Revenue Department appeared at my office with a search warrant, pawed my files and records for two hours, and hauled off boxes of personal papers. That was the first—and last—I heard of them for a long time. They immediately turned over my papers to the IRS.

In the spring of 1988 the IRS and the U.S. attorney's office leap-frogged their investigation from me to my church. There was nothing unusual about the church. It wasn't a "tax protest" church, just a member congregation of the conservative Presbyterian Church in America. The assistant U.S. attorney subpoenaed church members before the grand jury and grilled them about what the church taught. Did the pastor teach people how to not file income tax returns? Did the church have militia practice in the woods? Survival training? Did the church hand back contributions under the table? About the only thing they didn't accuse us of was trafficking in nuclear warheads.

We landed in the Catch 22 maelstrom of official suspicion. The more the pastor and the elders proved to the U.S. attorney's office that these accusations were lies, the more convinced they became that we were such clever conspirators that their suspicions must be true. The assistant U.S. attorney issued a subpoena to the church for all her records: counseling, sessional, financial, everything. The session of the church offered to consider any request for specific documents, but refused to open the Bride of Christ up to a fishing expedition.

SWAT RAID AND ARREST

On January 9, 1990, just at dawn, the IRS struck. Although the agent investigating me knew very well that I was not violent, IRS agents and

Tennessee Revenue Department agents roared in my driveway while the SWAT team in their black ninja suits poured out of the woods on either side of my house.

They attacked with reckless, malicious disregard for the safety of my wife and seven children. All they needed to do was pick up the phone and tell me I had been indicted, and I would have gone downtown. No, these IRS thugs wanted headlines from a sensational "predawn raid" to scare the sheep for tax season, and to make me and my wife, the mother of my seven children, look violent and dangerous.

After they arrested me and Susan, the IRS refused to leave my home. Contrary to the law and over the protest of my spunky 15-year-old daughter, Liberty, three IRS agents stayed and held my children hostage until the end of the day. They were waiting for a search warrant so they could come back and steal my records and my computer.

On the ride downtown I had no idea what was going on. Why would they arrest Susan? She had never done anything other than minor secretarial work in my business and spent all her waking hours home-schooling and raising children.

When I stepped into the jail cell, I began to understand. They had indicted her to blackmail me. My friends, customers of the gold and silver bank, and numerous church members were already there, including my pastor and assistant pastor. The indictment was an inch thick. In 72 pages it charged 26 defendants with conspiracy to defraud the government, willful failure to file, and diverse other malefactions.

The government claimed that the gold and silver bank was a tax evasion scheme to hide income. Not even two years in the U.S. Army had prepared me for stupidity of this magnitude. How could we hide income when almost everything we took in was in checks, and we deposited the checks into our bank account? Oh, yes, we did pass some of the checks along to other dealers to pay for gold or silver we bought for them, a common practice in the industry and perfectly legal. This, the government taught us, was "laundering checks," a sinister activity proving we were up to no good. But every bank deposit I had made was a count on the indictment! And Susan—poor home-making, home-schooling, never-stop-running Susan—was the Number Two conspirator, right after me!

My bond was set at $150,000, fully secured. For comparison, that same day they arrested a child molester and set his bond at $10,000, not secured. I stayed in jail from Tuesday until Friday, when my parents put up their house to get me out of jail. When the federal marshals released me at 5:00 P.M., sheriff's deputies were waiting to arrest me, and me alone, on state charges.

I believe but cannot yet prove that an ex-IRS agent had been sent to work for the Tennessee revenue department to get the search warrant the IRS couldn't get, and to figure out some way to charge me under state law. (You're not paranoid if somebody is really persecuting you.) I was charged with violating a statute that had been on the books 19 years: TCA 67-1-1440(d), "delaying and depriving the state of revenue to which it was lawfully entitled at the time it was lawfully entitled thereto." In all those 19 years, not a single Tennessean had discovered how to violate it, but I had. Truth to tell, I hadn't even figured it out, since I was accused of "delaying and depriving" the state of revenue, the amount of which was unknown and to which the state had never become lawfully entitled. They accused me of a crime I could not possibly have committed because I didn't know it existed. Never mind, due process just slows things down.

They were charging me with not collecting sales tax on exchanges of gold and silver money for paper money. You know—like when you go to the bank, and give the teller a twenty and she gives you back a ten and two fives, less sales tax. What? She doesn't charge you sales tax? Of course not, because it's an exchange of money for money.

But neither the state of Tennessee nor any other state can admit that gold and silver coin are money. If they do, they will admit they are operating outside the law. The monetary emperor is naked, and state officials from the Chief Justice of the Supreme Court to the governor to the second assistant tire checker are afraid to tell him. They should be afraid, because the monopoly on money creation is the jugular vein of the U.S. fascist state.

But in January 1990, I didn't have time to worry about state charges. Susan and I were both facing 19 years in jail if convicted in federal court. We knew the statistics, too. Humanly speaking, we had no chance. Ninety-eight percent of federal tax prosecutions end in guilty verdicts.

The next year and a half was a wretched struggle to persevere without despair. Only a survivor of a criminal prosecution could understand how it hammers your soul. Most defendants never make it to trial. Through the investigation alone, federal agents and prosecutors can destroy their businesses and their families and break their spirit. Stripped of business, money, family, and hope, most plead guilty just to end the nightmare. In our case one poor defendant pled guilty with no idea what it meant. When a defense attorney asked him who he had conspired with, he screwed up his face in confusion and paused several minutes. "I dunno. Myself, I guess!"

SECOND SET OF TRIALS

Our trial began on February 26, 1991, over a year after our arrest. Right after the noon break that first day, I received word that our sons Wright (10) and Christian (8) had been severely burned playing with gasoline. Susan spent the first two weeks of trial with them in the hospital.

Just when it seemed that things couldn't get worse, they did. Day after day I had to listen as the prosecutor hatefully twisted everything I had ever done into something evil—including the good things. This went on for four and a half long months. The government entered immaterial documents by the hundredweight.

The vast but tediously shallow silliness of the whole farce made me the maddest. Do you remember in C.S. Lewis's *Perelandra,* when the Unman is struggling to convince the Green Lady to disobey Maleldil's command not to spend the night on the land? Ransom notes with dismay the childish silliness of evil. Throughout the night while the Green Lady sleeps, the Unman repeats, "Ransom? Ransom?" When Ransom answers, "What?," the Unman responds, "Nothing." At its depths, evil is not noble or grand. It's merely a silly, spoiled child, flicking boogers at his betters.

To the charges of "willful failure to file income tax returns" we argued that no statute makes anyone liable for an income tax (except "foreign withholding agents"). No one—not the federal district court judge, not the assistant U.S. attorney, not the IRS, no one—was able to point out that statute, because it doesn't exist.

Here was a "man bites dog" story if ever there was one, but was the local media interested? Hardly. The first day of trial was covered by an old reporter for the Commercial Appeal who with great insight described issues and characters. Next day he was yanked off the case and replaced with a Stalinist "comrade" who loyally published whatever official line the U.S. attorney's office gave him.

But our jury was more open-minded. On July 9, 1991, the jury returned its verdict: 17 defendants not guilty on all counts! To God be the glory! We threw an enormous party and that Sunday had one bodacious worship service.

I still had to face a state trial. I no more than caught my breath when I had to dive back down into the sewage of the "justice system."

The trial started in May 1992, and lasted three weeks. The judge and the prosecution did their best to keep out my evidence—evidence that showed how many hundreds of hours I had haunted the law library to study out my position and make sure I was right.

It did little good. Remember the letter I wrote a friend when I escaped from Arkansas? The Revenue Department had seized it in 1986, and the prosecutrix used it to make me look like a hypocrite.

Even at that, three jurors held out for three days. I later talked to one of the holdouts, and he said that one of the women who gave up said, "Oh, well, he'll get another trial on appeal." Can people really be that ignorant, or will they just use any excuse to justify their own cowardice? On May 18, 1992, I was convicted on two counts of "delaying and depriving."

A month later the judge sentenced me to two years in jail, but he suspended all but 30 days, provided I would pay $1,000 a month for 73 months as "restitution" and do 1,000 hours (half a year's work) of community service. With seven children to support, it was a deal I couldn't refuse.

I appealed. In August 1994 the Court of Criminal Appeals overturned one count of the conviction for double jeopardy. I couldn't be guilty of one count of "delaying" and one count of "depriving" for the very same conduct. On the money issue, however, the real heart of the case, the court dodged and denied all my arguments.

We appealed to the Tennessee Supreme Court, and they heard the case on All Saints Day, 1995. Dr. Edwin Vieira, Jr., constitutional attorney and America's foremost expert on monetary law, prepared the briefs and argued the case. For over six months we heard nothing. Then on May 28, 1996, the Supreme Court affirmed my conviction, once again dodging the money issue.

I am still appealing, this time into the federal system, but the appeal couldn't be filed quickly enough to prevent my arrest on June 28, 1996. The petition for habeas corpus in federal district court was assigned to the same judge who had tried our federal case. She took jurisdiction of the appeal, but refused to order my release. From June 28 until July 23, I was a guest of the Shelby County Jail and the Shelby County Penal Farm.

The next hurdle is securing a stay of execution on the $72,000 fine. Failing that, I go back to jail for another 11 months while the appeal goes on.

WHY?

Why keep on fighting? After 15 years, why not just put down the load and forget it?

Because the fiat money system is both the strength and weakness of America's tyrants. It bleeds the people's wealth and labor, but it also threatens to collapse under its own weight—or whenever the scales fall off the people's eyes. With its green engravings of famous Americans, electrons whirling around in bank computers, and loans created out of thin air, it is one vast confidence game. As long as the people believe they can't see the emperor's naked pink flesh, his power and dignity will be preserved. But let one little boy holler, "Hey, he's nekkid!" and the tyranny collapses.

I didn't sally forth looking for dragons to slay. The dragon came to me. He came with a lie, and either you oppose a lie, or you become a liar. You can kid yourself and say I'm only going along because they have all the guns, but day by day, year by year, your integrity erodes. Finally, you become like the tyrants: just one more liar.

Even if you have no chance to win, you have to fight. Not many are willing, but even a few keep the tyrants from sleeping at night. If we don't fight, how many more Ruby Ridges and Wacos will there be? How many more SWAT team attacks? How many more police checkpoints? How many more bureaucrats watching your bank account and your finances? How many more children held hostage by IRS agents? The Bill of Rights is already dead. Will it be time to fight when your wife and children are dead, too?

The U.S. government spent millions of dollars trying to jail me and my wife and my pastor and assistant pastor. The assistant U.S. attorney here told one lawyer that I was "the most dangerous man in the mid-South." In a four and a half year investigation the government spent $5 to $10 million, maybe more. We heard they spent nearly two million on the trial alone.

We can't both be right. Either the government is right and gold and silver coin is not money, or I am right. This is not a gentlemen's "difference of opinion."

If I'm right, and if I win in the courts, then no state will ever be able to charge sales tax on gold and silver coin again. The greatest disability to free trade in gold and silver will have been removed. We will have broken down the last illegal roadblock to sound metallic money.

POSTSCRIPT

Because the conditions of probation were so burdensome on him and his family, Mr. Sanders returned to jail and was relocated to a medium-security prison on November 4, 1996. He was released on December 20, 1996. In May 1996 he appealed the Tennessee conviction into the federal court system. In March 1999 the Sixth Circuit Court of Appeals in Cincinnati affirmed his conviction. On November 27, 2000, the United States Supreme Court denied his petition for writ of *certiorari*.

Mr. Sanders lives with his wife, six of their seven children, and 12 grandchildren in Dogwood Mudhole, Tennessee, which is not near anywhere.

PART IV

THE MINERS

"Although gold and silver are not by nature money, money is by nature gold and silver."

—Karl Marx, philosopher and revolutionary (1818–1883)

There is little doubt in my mind that had I read *Diamond: A Journey to the Heart of an Obsession* by Mathew Hart back when I was in college 35 years ago, I would have been a geologist. While the book gives an excellent historical overview of the diamond trade, it was the geolo-gical overview and the lengths people go to obtain and find diamonds that fascinated me the most. The chapter on the recent Canadian Diamond Rush was particularly interesting, perhaps because of my interest in the Canadian mining industry.

The Canadian Venture Exchange (CDNX), which includes the old Vancouver Stock Exchange, is one of the greatest venture capital markets in the world, perhaps even rivaling Silicon Valley. Over the last five or six years, tens of billions of dollars have been raised on the CDNX by small mining companies, many of them gold mining companies. Rick Rule likes to point out that the primary asset of these companies is "intellectual capital," the knowledge, experience, and ideas about where to find a geologic resource. It is not property, mines, or processing facil-ities, features that one normally associates with mining companies.

This section of the book includes contributions from several of the finest geologists I know. Before investment advisors or investment newsletter writers or even I can make recommendations to you, we look to the miners and geologists to help gain an understanding of a geologic resource, an operating mine, or a mining company. Your advisors use their years of experience to assess their own "whos." As far as I'm concerned, the sage miners included in this section are some of the best in the business.

- **Bob Quartermain:** Is a geologist by trade. The company Bob founded and now runs, Silver Standard Resources, is one of the most successful precious metals resource companies in existence, and as he points out in this contribution, "gold and silver do move together." Like many of the other sages in this book, Bob "is very long on precious metals," including gold.
- **Louis James:** How do the pros evaluate a gold mining company? Louis James shows you how he used "the 8 Ps": People, Property, Paper, Phinancing, Politics, Push, Promotion, and Price to analyze his September 2008 "New Company Recommendation," International Tower Hill Mines, a stock that has risen sevenfold since his recommendation.
- **Brent Cook:** A contribution packed with gold mining facts, statistics, and analysis from a geologist with the experience that can make sense of it all arrives at the conclusion that "given the critical demand for new gold deposits, the most dramatic share price increases of all will accrue to the junior companies that are able to produce a real discovery."
- **Morgan Poliquin:** Beginning with the premise that "practically all civilizations over human history have gradually and spontaneously agreed upon gold to be money," this contribution presents a short history of money, the money monopoly, and a look at gold's role as a store of value. Great miners not only know how to find gold, they know the "gold standard has coincided with the most significant rises in real wealth."

CHAPTER 17

SILVER—"POOR MAN'S GOLD"

Bob Quartermain
Silver Standard

"Genius without education is like silver in the mine."

—Benjamin Franklin, American
statesman (1706–1790)

Bob Quartermain is the president and CEO of Silver Standard Inc., which has the largest in-ground silver resource of any publicly traded primary silver company. Bob joined Silver Standard as its president in 1985 and grew its market cap from C$1.5 million then to over $1.5 billion today. Silver Standard Resources is now considered a significant silver and gold resource company making the transition from explorer to producer while continuing to grow through exploration and developing its own projects. Although primarily a silver company, silver is a precious metal and it is often viewed as a gold substitute or "poor man's gold" by many.

Originally published in *The Gold Report* on June 20, 2008, as "The Outlook for Gold Is Still Sterling: An Interview with Robert Quartermain." *The Gold Report* is an online report that features investment coverage of precious metals, base metals, and gems that is published by Streetwise Inc.

Like many of the other sages in this book, Bob considers himself to be a "contrarian," going so far as to say that "we got into the silver business when no one else was in silver." This interview with Bob by The Gold Report *provides insights into both the silver and gold markets, why Bob believes silver prices will continue to rise, and then tells us where to look for good values.*

The Gold Report: *What's your outlook for silver in 2009 and, perhaps, beyond?*

Robert Quartermain: The outlook for silver remains positive. Since 1990, demand has exceeded supply every year, resulting in reduced stockpiles. Mine supply represents only about 75 percent of fabrication demand. The other 25 percent is made up of government sales or scrap, most of which is photographic scrap. As these secondary supplies dry up, current mine supply won't be able to keep up with demand. This will put upward pressure on silver prices.

Demand for silver has increased about 1 percent per year during the past seven years. During this same time, we've seen photographic consumption of silver drop about 39 percent. More significantly, industrial consumption of silver has increased about 36 percent during this period. That's an increase in demand, since 2001, of 110 million ounces per year. If we look at 2008 specifically, over 447 million ounces of silver were consumed in industrial applications, and those, of course, were across a wide range of products. Industrial demand now represents more than 50 percent of total annual silver demand. We expect that to continue through 2009, and going forward, to increase.

TGR: *That's a significant increase in industrial demand. Can you talk a little about that?*

RQ: Well, for instance, silver is used in cell phones, iPods, and Palm Pilots, many consumer products used in our everyday lives. The interesting thing is that while these products are produced in large quantities, each unit requires only a small amount of silver. It's not economic to recover the silver from each unit, so it's not being recycled. It's not coming back into the marketplace.

Silver is also being used in water purification for its antibacterial properties. It's used in clothing, and its health care applications are increasing in a more environmentally sensitive world. I think we're going to see a rise in its use in all of these areas. And then, with the recent increase in gold prices, we're seeing greater interest in high-end designer silver jewelry, which is replacing gold jewelry. I expect to see new electronic and industrial applications for silver, particularly in the energy field as well as other technological breakthroughs for its use that will continue to be drivers on the consumption side.

TGR: *What about from an investment standpoint?*

RQ: We've seen renewed interest in silver as an investment, both in terms of owning the physical metal, and through exchange-traded funds. iShares (SLV, http://seekingalpha.com/symbol/slv) holds over 280 million ounces of silver for investors. So, to use a bit of a pun, I would say that the outlook for this year and next year is going to be "sterling."

TGR: *What are the potential obstacles to this "sterling run"? I know gold and silver are not tied together, but there seems to be some correlation.*

RQ: That's true, gold and silver do move together but sometimes not to the same extent. Last year, 900 million ounces of silver were consumed at an average price of about $15 an ounce. So the total dollar amount of silver consumed last year was around $13.5 billion. This is a relatively small market, compared with gold or the base metals or many other commodities. Yet there's a lot more silver traded through the futures markets and futures contracts—these markets are much larger than the physical market. So we have a situation where what occurs in the paper trade market can influence price.

As you point out, a lot of the silver price movement has been dictated by gold and a lack of confidence in the U.S. dollar. With the U.S. dollar under pressure, silver has moved up over the last few years. Clearly, if there is some strengthening of the U.S. dollar, there could be some reduction in silver prices as people move out of it as an investment. As silver has such strong industrial demand, I think there will always be underlying investor interest.

TGR: *What should individual investors look for when they're investing in silver or silver stocks?*

RQ: Well, as we've discussed, the U.S. dollar is one of the key drivers. Silver is certainly acting in sympathy with gold. As the U.S. dollar index has fallen in the last few years, both gold and silver have increased in value. So investors need to watch the dollar.

Second, I think investors should focus on iShares. There continues to be strong movement of silver into iShares. Three years ago there was nothing; now there are 280 million ounces of silver in iShares alone. So long as there continues to be growth in the fund, investor sentiment for silver is likely to be strong.

Third, there's the consumption aspect. Silver's new uses in electronics, batteries, biocides, and other applications will be positive for the metal. So, it's often good to be watching what's going on in the press around new consumer products. The Silver Institute publishes a quarterly report that details the new uses for silver as they develop. It's worth keeping an eye out for potential new sources of demand.

TGR: *What about on the legislative side?*

RQ: That's a good question. As you may be aware, in many jurisdictions around the world, silver, unlike gold, is treated not as an investment but as a commodity that is taxed. For instance, in Switzerland, you can buy physical gold at market value. But if you buy physical silver, you have to pay a value-added tax on top of it. So, it makes it a less attractive investment than gold. Through the Silver Institute, we're looking at initiatives to try to level that playing field.

TGR: *Going back to new uses for silver as a commodity, have you heard of any talk of Mitsui working on a silver-based catalytic converter?*

RQ: Mitsui has looked at replacing platinum or palladium, which they use in their catalytic converters, with silver because silver is a great catalyst. So far they're looking at only diesel applications, primarily for farm equipment. That's a very small and specific market. But as we all know, once you develop a new use for a commodity, technological advances often follow, which can then lead to wider applications. Mitsui has talked about this initial small market, but using silver in catalytic converters creates a new inroad, and as we know, with higher oil prices and third world economies rapidly developing, there will be more vehicles on the road. If silver is another option for a better environment, I think that is positive.

TGR: *As the price of silver neared $21 an ounce, did you see an increase in the number of people recycling their silver possessions?*

RQ: We'd have to look at some research to answer this question. On a global basis, there's a lot of silver trade going on in India because India is a very large consumer of silver jewelry. When silver prices rise, jewelry consumption tends to dry up a little in India, and we may even see some of that silver come back into the market for recycling.

However, if you look at the actual price point of silver, which is very low relative to gold, the fabrication costs that go into silver jewelry often push the price point of the end product up significantly. If you take an ounce of silver and make it into silver jewelry, you're probably going to end up selling the jewelry at about five to ten times the value of the silver. It's different for gold, because the metal costs so much more per ounce than silver. The fabrication costs put the final gold product at only about two to three times the value of the gold itself. So while it may be worth melting down the gold and recycling it, that's often not the case for silver.

That's why we don't often see large movements of physical metal into recycling. Back in the late 1970s when the Hunt Brothers tried to corner the silver market, silver prices jumped from $3 to $50 per ounce. Silver scrap increased from 130 million ounces in 1979 to 165 million ounces in 1980, and back to 125 million ounces in 1981. So those high prices brought only another 25 percent of additional scrap into the marketplace.

TGR: *Would you say that most of the silver recycling now is related to photography?*

RQ: Yes, that's one of the largest sources of recycled silver. Hospitals or labs that have old photographs or x-rays on file will often dispose of them. The silver is recovered and becomes part of the scrap supply network.

Last year about 100 million ounces of silver were used in photography. We might see 50 percent or more of that recycled.

TGR: *On another topic, what's your thinking on nationalization and geopolitics as they relate to investing in silver?*

RQ: I think investors have to look at the entire political landscape, whether it's nationalization that occurs at the country level or regulatory changes at a state or provincial level. For example, in Alberta, which is considered the conservative bastion of the Canadian economy, they created an excess profits tax last year on fossil fuels. So you can't tell a developing country that it's wrong to do something similar. The same applies with respect to mining laws—developed countries can't expect developing countries to operate by a different set of laws. The resource industry can't control the regulatory environments of individual countries. There will always be the potential for international regulations that could have a negative impact on operations and profits.

So what do we do? At Silver Standard Resources Inc. (SSRI, http://seekingalpha.com/symbol/ssri), we carefully evaluate the geographic areas before we invest in them. We try to choose those countries where there's a long history of mining, such as Mexico, or Peru, or Chile. We look for countries that have an understanding of mining and a recognition of its contributions to the economy in providing jobs and providing the products we use in our everyday life.

TGR: *There's more regulation in developed countries, yet those are the countries where demand is highest, right?*

RQ: That's true. Here in North America we have our electronics, cell phones, flat-screen TV's, etc. that all require silver. We may regulate and shut down mining here from over regulation, but we still want these products. So we have to go to jurisdictions where mining laws support mining development. On the whole, the international mining fraternity operates at a very high environmental standard. Here in Canada and in the United States we have environmental laws that require us to make mining as benign as possible. We export and transport those same standards to all of our operations irrespective of the jurisdiction. We try to be good citizens with the local communities where our projects are located, and I think that if we're providing jobs and being socially responsible, then we don't have to be as concerned about nationalization.

But we all know that every four to six years politicians change. Mines, on the other hand, are much longer-term projects. So there's always the potential for shorter-term disruption from regulatory or tax law changes.

TGR: *Where do you think we are now in this bull market for precious metals? This run began in 2001, and back then, we could expect some big moves. Now, we seem to have hit a wall of worries. What are your thoughts?*

RQ: My background is in geology, not as much in macroeconomics. So my comments on this topic are more personal. They stem from my travels over the last year to China and Southeast Asia, in my recent role as head of The Silver Institute. With recent high oil prices and commodity prices, we are witnessing a transference of wealth from the West to the East. We've already seen a large transfer of U.S. dollars to China through trade because of China's low labor rates and less expensive products.

So what we're now seeing is a redistribution of capital as it moves out of the developed economies into those that are supplying cost competitive products as well as oil. The money is still there, it's just more heavily concentrated in some cases into fewer hands. It will ultimately be invested somewhere. Maybe it will be invested in U.S. dollars or euros. But I think there's a movement toward holding hard assets, such as commodities and certainly precious metals. If we look at precious metals separately, we have had a very good run up these last few years. We may well have some retrenchment in prices now, but then it continues to go forward again. I think we're seeing a substantial wealth creation because of natural resources, in economies that didn't have such wealth before. We're also seeing more people purchasing consumer goods. And as we've discussed, a lot of these consumer goods, especially electronics, contain silver. Ten years ago, China made up only a fraction of the U.S. GDP. And now China has become almost the third largest economy in the world—and growing. And its silver consumption has doubled in the last five years.

So to answer your question, I think we may see some volatility along the way as investors stop and reflect on which way the precious metals markets are headed. But from a personal point of view, I am very long on precious metals and base metals because I think the development that we're seeing in the new economies bodes well for consumer goods and ultimately for precious metals. There may be some short-term contraction in the world economies, when people stop buying consumer goods, and that will impact metal prices. But I suspect that this cycle will continue for some time yet.

TGR: *Let's talk about two of the companies you're involved with, beginning with Silver Standard. The company is transitioning from an exploration company to a production company. Could you give us a progress report?*

RQ: Silver Standard has been involved in silver since 1993 when we started acquiring silver projects. At that time, silver prices were low but we believed prices would rise to the point where it made sense to put our projects into production. Over the last 16 years, we have acquired the largest in-ground resources of any publicly traded company. We have 286 million ounces of reserves. We have 1,036 million ounces of measured and indicated resources. We have 457 million ounces of inferred resources in 16 projects around the world.

The first project we're advancing into production is the Pirquitas Project in northern Argentina. About 24 months ago we made the construction decision and we expect to achieve commercial production in the fourth quarter of this year. We're spending $233 million to place this project into production. It will be a sizable silver producer and will produce on average 10 million ounces of silver a year over what we see as a 14-year mine life based on the current reserves. We are now completing the transition from explorer to producer. This will allow us to focus on our 15 other projects, and bring them along the development pipeline so that Silver Standard can grow organically and become a significant silver producer.

TGR: *That's exciting. How about bringing us up to date on Canplats Resources Corporation [TSX.V: CPQ]?*

RQ: I had been a director of Canplats since 2000 but left the board a year ago to focus on Silver Standard. We had directed Canplats initially to look for platinum group metals in the Nipigon Lake area of Ontario. But we also had some good technical successes in Mexico, so the Board decided to focus on projects and areas in Mexico. Over the last few years, Canplats has picked up some properties and drilled them with some technical success.

Two years ago, Canplats was prospecting for grassroots opportunities and came up with a project called Camino Rojo where gold and silver, as well as base metals, were discovered near the surface. They trenched it and showed the values were there. The company staked a large area, drilled, and found extensive gold and silver mineralization, which continues to many hundreds of meters at depth. The market has reacted favorably to it, in part driven by the fact that the project is located about 50 kilometers south of the Penasquitos project that Goldcorp Inc. (GG, http://seekingalpha.com/symbol/gg) has, which is a very large tonnage gold, silver, and base metal project with grades not too dissimilar from those of Canplats. It's early stage, the results to date show a fairly consistent mineralized zone, and there's excellent potential in the land package that's over 1,300 square miles. Shareholders will continue to benefit from positive drill results.

TGR: *Let's finish up by talking about the Silver Institute.*

RQ: The Silver Institute is comprised of many companies—mining, fabrications, financial—focused on silver. The purpose of the Silver Institute is to promote the use of silver and to expand its range of applications through research and technological advances. We promote a better understanding of silver through our website and our annual World Silver Survey. Every year we have a conference in China where we hope to learn more about that market. This will be our eighth year in China. Our website, www.silverinstitute.org, posts a lot of good historical data on silver. We also publish a quarterly newsletter that describes some of our new initiatives.

CHAPTER 18

ANALYZING A GOLD MINING STOCK

Louis James
International Speculator

"Gold would have value if for no other reason than that it
enables a citizen to fashion his financial escape from the state."
                            —William F. Rickenbacker, author and U.S.
                                        Air Force pilot (1938–1995)

Louis James is the senior editor of the International Speculator *and*
Casey Investment Alert. *Louis constantly travels the world, visiting
promising prospective geologic targets, grilling management and company geologists for their expert opinions. On any given day he might be
pounding rocks in the Democratic Republic of Congo, examining drill
cores in Argentina, or sharing an exotic food dish with miners in China.
He evaluates dozens of companies every month, conducts due diligence
on only the best, and then compares notes with his colleagues.*

*In terms of how to analyze a prospective investment in a mining
stock in general or a gold mining stock in particular, Louis's contribution
is a must read. He uses what he calls the 8 Ps format to analyze the*

Originally published in *International Speculator* in November 2008 as "New Company
Recommendation."

most important aspects of such an investment: people, property, paper, phinancing, politics, push, promotion, and price. In this contribution, he recommends International Tower Hill Mines (ITH) noting that "a veteran explorer with almost 30 years in the field" is CEO of an "Alaska and Nevada gold explorer with over a dozen prospective projects" and that "ITH is a steal at current prices." If ITH's subsequent six-fold increase in price is any indication, Louis knows what he's talking about.

For those who still have cash for the speculative portions of their portfolios (or are liquidating formerly "safe" mainstream investments and now have more than one-third of their portfolios in cash), this is a market rife with amazing opportunities. There are known gold elephant deposits and even some monster deposits on the deep discount rack, right next to the juniors with nothing but a geologist's dream.

We're still looking over a couple of the more advanced of these; one has to wonder, if they are as good as they look, why a cash-rich major hasn't taken them out while their share prices are down. It's our fortune that we should have time to kick the tires on them hard and see if we can shake anything important loose. However, there's one we've been following as a Casey Investment Alert pick that has delivered on its promise without market recognition, and that gives you the opportunity we're bringing to your attention today.

Just remember the tactics of the day: Buy in tranches, buy on days when gold retreats, use aggressive stink bids.

BUY—ITH is a cashed-up company with a new 4.0-million-ounce resource in the 43–101-compliant bag, currently selling for $13.16/ounce. The company has the potential to double that resource again by the end of 2009, and the deposit is in mine-friendly Alaska, 80 kilometers from another producing open pit mine. The 8 Ps are pretty straightforward. . . .

PEOPLE

The president and CEO of ITH is Jeffrey A. Pontius, a veteran explorer with almost 30 years in the field. Jeff was exploration manager of Pikes Peak Mining Company, where he managed the exploration program resulting in the discovery of the Cresson Deposit at Cripple Creek, Colorado, containing over five million ounces of gold. Before taking on ITH, Jeff spent seven years at AngloGold Ashanti (USA) Exploration Inc., ending up as North American exploration manager and also a director of Anglo American (USA) Exploration Inc. While with Anglo, Jeff led the exploration team that spent US$10 million developing an extensive database and acquiring all of the Alaskan projects vended into ITH. No one knows these projects better than Jeff.

Many people have impressive resumes, of course, so we checked up on Jeff when we first heard this story about a year ago and heard from more than one source that he's a technically competent geo and a straight shooter—our favorite combination. Since then, Jeff has calmly delivered exactly as he said he would, and that counts for a lot in our view.

Also in the rock-kicking department is VP for exploration Dr. Russell Myers, a 25-year veteran who also comes from Anglo, where he was part of the team of geologists that evaluated the potential for deep targets at the Cripple Creek gold mine.

As usual, there are many other members of the team, which Jeff basically brought with him from Anglo. But the essential player is definitely Jeff, and we think he's got the Right Stuff.

PROPERTY

ITH is an Alaska and Nevada gold explorer with over a dozen prospective projects, all but two in Alaska. As per Jeff's bio, these are projects Anglo had been bringing along from the earliest stages and decided to farm out—along with Jeff—in 2006. One upside of this is that if ITH does find something that looks good to a major (and we think they may already have), Anglo is one big company that will obviously be interested . . . if another doesn't scoop it up first.

The "something that may already interest a major" is a potentially heap-leachable, open-pit project called Livengood, about 120 kilometers northwest of Fairbanks, Alaska. The infrastructure is excellent, with the project just off the Alaskan pipeline corridor and a paved highway right through the property. Management reports that the location gets as cold as you'd expect of an Alaskan winter, and that will be a cost factor, but as it's in the Alaskan interior, there's only an average of 14 inches of snow annually—a major advantage. Topography is gentle and there are roads all over the property—which is about 80 kilometers from the producing Fort Knox mine near Fairbanks (Kinross, 330,000 ounces per year).

Here's a real plus: The property is 100 percent on Alaskan state lands—lands specifically acquired by the Alaska Department of Mental Health for the purpose of generating revenue from mineral development. This not only means that the Alaskan state government wants to see the minerals resources developed, but that if there is a U.S. federal royalty at some point in the future, it won't affect Livengood.

That's important because Livengood is a bulk-tonnage project, with margins that wouldn't likely take a large federal royalty. How big is it? The company just published a new resource calculation, including 69.5 million Indicated tonnes averaging 0.83 g/t gold, containing 1.9 million ounces of gold, plus 87.9 million Inferred tonnes at 0.77 g/t, containing 2.2 million ounces of gold. That's good but not great bulk tonnage grade—and everything costs more in Alaska. However, there's a higher-grade core of 1.2 million Indicated ounces at 1.06 g/t and 1.3 million Inferred ounces at 0.96 g/t gold.

That's better, but still not terrific grade. We still love the deposit. Why? Early metallurgy work is encouraging for a low-cost heap leach operation (recoveries ranging from 90.2 to 99.9 percent, with even the primary sulfide ore at depth appearing to be leachable; 42.3 to 60.9 percent recoveries), and there are other factors, with perhaps the most important one being that the deposit is basically a gentle hill. That's key for two reasons: (A) the strip ratio early on (when you're in a hurry to pay back your mine-building capital expenditures) will be very low and that's a major cost saving, and (B) there's plenty of room for leach pads, a mill, tailing dams, etc., right next to the deposit.

Furthermore, Livengood remains open, with assays pending on areas outside the new resource (see: http://media3.marketwire.com/docs/ith1029.jpg). And there are other areas on the property with similar surface characteristics as those of the current resource area.

Another resource calculation is due in early 2009, which will include all 2008 drill results. Five-plus million ounces with a higher-grade core is not at all out of the question by then, and the company has the targets and the cash to increase the resource much farther by the end of 2009.

How big could it get? The normally calm Jeff Pontius gets visibly excited on this subject. He sees the potential at Livengood as being similar to that at Cripple Creek—that district has seen production of more than 23.5 million ounces of gold, as of 2005. That may be pie-in-the-sky, but Jeff has targets he hasn't even started drilling yet. There's no question in our minds that Livengood will get bigger, it's only a question of how much bigger.

Good infrastructure, good metallurgy, and pro-mining politics—all of this coupled with an emerging elephant deposit big enough to interest a major . . . we like this one a lot.

PAPER AND PHINANCING

The share structure is relatively clean and tight. All shares are free trading, and there is no paper about to expire. All the 2009 paper is out of the money—actually, *all* of the warrants and options are out of the money—so we'd have to already have substantial gains before any of it might become a worry in the future. Should our speculation work out and the shares trade higher than C$3 next May (or US$— we'd still have a double), the warrants would bring in another C$24 million without new dilution—a good thing at that stage.

But even if not, as already noted, ITH has enough money to complete its exploration programs for this year and next year.

Management, by the way, owns about 7.7 percent of the shares. Anglo still owns 14.8 percent of the shares. Insider trading reports show some selling before tax season, but also steady buying throughout the year—a good sign.

The company gets an all-around clean bill of financial health.

POLITICS

Alaska has long been a pro-mining jurisdiction, almost as good as Nevada. But it just got better a couple months ago, when voters rejected a ballot initiative that would have killed large-scale mining in the state (it was targeting T.NDM's giant Pebble gold project, but would have affected others as well). With most of the world making mining more difficult, Alaska's move in the opposite direction was a breath of very fresh air.

PUSH

ITH has plenty of major Push ahead:

1. Drills are still turning. Recent highlights include: 25.91 meters of 3.35 g/t gold, 143.26 meters of 1.32 g/t gold, 123.45 meters of 1.04 g/t gold, 79.25 meters of 1.16 g/t gold. Last June, ITH reported 202.7 meters of 1.37 g/t gold. As consistently good as the results have been, we expect more good bulk-grade intercepts like these ahead.
2. A new resource calculation is due out in Q109, and then another by the end of the year.
3. If the company does outline five million ounces of potentially economic gold (they already have over 6.37 million if you take the cutoff down to 0.3 g/t gold, but that's pushing the economic envelope pretty hard), expect the majors to start taking serious interest.

PROMOTION

The company has a genuine U.S. listing (AMEX) and employs an investor relations firm we know to be effective. We don't think a new elephant deposit will need much promotion if it gets as big as fast as we think it might, but as many emails as we've had from them over the last year, we're confident the team will get the story out.

PRICE

ITH is a steal at current prices, but that doesn't mean the shares couldn't get cheaper before they go up again. Stick with the program;

try to get an initial position filled under market, then look for big corrections without company-specific bad news for opportunities to increase your position, and keep those nasty stink bids on the table! The shares dropped as low as US$0.86 in the last bout of weakness, so we'd shoot for that range, or for a larger block at a lower price.

CHAPTER 19

LET'S TALK A BIT ABOUT GOLD AND GOLD EXPLORATION

Brent Cook
Exploration Insights

"No gold-digging for me . . . I take diamonds! We may be off the gold standard someday."

—Mae West, American actress and
sex symbol (1892–1980)

Brent Cook inherited Exploration Insights *from investor/analyst Paul van Eeden in early 2008 and with a little tweaking repurposed it into a mining and exploration investment newsletter. With over twenty-five years of experience—with a good deal of it as Principal Mining and Exploration Analyst at Global Resource Investments, Ltd.—providing economic and geologic evaluations to major mining companies, resource funds, and investors, Brent's insights into gold and gold stocks are invaluable. Brent has worked in over 50 countries on virtually every mineral deposit type, ranging from grassroots projects through feasibility studies and bank audits.*

As his contribution shows, not only does Brent know rocks, he understands gold mining's big picture. As he points out, assuming you can even get the environmental and political issues resolved on any given project, it can often take "decades from discovery to production." In the piece below, Brent explains some of the ingredients necessary to turn a "prospector's pipe dream to reality," including requiring "assessment of gold recovery issues, mineralization continuity, strip ratios, infrastructure and power costs, ore dilution and mining methods, and ultimately a risk adjusted economic assessment of the gold deposit." Brent's contribution and analysis will give you an appreciation of how the right "who" matters in any decision involving an investment in a gold mining stock. Brent Cook knows rocks.

The gold price in U.S. dollars has risen more than $700 since 2001, yet world gold mine production has consistently declined since 2002. Last year (2008) total mined gold production was about 78 million ounces. Total historical world gold production since man began mining gold is estimated by various sources at around 4.4 billion ounces (~US$4.4 trillion at $1,000/oz gold), most of which is still around today. Approximately 25 percent of the 4.4 billion ounces is officially held as gold reserves by 107 countries or funds. If gold is money, and I believe it is, then the "gold inflation rate" is the annual amount of new gold added to the system by mining.

The long-term gold inflation rate has averaged about 2.2 percent over the past 110 years. The past eight years have seen the gold inflation rate average about 1.76 percent (1.5 percent in 2008), and all indications are that this declining gold production profile will continue into the foreseeable future. The obvious implication from this data is that as the inflation rate of gold (gold production) declines and global monetary inflation accelerates the value of gold will increase.

There are more or less 32 major gold mining companies and untold junior mining companies that contribute to the roughly 78 million ounces of annual gold production. Most of the major mining companies show steady to declining production and reserve profiles. They have been able to add ounces predominantly by (1) raising the gold price used in their reserve calculations and (2) acquisitions.

By raising the gold price used in their reserve calculations, material that was formerly waste rock becomes gold ore. The increased gold price assumption directly translates into a lower average recovered grade, and by default higher production costs. CIBC World Markets calculates that world recovered gold grade declined from 1.7g/t in 2006 to 1.4g/t in 2008. This is a trend that will continue as long as the gold price remains high: Marginal mines become economic.

The second method of maintaining a gold mining company's production profile has been to acquire large base metal (copper, lead, and zinc) deposits that contain some gold. When base metal prices are high, gold company production costs are lower and earnings strong due to the base metal credits. The collapse in base metal prices at the end of 2008 resulted in a remarkable 31 percent increase in gold production costs, according to World Gold Council figures. Lesson learned: Henceforth, gold-dominant deposits will command a premium.

LET'S CONSIDER HOW MUCH METAL IS ACTUALLY BEING MINED AND FOUND

The mining industry desperately needs the next big discovery because even during a recession, the world is consuming enormous quantities of base and precious metals. To wit, global gold mine production in 2007 was approximately 81 million ounces. That's the equivalent of nearly all the gold ever mined from the 40 individual deposits on Nevada's world-class Carlin Gold Trend. In 2007, copper mine production totaled about 15 million tonnes. That is roughly equal to all the copper produced from Kennecott's Bingham deposit in Utah. Think about it: We are exhausting the equivalent of one of the largest gold districts and one of the largest copper deposits in the world on an annual basis. To varying degrees, this same story holds true for all metals.

Further exacerbating the production expansion problem is the time frame and costs to turn successful new discoveries into mines. The costs have been blown way out of the water, almost doubling since 2007. Social and political issues associated with getting a new mine permitted can take years, if not decades to resolve. Take a look at Ivanhoe's Oyu Tolgoi, Northern Dynasty's Pebble, and Freeport's Tenke deposits if you doubt this statement. It will probably be years, maybe even decades, from discovery to production *if* the local political and environmental issues can be resolved. The uncertainties of permitting, politics, and capital cost increases, coupled with the near impossibility of accurately estimating metal prices, force mining companies to use very conservative estimates in their financial models. This financially conservative bias in turn adds to the dearth of new mine production by keeping new projects on the drawing board. One notable example is the Galore Creek copper-gold deposit where NovaGold's original capital costs estimate of $2.5 billion increased to over $4 billion. The new cost estimates forced its partner, Teck-Cominco, to halt development and attempt a rejig of the whole project.

The final and ultimately most important aspect of any investigation of a mining or exploration company comes down to economic geology. Without an economic deposit, or the ability to differentiate ore from waste, your research is for naught. A good drill hole does not make a discovery and a resource does not make an economic reserve. Getting from a prospector's or promoter's pipe dream to reality requires turning the rocks into money. To do so requires the assessment of gold recovery issues, mineralization continuity, strip ratios, infrastructure and power costs, ore dilution and mining methods, and ultimately a risk-adjusted economic assessment of the gold deposit. Again, selectivity and skepticism need to be brought to the table.

This dearth of new discoveries is not for want of trying. There are over 2,000 publicly traded junior mining and exploration companies listed on the Canadian and Australian exchanges. The overwhelming majority of junior companies reside on the Toronto Venture exchange where they raised roughly C$34 billion between 2002 and 2008. Despite this rather stunning sum of speculative money and an estimated US$30 billion being devoted to global gold exploration alone, both the quality and number of new gold deposits dropped. Concurrent with the lack of success, speculative money comes and goes at the will of the market, and many junior exploration companies are headed for the graveyard: with their investors' money.

This poor record of success makes minerals exploration and mining one of the riskiest investment sectors you can investigate. Unfortunately, the average investor is ill equipped to sort through the idiosyncratic and vague lingo of this industry in order to differentiate the good from the bad. Compounding this difficulty is the fact that nearly every junior exploration company out there claims to have the next big thing. My goal in *Exploration Insights* has been to identify developing discoveries before the market or industry does with as little risk as possible. To do so requires using hard economic- and geologic-based analysis based on factual data and interpretations. In a rising gold price environment solid gold companies will be some of the best performing stocks. Given the critical demand for new gold deposits, the most dramatic share price increases of all will accrue to the junior companies that are able to produce a real discovery. Making money then only involves positioning yourself in the way of a gold discovery. There is no doubt that the major and mid-tier gold mining companies need new gold resources— regardless of the gold price.

Positioning yourself is, of course, easier said than done. Economically viable gold deposits are very rare indeed. Environmentally and socially permitable gold deposits *in politically stable countries* are even scarcer— hence the high price of gold. Finding them takes experienced people, money, and time. These are the three most valuable assets in the business: They are almost as scarce as gold. Therefore, a speculator in the junior exploration and mining sector needs to focus on these factors with a high degree of selectivity and skepticism.

CHAPTER 20

MONEY IS GOLD, AND GOLD IS A NOBLE METAL

Morgan Poliquin
Almaden Minerals

"Gold is Money. That's it."

—J.P. Morgan, American financier (1837–1913)

Morgan Poliquin is president and COO of British Columbia–based Almaden Minerals while his father, Duane, is chairman and founder. In 1996, Morgan came to work with his father at Almaden, and since 2000 he has planned, instituted, managed, and personally led country-wide exploration programs for them. He also manages Almaden's copper/ gold BHP Billiton joint venture and their base metals Mexican-based Japan Oil Gas joint venture. Morgan specializes in studying and finding geothermal systems and gold deposits.

Almaden Minerals is considered by many to be one of the premier prospect generators in the mining field. Mining firms that use the prospect generator business model reduce the risk and cost of exploration by joint venturing their ideas to larger, better capitalized mining companies that then fund further exploration of the company's projects/

prospects in order to earn an interest in the project. With over 40 projects underway in Canada, Mexico, and the United States, Almaden has perfected the model.

In the contribution below, Morgan takes a comprehensive look at gold's role in society at large. This is not a piece that analyzes a deposit; rather, it's about the crucial role that sound money plays in society and what happens when gold money is replaced with fiat money. As Morgan points out, fiat currency enables "politicians to print money at random to finance war, special interests and political ambition," whereas gold shines in a thriving and healthy society.

Civilization must involve more than one person. Indeed, the greater number of people and the diversity of what each one does and produces determines the "level" of civilization by virtually anybody's standards. Money is what enables people to cooperate by doing and making many things for each other. Practically all civilizations over human history have gradually and spontaneously agreed that gold is money.

A SHORT HISTORY OF MONEY

If an enormous chest of money washed up on his desert island, it is obvious that it would have been useless to Robinson Crusoe, even after he had met Friday. Those two eventually decided to exchange goods and services with each other; the alternative being that they each would have had to do everything for themselves. Both parties engaging in voluntary exchange do so because they both expect to benefit from it. This is because each party values the goods or services differently, a point lost on many people, notably Adam Smith and Karl Marx. Value is subjective and depends on each person's unique tastes and circumstances; a person dying of thirst in the desert might trade all his possessions for water, but would only pay a dollar for a bottle of French spring water in New York. As a result of their exchange, Friday and Crusoe are better off than they were before, but they didn't need money to do it; they bartered.

But barter or direct exchange doesn't allow people to cooperate above a very primitive level. This is largely because of "indivisibility" and a "lack of coincidence of wants"[1] If a furniture maker wants to exchange a table for milk and a shirt, how does he divide the table to pay the farmer and the tailor? What if a music teacher wanted eggs, but couldn't find a chicken farmer interested in music? The music teacher would have to find out what the chicken farmer did want and then find somebody with this good who wanted music lessons, and through exchange obtain it to trade for eggs. This is called indirect trade, a quite cumbersome affair. Gradually some goods, as a result of their higher utility or beauty, are valued by enough people that they become mediums of exchange, or money. These more marketable items have ranged from feathers in pre-Columbian Mexico, cigarettes in prisons, seashells and fishhooks in fishermen's villages and even, horrifically, potato peelings in Nazi concentration camps. Eventually, the rarest, most desired, storable, and divisible goods displace all others as mediums of exchange. Over history, gold has been elected spontaneously by humankind as the most universally valued good in the world. This is because gold is unique and highly sought after. Gold can be stored for future exchange, is indestructible, doesn't tarnish, conducts better than most other metals, is the only naturally occurring yellow-colored metal, is highly malleable and divisible, is extremely rare (out of 92 naturally occurring elements, gold is the 73rd most common), is resistant to bacteria, and is non–allergenic to the human skin against which it can be breathtaking. No wonder humankind values it so much.

THE MONEY MONOPOLY

Throughout history, governments have often tried to monopolize money by making all forms of money, except what the state mints, illegal. For those who represent the government, controlling money means that you have the power to make as much as you want for your own purposes. Consequently, at all times, people possessing that power have abused it. The rulers of the Roman Empire made more gold coins

---

[1]Rothbard, M., *What Has Government Done to Our Money?* Auburn, AL: Ludwig von Mises Institute, 1990.

by clipping bits off the edges and adding copper. The nation state of today insists that the bits of paper it prints are legal tender, all the while frantically printing more of them. Lyndon B. Johnson printed money to fight a war in Vietnam and a war on poverty, creating yet another welfare-warfare state not unlike that of the Romans, which doled out free bread and bloodthirsty entertainment while simultaneously engaging in expensive military actions. As we know, their empire collapsed under the weight of this monetary decadence and the raiding peoples who took advantage of it.

But making more money comes with a heavy cost: With more money, the proverbial pie is bigger and the slice in your bank account is smaller. This means that prices go up, which is called inflation. People aren't stupid; they gauge very quickly that there is more money in the same world with the same amount of people and the goods and services. The people who get the new money first obviously profit the most as everyone else hasn't yet recognized the change. These people are inevitably the closest to those printing the new money. In this way, state monetary policy finances deficits, fixes elections, wages war, rewards special interests, and enslaves us by destroying our savings and forcing us to invest aggressively in order to save what we do have left. Injecting artificial money into the economy also results in less scrupulous investments, which together with the inevitable resulting collapse in their value, is a process better known as the business cycle. The worst part is that the average person thinks he or she is getting something out of the deal. But the question is would people, for example, really want government-funded day care paid for with created money if they knew that the cost was that their savings would lose practically all value in twenty years? Despite these outcomes, no politician, regardless of politics, wants to end this system of political money because he or she wants the machine for his or her purposes, goals, schemes, and friends. Inflation also affects the way we consume. Some people have the mistaken belief that prosperity correlates directly and positively with consumption. The truth is that consumption is possible only from real prosperity resulting from saving and investment, rather than the creation of fictional paper wealth. People today may be forced into consumption because inflation has made it very difficult to save.

GOLD FOR THE POOR AND THE WORKING PERSON

Money is only useful if we want the goods and services of other people. If we didn't want the goods and services of other people, we could try and survive by living off the land on our own. Obviously, that is an existence few of us want to lead; we enjoy the prosperity and even the nonessential goods and services that we provide for each other. Over history, as people exchanged with each other to a greater degree, the survival rate rose, people prospered and had more children. With a greater population came more goods and services for everyone. But what if we don't want these goods or services immediately but some time in the future for retirement, our children's education, or for a larger item we can't afford today? In this case we need to save. In fact, saving is what has elevated countless people out of poverty over human history. As population expanded with the same amount of gold in the world, the amount of money decreased. Known as deflation, it resulted in the decrease of prices. But these new people and newly prosperous people want to store or save as well.[2]

This ongoing process has led to an increased demand for money, which over the centuries has stimulated the mining of gold in order to meet it. Unlike printing little bits of paper at the arbitrary whims of politicians, mining gold is directed by the returns of mining, which are in turn directed by people's demand for new money. Being a substance of real value, gold stimulates real and prudent saving and investment. Of course, a component of the demand for gold is the demand for its use as a commodity. Gold's unique qualities mean that its uses are constantly expanding as new entrepreneurship seeks better, cheaper, and more efficient ways to serve mankind. Industrial uses make up about 300 tonnes of the roughly 2,500 tonnes that are produced annually. These uses vary from plating on Buddhist temples to electronics. The average pushbutton telephone has 33 gold-plated electric points, for example.[3]

---

[2]Mises, L., von, *Human Action: Scholars Edition*. Auburn, AL: Mises Institute, 1999.; Rothbard, M., *Man, Economy and State with Power and Market*. Auburn, AL.: Mises Institute, 2004 (1962, 1970).

[3]Taken from the World Gold Council's website: www.gold.org.

There is another important factor, however. Over history, gold has been owned by monarchs and, more recently, the central banks of the nation state. Most people in the world today are permitted by their governments to own gold, and gradually this gold is moving from state vaults to their pockets. All the gold produced in the world through history totals 140,000 tonnes.[4] Divided by today's world population, this equates to less than one ounce of gold per person. In a free market, price dictates the demand. People's demand for gold is signaled to the mining industry by its price, determining whether gold mining entrepreneurs should engage in the risk of exploring for and developing gold mines.

But governments have united, forming organizations and agreements designed to protect paper currencies and, some claim, to hinder or dissuade people from selling their paper currencies to buy gold. Government banks are the largest holders of gold, and it is argued that these banks repress the price of gold by selling their stocks of gold. Conspiracy theory or not, one can certainly concede that it would be in the interest of governments to prop up their currencies by doing so. GATA (the Gold Anti-Trust Action Committee) believes that they have sufficient evidence of the manipulation of gold to undertake litigation.[5]

CONCLUSION

It used to be that the government needed to tax its citizens in order to achieve its objectives, whether that is wealth redistribution or war. But taxation has limitations; when people are taxed too much, they move elsewhere or stop working. The original paper monies created by states could be redeemed for gold. This so-called gold standard has coincided with the most significant rises in real wealth. In the twentieth century, states have reneged on their promises of gold redemption, divorcing legal tender from gold. This has enabled politicians to print money at random to finance war, special interests, and political ambition. We have

---

[4]Baker, L.M., "From the Gold Standard to the Credit Bubble: Gold's Evolution as a Store of Value," Austrian Scholars Conference 9, 2003.
[5]See the Gold Anti-Trust Action Committee (GATA) website, www.gata.org

borne the results in the form of devastating losses of life, the destruction of savings, and massive debt. It's the state's new means of taxation: grabbing our savings through inflation by printing money. There is one gleaming (and nonallergenic) hope, however. Just as Indonesians ran to their rivers to pan for gold during the last collapse of Indonesian paper currency, people, where and when they are allowed to, have turned to gold as a store of wealth. Lord Keynes may have viewed this as "hoarding," but most know it to be saving for the future. The Chinese, in their march to becoming an open society, have just been allowed by their state to own gold.[6] Thankfully, most peoples of the world can now own gold, and the world's mining industry is providing us with a means of saving as we all move together toward greater prosperity. If people who wish to stop gold mining succeed to any degree, they should be aware that it is the poor and working people of the world they are hurting, who will have a much more difficult time saving.

---

[6]"China Opens Up Gold Trade," The Standard, September 8, 2004.

PART V

GAME-CHANGING EDUCATORS

"Intelligence plus character—that is the goal of true education."

—Martin Luther King, Jr., American clergyman
and civil rights activist (1929–1968)

My wife, Mary, is a doctor and a lot smarter than I am. At least that's what I tell the kids. However, she does say that I am the best researcher she knows. I think the reason I am such a good researcher is because I recognize the value and importance of education. Not only do I enjoy learning new things, I know from experience that new knowledge can pay off later.

While they are rare, great educators and writers can change the rules of understanding on a topic thought their communication. I have learned an immense amount of information from the three contributors below who have been educating readers with valuable information about surviving tough economic times for many, many years. The three contributions below are so non-mainstream, so game-changing that the contributors almost come across as being revolutionary in their thinking.

- **Ron Paul:** A Washington, D.C. insider points out in his contribution that "ultimately, the gold price is a measurement of trust in currency . . ." and unfortunately, "the belief that money created out of thin air can work economic miracles, if only properly 'managed,' is pervasive in D.C." Reinforcing a repeated message of this book, Ron Paul emphatically believes that "holding gold is protection or insurance against government's proclivity to debase its currency."

- **Paul van Eeden:** In the most thorough and concise analysis in this book on the price of gold, Paul explains "why a historic rise in the gold price has already commenced" and more important, "why it's not too late to get positioned."
- **Kenneth W. Royce:** Ken's contribution literally shouts, "If you haven't any gold, start buying NOW." And what he talks about is physical gold, "gold coins held . . . in . . . your . . . own . . . hand. Totally private and portable wealth. No reporting. No tracking." As he says, "Gold is cheap at any price."

CHAPTER 21

WHAT THE PRICE OF GOLD IS TELLING US

Ron Paul
Congressman

"Most Americans have no real understanding of the operation of the international money lenders. The accounts of the Federal Reserve System have never been audited. It operates outside of the control of Congress and manipulates the credit of the United States."

—Barry Goldwater, U.S. Senator (1909–1998)

With 11 terms in Washington, Ron Paul has been serving in Congress off and on since the late 1970s, although he has been continuously serving since 1996. Because of his role in Congress, many believe Ron Paul to be the leading U.S. voice for limited constitutional government, low taxes, free markets, and a return to sound monetary policies. After his 2008 presidential run, he set up a new political action and advocacy

---

This is a copy of a speech given before the U.S. House of Representatives on April 25, 2006.

group called Ron Paul's Campaign for Liberty *to "spread the message of the Constitution and limited government."*

He is also the author of several books, including Challenge to Liberty; The Case for Gold; A Republic, If You Can Keep It; *and, more recently,* The Revolution: A Manifesto *and* End the Fed. *In addition to his avowed goal of ending the Federal Reserve System, Congressman Paul has been a staunch advocate of sound money policy, including advocating a return by the United States to a gold standard for its currency.*

In a very methodical way Ron Paul's contribution lays out ways a "fiat monetary system encourages speculation and unsound banking" and why the "discipline of gold" or another hard currency "serves as a check on the government size and power." For the United States, the result of not having such discipline will continue to be ever-growing federal deficits, trade imbalances, recurring economic downturns, and ultimately massive inflation. "A sharply rising gold price is a vote of 'no confidence' in Congress's ability to control the budget, the Fed's ability to control the money supply, and the administration's ability to bring stability to the Middle East."

The financial press and even the network news shows have begun reporting the price of gold regularly. For twenty years, between 1980 and 2000, the price of gold was rarely mentioned. There was little interest, and the price was either falling or remaining steady.

Since 2001, however, interest in gold has soared along with its price. With the price now over $600 an ounce, a lot more people are becoming interested in gold as an investment and an economic indicator. Much can be learned by understanding what the rising dollar price of gold means.

The rise in gold prices from $250 per ounce in 2001 to over $600 today has drawn investors and speculators into the precious metals market. Although many already have made handsome profits, buying gold per se should not be touted as a good investment. After all, gold earns no interest and its quality never changes. It's static and does not grow as sound investments should.

It's more accurate to say that one might invest in a gold or silver mining company, where management, labor costs, and the nature of new discoveries all play a vital role in determining the quality of the investment and the profits made.

Buying gold and holding it is somewhat analogous to converting one's savings into 100-dollar bills and hiding them under the mattress—yet not exactly the same. Both gold and dollars are considered money, and holding money does not qualify as an investment. There's a big difference between the two, however, since by holding paper money one loses purchasing power. The purchasing power of commodity money—i.e., gold—however, goes up if the government devalues the circulating fiat currency.

Holding gold is protection or insurance against government's proclivity to debase its currency. The purchasing power of gold goes up not because it's a so-called good investment; it goes up in value only because the paper currency goes down in value. In our current situation, that means the dollar.

One of the characteristics of commodity money—one that originated naturally in the marketplace—is that it must serve as a store of value. Gold and silver meet that test—paper does not. Because of this profound difference, the incentive and wisdom of holding emergency funds in the form of gold becomes attractive when the official currency is being devalued. It's more attractive than trying to save wealth in the form of a fiat currency, even when earning some nominal interest. The lack of earned interest on gold is not a problem once people realize the purchasing power of their currency is declining faster than the interest rates they might earn. The purchasing power of gold can rise even faster than increases in the cost of living.

The point is that most who buy gold do so to protect against a depreciating currency rather than as an investment in the classical sense. Americans understand this less than citizens of other countries; some nations have suffered from severe monetary inflation that literally led to the destruction of their national currency. Although our inflation—i.e., the depreciation of the U.S. dollar—has been insidious, average Americans are unaware of how this occurs. For instance, few Americans know nor seem concerned that the 1913 pre-Federal Reserve dollar is now worth only four cents. Officially, our central bankers and our politicians express no fear that the course on which we are set is fraught with great danger to our economy and our political system. The belief that money created out of thin air can work economic miracles, if only properly "managed," is pervasive in D.C.

In many ways we shouldn't be surprised about this trust in such an unsound system. For at least four generations our government-run universities have systematically preached a monetary doctrine justifying the so-called wisdom of paper money over the "foolishness" of sound money. Not only that, paper money has worked surprisingly well in the past 35 years—the years the world has accepted pure paper money as currency. Alan Greenspan bragged that central bankers in these several decades have gained the knowledge necessary to make paper money respond as if it were gold. This removes the problem of obtaining gold to back currency, and hence frees politicians from the rigid discipline a gold standard imposes.

Many central bankers in the last 15 years became so confident they had achieved this milestone that they sold off large hoards of their gold reserves. At other times they tried to prove that paper works better than gold by artificially propping up the dollar by suppressing market gold prices. This recent deception failed just as it did in the 1960s, when our government tried to hold gold artificially low at $35 an ounce. But since they could not truly repeal the economic laws regarding money, just as many central bankers sold, others bought. It's fascinating that the European central banks sold gold while Asian central banks bought it over the last several years.

Since gold has proven to be the real money of the ages, we see once again a shift in wealth from the West to the East, just as we saw a loss of our industrial base in the same direction. Although Treasury officials deny any U.S. sales or loans of our official gold holdings, no audits are permitted so no one can be certain.

The special nature of the dollar as the reserve currency of the world has allowed this game to last longer than it would have otherwise. But the fact that gold has gone from $252 per ounce to over $600 means there is concern about the future of the dollar. The higher the price for gold, the greater the concern for the dollar. Instead of dwelling on the dollar price of gold, we should be talking about the depreciation of the dollar. In 1934 a dollar was worth 1/20th of an ounce of gold; $20 bought an ounce of gold. Today a dollar is worth 1/600th of an ounce of gold, meaning it takes $600 to buy one ounce of gold.

The number of dollars created by the Federal Reserve, and through the fractional reserve banking system, is crucial in determining how the market assesses the relationship of the dollar and gold. Although there's a strong correlation, it's not instantaneous or perfectly predictable. There are many variables to consider, but in the long term the dollar price of gold represents past inflation of the money supply. Equally important, it represents the anticipation of how much new money will be created in the future. This introduces the factor of trust and confidence in our monetary authorities and our politicians. And these days the American people are casting a vote of "no confidence" in this regard, and for good reasons.

The incentive for central bankers to create new money out of thin air is twofold. One is to practice central economic planning through the manipulation of interest rates. The second is to monetize the escalating federal debt politicians create and thrive on.

Today no one in Washington believes for a minute that runaway deficits are going to be curtailed. In March alone, the federal government created a historic $85 billion deficit. The current supplemental bill going through Congress has grown from $92 billion to over $106 billion, and everyone knows it will not draw President Bush's first veto. Most knowledgeable people therefore assume that inflation of the money supply is not only going to continue, but accelerate. This anticipation, plus the fact that many new dollars have been created over the past 15 years that have not yet been fully discounted, guarantees the further depreciation of the dollar in terms of gold.

There's no single measurement that reveals what the Fed has done in the recent past or tells us exactly what it's about to do in the future. Forget about the lip service given to transparency by new Fed Chairman Bernanke. Not only is this administration one of the most secretive across the board in our history, the current Fed firmly supports denying the most important measurement of current monetary policy to Congress, the financial community, and the American public. Because of a lack of interest and poor understanding of monetary policy, Congress has expressed essentially no concern about the significant change in reporting statistics on the money supply.

Beginning in March, although planned before Bernanke arrived at the Fed, the central bank discontinued compiling and reporting the monetary aggregate known as M3. M3 is the best description of how quickly the Fed is creating new money and credit. Common sense tells us that a government central bank creating new money out of thin air depreciates the value of each dollar in circulation. Yet this report is no longer available to us and Congress makes no demands to receive it.

Although M3 is the most helpful statistic to track Fed activity, it by no means tells us everything we need to know about trends in monetary policy. Total bank credit, still available to us, gives us indirect information reflecting the Fed's inflationary policies. But ultimately the markets will figure out exactly what the Fed is up to, and then individuals, financial institutions, governments, and other central bankers will act accordingly. The fact that our money supply is rising significantly cannot be hidden from the markets.

The response in time will drive the dollar down, while driving interest rates and commodity prices up. Already we see this trend developing, which surely will accelerate in the not too distant future. Part of this reaction will be from those who seek a haven to protect their wealth—not invest—by treating gold and silver as universal and historic money. This means holding fewer dollars that are decreasing in value while holding gold as it increases in value.

A soaring gold price is a vote of "no confidence" in the central bank and the dollar. This certainly was the case in 1979 and 1980. Today, gold prices reflect a growing restlessness with the increasing money supply, our budgetary and trade deficits, our unfunded liabilities, and the inability of Congress and the administration to rein in runaway spending.

Denying us statistical information, manipulating interest rates, and artificially trying to keep gold prices in check won't help in the long run. If the markets are fooled short term, it only means the adjustments will be much more dramatic later on. And in the meantime, other market imbalances develop.

The Fed tries to keep the consumer spending spree going, not through hard work and savings, but by creating artificial wealth in stock markets bubbles and housing bubbles. When these distortions run their course and are discovered, the corrections will be quite painful.

Likewise, a fiat monetary system encourages speculation and unsound borrowing. As problems develop, scapegoats are sought and frequently found in foreign nations. This prompts many to demand altering exchange rates and protectionist measures. The sentiment for this type of solution is growing each day.

Although everyone decries inflation, trade imbalances, economic downturns, and federal deficits, few attempt a closer study of our monetary system and how these events are interrelated. Even if it were recognized that a gold standard without monetary inflation would be advantageous, few in Washington would accept the political disadvantages of living with the discipline of gold, since it serves as a check on government size and power. This is a sad commentary on the politics of today. The best analogy to our affinity for government spending, borrowing, and inflating is that of a drug addict who knows if he doesn't quit he'll die; yet he can't quit because of the heavy price required to overcome the dependency. The right choice is very difficult, but remaining addicted to drugs guarantees the death of the patient, while our addiction to deficit spending, debt, and inflation guarantees the collapse of our economy.

Special interest groups, who vigorously compete for federal dollars, want to perpetuate the system rather than admit to a dangerous addiction. Those who champion welfare for the poor, entitlements for the middle class, or war contracts for the military industrial corporations all agree on the so-called benefits bestowed by the Fed's power to counterfeit fiat money. Bankers, who benefit from our fractional reserve system, likewise never criticize the Fed, especially since it's the lender of last resort that bails out financial institutions when crises arise. And it's true, special interests and bankers do benefit from the Fed, and may well get bailed out, just as we saw with the Long-Term Capital Management fund crisis a few years ago. In the past, companies like Lockheed and Chrysler benefited as well. But what the Fed cannot do is guarantee the market will maintain trust in the worthiness of the dollar. Current policy guarantees that the integrity of the dollar will be undermined. Exactly when this will occur, and the extent of the resulting damage to financial system, cannot be known for sure—but it is coming. There are plenty of indications already on the horizon.

Foreign policy plays a significant role in the economy and the value of the dollar. A foreign policy of militarism and empire building cannot be supported through direct taxation. The American people would never tolerate the taxes required to pay immediately for overseas wars under the discipline of a gold standard. Borrowing and creating new money is much more politically palatable. It hides and delays the real costs of war, and the people are lulled into complacency—especially since the wars we fight are couched in terms of patriotism, spreading the ideas of freedom, and stamping out terrorism. Unnecessary wars and fiat currencies go hand-in-hand, while a gold standard encourages a sensible foreign policy.

The cost of war is enormously detrimental; it significantly contributes to the economic instability of the nation by boosting spending, deficits, and inflation. Funds used for war are funds that could have remained in the productive economy to raise the standard of living of Americans now unemployed, underemployed, or barely living on the margin.

Yet even these costs may be preferable to paying for war with huge tax increases. This is because although fiat dollars are theoretically worthless, value is imbued by the trust placed in them by the world's financial community. Subjective trust in a currency can override objective knowledge about government policies, but only for a limited time.

Economic strength and military power contribute to the trust in a currency; in today's world trust in the U.S. dollar is not earned and therefore fragile. The history of the dollar, being as good as gold up until 1971, is helpful in maintaining an artificially higher value for the dollar than deserved.

Foreign policy contributes to the crisis when the spending to maintain our worldwide military commitments becomes prohibitive, and inflationary pressures accelerate. But the real crisis hits when the world realizes the king has no clothes, in that the dollar has no backing, and we face a military setback even greater than we already are experiencing in Iraq. Our token friends may quickly transform into vocal enemies once the attack on the dollar begins.

False trust placed in the dollar once was helpful to us, but panic and rejection of the dollar will develop into a real financial crisis. Then we will have no other option but to tighten our belts, go back to work, stop borrowing, start saving, and rebuild our industrial base, while adjusting to a lower standard of living for most Americans.

Counterfeiting the nation's money is a serious offense. The founders were especially adamant about avoiding the chaos, inflation, and destruction associated with the Continental dollar. That's why the Constitution is clear that only gold and silver should be legal tender in the United States. In 1792 the Coinage Act authorized the death penalty for any private citizen who counterfeited the currency. Too bad the founders weren't explicit that counterfeiting by government officials is just as detrimental to the economy and the value of the dollar.

In wartime, many nations actually operated counterfeiting programs to undermine our dollar, but never to a disastrous level. The enemy knew how harmful excessive creation of new money could be to the dollar and our economy. But it seems we never learned the dangers of creating new money out of thin air. We don't need an Arab nation or the Chinese to undermine our system with a counterfeiting operation. We do it ourselves, with all the disadvantages that would occur if others did it to us. Today we hear threats from some Arab, Muslim, and Far Eastern countries about undermining the dollar system—not by dishonest counterfeiting, but by initiating an alternative monetary system based on gold. Wouldn't that be ironic? Such an event theoretically could do great harm to us. This day may well come, not so much as a direct political attack on the dollar system but out of necessity to restore confidence in money once again.

Historically, paper money never has lasted for long periods of time, while gold has survived thousands of years of attacks by political interests and big government. In time, the world once again will restore trust in the monetary system by making some currency as good as gold.

Gold, or any acceptable market commodity money, is required to preserve liberty. Monopoly control by government of a system that creates fiat money out of thin air guarantees the loss of liberty. No matter how well-intended our militarism is portrayed, or how happily the promises of wonderful programs for the poor are promoted, inflating the money supply to pay these bills makes government bigger. Empires always fail, and expenses always exceed projections. Harmful unintended consequences are the rule, not the exception. Welfare for the poor is inefficient and wasteful. The beneficiaries are rarely the poor themselves, but instead the politicians, bureaucrats, or the wealthy. The same is true of all foreign aid—it's nothing more than a program that steals from the poor in a rich country and gives to the rich leaders of a poor country. Whether it's war or welfare payments, it always means higher taxes, inflation, and debt. Whether it's the extraction of wealth from the productive economy, the distortion of the market by interest rate manipulation, or spending for war and welfare, it can't happen without infringing upon personal liberty.

At home the war on poverty, terrorism, drugs, or foreign rulers provides an opportunity for authoritarians to rise to power, individuals who think nothing of violating the people's rights to privacy and freedom of speech. They believe their role is to protect the secrecy of government, rather than protect the privacy of citizens. Unfortunately, that is the atmosphere under which we live today, with essentially no respect for the Bill of Rights.

Although great economic harm comes from a government monopoly fiat monetary system, the loss of liberty associated with it is equally troubling. Just as empires are self-limiting in terms of money and manpower, so too is a monetary system based on illusion and fraud. When the end comes, we will be given an opportunity to choose once again between honest money and liberty on one hand; chaos, poverty, and authoritarianism on the other.

The economic harm done by a fiat monetary system is pervasive, dangerous, and unfair. Although runaway inflation is injurious to almost everyone, it is more insidious for certain groups. Once inflation is recognized as a tax, it becomes clear the tax is regressive: penalizing the poor and middle class more than the rich and politically privileged. Price inflation, a consequence of inflating the money supply by the central bank, hits poor and marginal workers first and foremost. It especially penalizes savers, retirees, those on fixed incomes, and anyone who trusts government promises. Small businesses and individual enterprises suffer more than the financial elite, who borrow large sums before the money loses value. Those who are on the receiving end of government contracts—especially in the military industrial complex during wartime—receive undeserved benefits.

It's a mistake to blame high gasoline and oil prices on price gouging. If we impose new taxes or fix prices while ignoring monetary inflation, corporate subsidies, and excessive regulations, shortages will result. The market is the only way to determine the best price for any commodity. The law of supply and demand cannot be repealed. The real problems arise when government planners give subsidies to energy companies and favor one form of energy over another.

Energy prices are rising for many reasons: inflation, increased demand from China and India, decreased supply resulting from our invasion of Iraq, anticipated disruption of supply as we push regime change in Iran, regulatory restrictions on gasoline production, government interference in the free market development of alternative fuels, and subsidies to big oil such as free leases and grants for research and development.

Interestingly, the cost of oil and gas is actually much higher than we pay at the retail level. Much of the DOD budget is spent protecting "our" oil supplies, and if such spending is factored in gasoline probably costs us more than $5 a gallon. The sad irony is that this military effort to secure cheap oil supplies inevitably backfires and actually curtails supplies and boosts prices at the pump. The waste and fraud in issuing contracts to large corporations for work in Iraq only add to price increases.

When problems arise under conditions that exist today, it's a serious error to blame the little bit of the free market that still functions. Last summer the market worked efficiently after Katrina—gas hit $3 a gallon, but soon supplies increased, usage went down, and the price returned to $2. In the 1980s, market forces took oil from $40 per barrel to $10 per barrel, and no one cried for the oil companies that went bankrupt. Today's increases are for the reasons mentioned above. It's natural for labor to seek its highest wage and businesses to strive for the greatest profit. That's the way the market works. When the free market is allowed to work, it's the consumer who ultimately determines price and quality, with labor and business accommodating consumer choices. Once this process is distorted by government, prices rise excessively, labor costs and profits are negatively affected, and problems emerge. Instead of fixing the problem, politicians and demagogues respond by demanding windfall profits taxes and price controls, while never questioning how previous government interference caused the whole mess in the first place. Never let it be said that higher oil prices and profits cause inflation; inflation of the money supply causes higher prices!

Since keeping interest rates below market levels is synonymous with new money creation by the Fed, the resulting business cycle, higher cost of living, and job losses all can be laid at the doorstep of the Fed. This burden hits the poor the most, making Fed taxation by inflation the worst of all regressive taxes. Statistics about revenues generated by the income tax are grossly misleading; in reality much harm is done by our welfare/warfare system supposedly designed to help the poor and tax the rich. Only sound money can rectify the blatant injustice of this destructive system.

The founders understood this great danger and voted overwhelmingly to reject "emitting bills of credit," the term they used for paper or fiat money. It's too bad the knowledge and advice of our founders, and their mandate in the Constitution, are ignored today at our great peril. The current surge in gold prices—which reflects our dollar's devaluation—is warning us to pay closer attention to our fiscal, monetary, entitlement, and foreign policy.

MEANING OF THE GOLD PRICE—SUMMATION

A recent headline in the financial press announced that gold prices surged over concern that confrontation with Iran will further push oil prices higher. This may well reflect the current situation, but higher gold prices mainly reflect monetary expansion by the Federal Reserve. Dwelling on current events and their effect on gold prices reflects concern for symptoms rather than an understanding of the actual cause of these price increases. Without an enormous increase in the money supply over the past 35 years and a worldwide paper monetary system, this increase in the price of gold would not have occurred.

Certainly geopolitical events in the Middle East under a gold standard would not alter its price, although they could affect the supply of oil and cause oil prices to rise. Only under conditions created by excessive paper money would one expect all or most prices to rise. This is a mere reflection of the devaluation of the dollar.

Particular things to remember:

- If one endorses small government and maximum liberty, one must support commodity money.
- One of the strongest restraints against unnecessary war is a gold standard.
- Deficit financing by government is severely restricted by sound money.
- The harmful effects of the business cycle are virtually eliminated with an honest gold standard.

- Saving and thrift are encouraged by a gold standard and discouraged by paper money.
- Price inflation, with generally rising price levels, is characteristic of paper money. Reports that the consumer price index and the producer price index are rising are distractions: The real cause of inflation is the Fed's creation of new money.
- Interest rate manipulation by central bank helps the rich, the banks, the government, and the politicians.
- Paper money permits the regressive inflation tax to be passed off on the poor and the middle class.
- Speculative financial bubbles are characteristic of paper money— not gold.
- Paper money encourages economic and political chaos, which subsequently causes a search for scapegoats rather than blaming the central bank.
- Dangerous protectionist measures frequently are implemented to compensate for the dislocations caused by fiat money.
- Paper money, inflation, and the conditions they create contribute to the problems of illegal immigration.
- The value of gold is remarkably stable.
- The dollar price of gold reflects dollar depreciation.
- Holding gold helps preserve and store wealth, but technically gold is not a true investment.

Since 2001 the dollar has been devalued by 60 percent.

- In 1934 FDR devalued the dollar by 41 percent.
- In 1971 Nixon devalued the dollar by 7.9 percent.
- In 1973 Nixon devalued the dollar by 10 percent.

These were momentous monetary events, and every knowledgeable person worldwide paid close attention. Major changes were endured in 1979 and 1980 to save the dollar from disintegration. This involved a severe recession, interest rates over 21 percent, and general price inflation of 15 percent.

Today we face a 60 percent devaluation and counting, yet no one seems to care. It's of greater significance than the three events mentioned above. And yet the one measurement that best reflects the degree of inflation, the Fed and our government deny us. Since March, M3 reporting has been discontinued. For starters, I'd like to see Congress demand that this report be resumed. I fully believe the American people and Congress are entitled to this information. Will we one day complain about false intelligence, as we have with the Iraq war? Will we complain about not having enough information to address monetary policy after it's too late?

If ever there was a time to get a handle on what sound money is and what it means, that time is today.

Inflation, as exposed by high gold prices, transfers wealth from the middle class to the rich, as real wages decline while the salaries of CEOs, movie stars, and athletes skyrocket—along with the profits of the military industrial complex, the oil industry, and other special interests.

A sharply rising gold price is a vote of "no confidence" in Congress's ability to control the budget, the Fed's ability to control the money supply, and the administration's ability to bring stability to the Middle East.

Ultimately, the gold price is a measurement of trust in the currency and the politicians who run the country. It's been that way for a long time and is not about to change.

If we care about the financial system, the tax system, and the monumental debt we're accumulating, we must start talking about the benefits and discipline that come only with a commodity standard of money—money the government and central banks absolutely cannot create out of thin air.

Economic law dictates reform at some point. But should we wait until the dollar is 1/1,000 of an ounce of gold or 1/2,000 of an ounce of gold? The longer we wait, the more people suffer and the more difficult reforms become. Runaway inflation inevitably leads to political chaos, something numerous countries have suffered throughout the twentieth century. The worst example, of course, was the German inflation of the 1920s that led to the rise of Hitler. Even the communist takeover of China was associated with runaway inflation brought on by Chinese Nationalists. The time for action is now, and it is up to the American people and the U.S. Congress to demand it.

CHAPTER 22

THE GOLD PRICE

Paul van Eeden
Cranberry Capital

"It is well that the people of the nation do not understand our banking and monetary system, for if they did, I believe there would be a revolution before tomorrow morning."

—Henry Ford, industrialist and inventor (1863–1947)

Paul is the president of Cranberry Capital Inc., a private holding and investment company based in Toronto. Originally from South Africa, he has an international perspective on markets, gold in particular. In addition to his expertise in gold, Paul has an insider's understanding of mineral exploration, having been intimately involved in the financing and evaluation of resource companies since 1995.

Although the article below was written and published in International Speculator *in early 2003, it is timeless in scope because of the historical and economic analysis that van Eeden covers. In it, he not only predicted the magnitude of the rise in the gold price but also gave the reasons why it would rise. He also provides readers with enough research and a model such that they can easily decipher whether gold is overvalued or undervalued today. His sobering conclusion regarding fiat*

Originally published in *International Speculator*, Volume XXIV, No. 4, on April 1, 2003, as "The Gold Price."

currencies having all "ended in disaster" and that "our current experiment with a monetary system based entirely on fiat currencies is unlikely to end any different" needs to be understood by every investor. (Since the article was written, Paul has substantially refined his model and ideas regarding gold and such updates can now be found on his website, www .Paulvaneeden.com.)

Attempts at predicting the future invariably lead to embarrassment; so why would I even bother trying to figure out what the gold price is likely to do?

Because, contrary to popular belief, the market is not efficient. What's more, the market acts like a manic-depressive, and the greatest opportunities occur when the market is either manic, as with Internet stocks a few years back when Doug Casey was shorting them, or depressive, as the gold market is right now.

I believe a historic rise in the gold price has already commenced, but it's not too late to get positioned, as the best is yet to come. Here's why.

Using only first principles (as opposed to witchcraft, conspiracy theories, and evil cartels), it is possible to explain why the gold price averaged $378.04 an ounce for 13 years from 1984 to 1996; why the gold price declined from 1996 to 2001; and why the gold price spiked from 1979 to 1980, but crashed again from 1980 to 1982.

Based on the same principles, you will see why the gold price is going to at least double in the next few years, and possibly triple within five.

It might surprise you to see how simple the methodology really is. But then, most complex problems can be broken up into simple, easy-to-understand components. It is most often those who don't understand what they are talking about that resort to complex theories that don't make sense or unquantifiable forces such as conspiracies.

My intention is not to bore you into a comatose state with mundane history, but it is really important that we synchronize our thoughts. Let's start at the Gold Standard, since we know what an ounce of gold was worth then, and continue to why it is trading for $325 an ounce today, and why I think it will be over $700 an ounce in the near future.

FLOATING CURRENCIES

During the Gold Standard, gold's value was determined by its purchasing power; the value of paper currencies, when they existed, was measured against gold. As a result of paper currency inflation to finance both World Wars, all countries abandoned the Gold Standard and gold lost its role as currency.

The Bretton Woods Accord of 1944 briefly assured stability for a world without hard money by making the U.S. dollar convertible into gold at a fixed rate, and then using the dollar as the world's reserve currency, against which all other currencies were measured. The deficiency embedded in the Bretton Woods Accord was that it allowed the United States to inflate the dollar without recourse, since the ratio between it and gold was fixed, and set by decree. Therefore, from 1934 to 1971 gold was "worth" $35 an ounce only because Franklin Roosevelt decreed that it be so, in 1934.

The fallacy that the United States could create reserve currency (dollars) at will, without impacting the dollar's value, while the rest of the world had to produce goods and services to earn dollars, came to an end in 1971 when Richard Nixon was forced to abandon the fixed exchange rate between the dollar and gold.

So what is an ounce of gold "worth" today? Because most currencies in the world are floating, meaning their exchange rates relative to each other are determined by market forces, as opposed to declared by governments, you have to specify in which currency you want to measure the gold price. For our purposes we will restrict ourselves to the U.S. dollar. The question therefore becomes, what is an ounce of gold worth in dollars today?

Two factors always influence the relative value of gold in any currency. The first is the increase in the amount of currency (inflation of dollars) and the second is the increase in the amount of gold (inflation of gold).

When the amount of dollars increases (inflation), the dollar loses buying power and that typically shows up as an increase in the prices of goods and services. It stands to reason that as the dollar is inflated, it also increases the price of gold, in dollars, even though gold's inherent worth (buying power) is not affected.

Similarly, if the amount of gold increases, the value of gold will decrease. Due to its physical properties, almost all of the gold ever mined is still around in one form or another, which is one of the reasons why gold is so suitable to be money in the first place. The amount of gold mined on an annual basis is nothing other than inflation of the total amount of gold ever mined. The inflation rate of gold is thus new mine production as a percentage of above ground gold stock, which in turn is equal to the total amount of gold mined since the beginning of time.

Consequently, the change in the gold price, in dollars, over time will be in proportion to the inflation of the dollar and inversely proportional to the inflation of gold. We can calculate the theoretical gold price (Au[n]) as follows:

$$Au[n] = Au[n-1](M3[n]/M3[n-1])(GP[n-1]/GP[n]) \quad \{Au = \text{gold price;} \\ M3 = \text{money supply; } GP = \text{gold production}\}$$

But for this to work we need to establish a time at which gold was priced correctly. This means we have to go back to the Gold Standard and work forward from there.

RESERVE CURRENCIES

World War I destroyed both physical property and, through inflation, the European currencies as well. After the war most countries were up to their eyeballs in debt with little or no hope of ever repaying it.

Prior to World War I the gold-backed British pound was the world's primary reserve currency because London was the largest financial center and Britain the largest trading nation in the world. But monetary expansion to finance World War I forced most countries, including Britain, to abandon the Gold Standard temporarily.

In 1923 Britain announced that it would honor all war debts in an attempt to restore confidence in the British economy and the pound. To accomplish this Britain had to raise taxes and that only hurt its already crippled economy.

In a second attempt at trying to boost confidence, Britain reinstated the Gold Standard in 1925, at prewar parity. At the same time many other nations devalued their currencies in an effort to reduce the burden of war debts and to stimulate their economies. Britain's return to the Gold Standard therefore pushed up the relative value of the pound, diminishing British exports while promoting imports, and led to further erosion of its economy. By 1931 Britain was forced to abandon the Gold Standard again.

As opposed to Britain, the United States returned to the Gold Standard in 1919. That, and its increasing importance in global trade, put the dollar in a position to replace the British pound as the world's reserve currency.

THE END OF THE GOLD STANDARD

The crash of 1929 precipitated a deflationary economic contraction. The combination of a series of bank and brokerage failures, losses on Wall Street, increased unemployment, and decreased confidence in the economy led to an increase in the savings rate as people attempted to preserve their capital. Because they were saving, they were not spending, resulting in a reduction in demand for goods and services and leading to reduced economic activity: the Great Depression.

The government needed increased spending to stimulate the economy, but how do you get people to spend if they are saving? People tend to spend more during inflationary times because their paper money is losing value relative to goods. So they are better off spending it as soon as possible, before it devalues any further. Hence, the government wanted to create inflation.

To create inflation and stimulate spending, the government needed to devalue the dollar. But it couldn't just print more paper dollars because gold was also a component of the monetary system. If the government devalued paper dollars by printing more of them, people would switch their savings to gold without a net increase in spending. Individuals were already hoarding gold and savings in the banking system tied up gold too, since banks had to maintain reserves, which were mostly in the form of gold.

As long as gold was money, devaluation of the dollar would not necessarily lead to an increase in spending. To resolve this dilemma, Roosevelt declared private gold ownership illegal in 1933, freeing him to print as many paper dollars as he saw fit.

> By virtue of the authority vested in me by Section 5 (b) of the Act of October 6, 1917, as amended by Section 2 of the Act of March 9,

1933 . . . in which Congress declared that a serious emergency exists, I as President, do declare that the national emergency still exists; that the continued private hoarding of gold and silver by subjects of the United States poses a grave threat to the peace, equal justice, and well-being of the United States; and that appropriate measures must be taken immediately to protect the interests of our people.

Franklin Roosevelt, March 9, 1933

This did not affect the dollar's status as an international reserve currency, as foreigners could still convert their dollars into gold at a fixed rate.

In 1933 a $20 gold coin contained 0.9675 ounces of gold. So the gold price was $20.67 ($20/0.9675) an ounce by definition, as it had been since 1879 when the United States joined the Gold Standard. The Executive Order of March 9, 1933, forced citizens (in their own best interest, of course) to exchange their gold for paper dollars at the rate of $20.67 per ounce.

The very next year Roosevelt increased the gold price by 69 percent to $35 an ounce, thereby instantaneously devaluing these same paper dollars by 41 percent—in the best interest of the people, of course.

DOLLARS FOR GOLD

Back in 1933, when gold was money, an ounce of it was worth $20.67. Therefore, we can safely say that gold was overpriced the following year when Roosevelt arbitrarily set it at $35 an ounce. But if gold was overpriced at $35 an ounce in 1934, at what time was it actually worth $35 an ounce? We can get an answer by looking at the movement of physical gold into, and out of, the United States Treasury, and the purchasing power of the dollar.

Because the gold price was arbitrarily raised to $35 an ounce in 1934, which meant it was significantly overpriced at the time, and due to the demand for dollars as reserve currency, the Unites States' gold reserves expanded from 8,998 tonnes in 1935 to 19,543 tonnes in 1940, as many foreigners cashed in on the overnight gain that the U.S. government handed them. Gold was happily sold to the Treasury in exchange for dollars, which could then be converted into local currency abroad for a 69 percent windfall, less transaction costs of course.

By 1952 gold reserves had reached 20,663 tonnes and the United States owned approximately 33 percent of all the gold in the world and more than 65 percent of the Official Gold Reserves, i.e., gold owned by governments.

But after 1952 the incessant inflation of U.S. dollars made the rest of the world realize that 35 of them just weren't worth an ounce of gold any more. Massive redemptions of dollars, in exchange for gold, depleted the Treasury's gold reserves by 58 percent, to 8,584 tonnes by 1972. In 1972 the United States had less gold than in 1935, but it had approximately ten times more dollars outstanding as measured by the change in M1 (currency held by the public plus demand deposits, checkable deposits, and travelers' checks).

We know that gold was overvalued at least up to 1940 because the world was converting gold into dollars as fast as it could. We also know that gold was undervalued after 1952 because dollars were now being redeemed for gold at a rapid pace. U.S. gold reserves stayed roughly at 20,000 tonnes from 1940, when gold was overvalued, to 1952, when it was undervalued. So somewhere between 1940 and 1952 one would expect gold to have been "worth" $35 an ounce.

Changes in the Consumer Price Index (CPI) give us a measure of how the dollar's inflation impacts its purchasing power. That means we can determine when gold was really worth $35 an ounce by looking at how the CPI (Reserve Bank of Minneapolis) changed since 1933, when we know gold was correctly priced at $20.67. From 1933 to 1947 there was a 69 percent increase in the CPI, so $20.67 in 1933 would have been worth $35 in 1947.

This coincides with the flow of gold into the Treasury up to 1950 (20,279 tonnes), peaking in 1952 (20,663 tonnes), then declining rapidly as the realization that inflation had caught up with the gold price led to the redemption of dollars. That gold was worth $35 an ounce in 1947 is thus plausible, as judged by the flow of gold, and validated by the change in the dollar's purchasing power, as measured by the CPI. We can therefore conclude that gold was actually worth $35 an ounce in 1947.

We did not consider gold inflation between 1933 and 1947, as the implied assumption is that gold production was in line with general economic growth in the United States, and thus the increase of goods

Figure 22.1   Theoretical versus Actual Gold Price

and services implicitly accounted for by the CPI also accommodated the increase in gold. This is obviously not ideal. Unfortunately, M3 data only goes back to 1959, although we did find a study that extrapolated M3 to 1948. The CPI we used goes back to 1913.

From 1947 onwards, however, M3 (dollar inflation) and mine production (gold inflation) were used to calculate what the gold price should have been (theoretical gold price), according to the preceding formula. The results from 1971 onwards are shown in Figure 22.1.

Following is a comparison between the theoretical gold price and the actual gold price to see how well the model stands up to reality.

CLOSING THE GOLD WINDOW

The massive redemption of dollars forced Nixon to close the gold window in 1971, in a desperate attempt to retain some gold in the Treasury. When forced to choose between holding gold or his own dollars, Nixon chose gold. That, in and of itself, should tell us something about the value of gold.

Gold was now officially demonetized, and since it could no longer be acquired at a price of $35 an ounce, the market was left to determine what the actual price should be. Since we know that gold was worth $35 an ounce in 1947, we can calculate what the price of gold should have been in 1971 and compare it to what actually happened in the market.

Dollar inflation from 1947 to 1971, offset by gold inflation, meant that the gold price should have been $103 an ounce when the gold window was closed, almost three times its official price of $35 an ounce. With the gold price at only a third of its value, it just had to go up.

Not only was this upward force at work, but inflation during the 1970s also lit a fire under the gold price. M3 more than doubled from 1971 to 1978. By 1978 the gold price should have been $199 an ounce and, in fact, its average price for that year was $193 an ounce.

It's very reassuring that the theoretical gold price coincides this well with the actual price for 1978: It confirms that the establishment of 1947 as the year during which gold was actually worth $35 an ounce is most probably right on the mark and that the model is working.

But if you look at Figure 22.1, you will notice that the gold price continued to rise far beyond what the model predicts and remained above the theoretical price until 1984. Why?

1978–1984

The gold price's deviation from its fair value between 1978 and 1984 can be explained by looking at what else went on during that time.

In retaliation for the Western world's support of Israel, during the Arab-Israeli War of 1973, Arab members of OPEC took control of the organization, cut oil production, and increased the oil price from $3.00 a barrel in October 1973 to $11.65 in January 1974, a 288 percent increase in just four months. In addition, the United States and the Netherlands were cut off from OPEC oil supply due to their close relationships with Israel.

This did not, however, push the price of gold up. In fact, the gold price had reached fair value in 1974, remained essentially flat during 1975, and fell 22 percent in 1976. By 1978 the gold price had reached fair value again. This market action seems normal and does not indicate any gold price premium as a result of the oil embargo or the increase in the oil price.

But on the backdrop of this tension between the United States and the Arab World, the Iranian Hostage Crisis in 1979 did cause a dramatic rise in the gold price. When 52 Americans were taken hostage by Iranian students in November 1979 at the American Embassy in Tehran, the gold price shot up from an average price of $305 to $615 in 1980, briefly trading over $800 an ounce in January of that year. The hostages were finally released on January 20, 1981, 444 days after their capture, and the gold price was on its way down again, to find its theoretical level of $236 an ounce.

From 1980 to 1984 the gold price declined by 41 percent to $361 an ounce, which differs by only $25, or 7 percent, from its theoretical price of $336 an ounce.

1984–1988

With the oil crisis over, the hostages released, and the status quo of the Cold War casting an eerie calm over the world, not much happened between 1984 and 1988 to upset the gold price. The actual gold price differed, on average, by only 7 percent from its theoretical price during those four years. This is a remarkable correlation, especially considering that we started with gold at $20.67 in 1933 and relied only on a logical adaptation of the gold price based on sound economic reasoning, without in any way modifying the results to better "fit" reality.

1988–1996

On the surface, the gold market between 1990 and 1996 was about as exciting as watching paint dry, but a lot was happening in the undercurrent.

Notice that the actual gold price started to deviate from its theoretical price in 1998. The reason, this time, may not be so obvious to those not intimately familiar with the gold market.

In 1983 a new financial risk management tool was developed to mitigate the impact of gold price volatility on mining companies: hedging. Total gold hedging increased from four tonnes in 1983 to 45 tonnes in 1986. But from 1987 to 1990 a total of 876 tonnes were hedged.

Whether it had anything to do with George Bush Senior's term as president or not, M3 growth increased only 6 percent between 1989 and 1993. Gold inflation on the other hand was 8 percent during that period, and so the gold price should have declined by 2 percent over those four years.

This downward pressure on the gold price, coupled to the expansion of hedging, decreased the actual gold price by 19 percent between 1987 and 1993. The gold price was now more than 15 percent below its theoretical value and the upward pressure again began to show.

The vigorous resumption of dollar inflation in 1994, and the already undervalued gold price, exerted strong upward pressure on the Midas metal. Yet in 1996 the gold price began a 30 percent decline, to $273 an ounce, which it reached in 2001. This occurred despite the increase in M3, which drove up the theoretical gold price to $659 an ounce over the same period.

Before we examine what happened since 1996, it is important to note that even with the advent of hedging between 1984 and 1996, the actual gold price differed, on average, by only 12 percent from its theoretical price during those years. This is five decades after we began our theoretical calculations and once again validates the concepts on which the theoretical price is based.

THE DOLLAR EXCHANGE RATE

Gold is quoted in U.S. dollars as a remnant of the period between 1944 and 1971, when the U.S. Treasury owned most of the official gold reserves, and an ounce of gold was convertible into $35.

Prior to 1971 most currencies were pegged against the dollar at fixed exchange rates, so the price of gold in other currencies did not change much between 1944 and 1971 either. After 1971 the exchange rates between most currencies started to fluctuate. Nothing was convertible into gold anymore, so there really wasn't any standard to measure a currency's "value" against.

The dollar was still regarded as one of the most stable currencies in the world as the United States had both the largest economy and the most foreign trade. It was therefore natural to continue to use the dollar as the de facto reserve currency. But as the dollar was now also floating against most other currencies, it was possible for the dollar's exchange rate to increase in response to the demand for dollars and decrease in response to supply.

To determine the price of gold in any other currency one would still just multiply the dollar denominated gold price by the relevant exchange rate. The difference is that the gold price now fluctuates in dollar terms (due to dollar inflation and gold inflation), and the dollar itself fluctuates against other currencies. So the gold price in Japanese yen, for example, would behave quite differently than the gold price in dollars—as we will see later.

From 1988 to 1992 the dollar exchange rate was relatively stable. But it has not been so since 1992.

CURRENCY CRISES

Recall that the upward pressure on the gold price predicted by the model since 1994, due to increased M3, was not reflected in the actual gold price, and that from 1996 to 2001 the gold price actually declined. The reason lies in the phenomenal increase in the demand for dollars following a series of currency crises, each one compounding the demand further, tightening the supply, and strengthening the dollar against almost all other currencies.

During a currency crisis, capital, seeking a safe haven, typically flows out of the troubled country. Between 1992 and 1994 the Brazilian real lost essentially all its value. The capital flight from Brazil created demand for dollars and some of it found a home in the United States. In response, the dollar increased by about 10 percent against a Gross Domestic Product (GDP)–weighted index of 35 currencies we monitor.

From 1994 to 1995 the Mexican peso declined by over 50 percent against the dollar, the worst financial crisis in Mexico since the Revolution. More capital moved into the United States and this further increased demand for dollars.

The Japanese yen lost 24 percent against the dollar from 1995 to 1996, and still more capital fled to the United States, but the "Big One"—the South East Asian Crisis—didn't hit until 1996.

From 1996 to 1998 the Indonesian rupiah lost 76 percent of its value against the dollar, setting off a domino effect that dragged the South

Korean won down 56 percent, the Malaysian ringgit down 40 percent, and the Philippine peso down by 40 percent. A truly massive flight of capital ensued, most of it destined for the United States, and increased the dollar by almost 30 percent against our GDP-weighted index.

In 1998 Russia defaulted on its foreign debt, sending the ruble down over 70 percent in 1998 alone. The euro's launch in 1999 was also the beginning of its 28 percent decline against the dollar. Back in 1998 the "new" Brazilian real collapsed again, the Turkish lira fell in 2000 and the Argentine peso followed in 2002 . . . you get the picture.

In all these cases capital fled to the United States. As a result, the dollar increased by more than 120 percent from 1990 to 2002 against our GDP-weighted index currencies.

Regardless of what the gold price is doing in other currencies, the gold price in dollars is inversely related to the dollar exchange rate. Just like any other import, if the dollar gets stronger, the price goes lower. There is an almost perfect correlation between the decline in the gold price, between 1996 and 1998, and the increase in the dollar exchange rate as a result of capital influx from abroad.

This explains the deviation from gold's theoretical price up to 1998, but it does not explain why the actual gold price stabilized between 1998 and 2001, and then commenced a 30 percent increase in 2002, while the dollar exchange rate did not decline.

The consolidation in the actual gold price from 1998 to 2001, and the ensuing increase in 2002, is a result of the raging, worldwide, bull market in gold that is finally affecting its price in dollars.

GOLD IN OTHER CURRENCIES

We can calculate the gold price in any currency by multiplying the dollar gold price by the currency's exchange rate. If we do this for all 35 currencies in our GDP-weighted index, we can actually calculate the weighted average gold price in the world, excluding the U.S. dollar. The currencies are weighted by GDP so as not to give too much influence to small, volatile currencies.

Doing exactly that, the astonishing fact that gold has been in a bull market for more than five years is blatantly apparent. On average the gold price worldwide has increased by more than 70 percent, and no one knows it, because most people are too fixated by the U.S. dollar–denominated gold price.

THE THEORETICAL GOLD PRICE

Our model shows that, given the increase in M3 and gold inflation since 1947, gold is worth $700 an ounce as of 2002. The gold price is currently $325 an ounce. What is this telling us?

Just as the actual gold price did not deviate from its theoretical price for very long after the Iranian Hostage Crisis, the current gold price cannot remain below its theoretical price for much longer.

In fact, were it not for the dollar exchange rate's tremendous increase over the past decade, the actual gold price would differ by less than 10 percent from its theoretical price. This can be shown by going back to 1990 and backing out the dollar exchange rate from the actual gold price; in other words, essentially keeping the dollar constant.

You can see the result of this exercise represented in Figure 22.1 by the modified gold price line. Notice how well it tracks the theoretical gold price, and keep in mind that these two lines were derived independently of each other. The theoretical price is based on gold being $20.67 in 1933 and adjusting for inflation. The adjusted gold price is merely backing out the exchange rate from the actual gold price since 1990.

The undeniable correlation is no coincidence and begs the question whether the dollar can sustain its current exchange rate.

TRADE DEFICITS

The influx of capital into the United States had a broader impact on America's economy than just increasing the dollar's exchange rate. This was discussed in the February 2003 issue, so suffice it to say here that the trade deficit is directly related to the strengthening of the dollar because it made imports cheaper and exports more expensive during an economic boom that was itself propagated by the influx of capital from abroad.

Barry Eichengreen, from the University of California at Berkeley, has shown using historical data that First World countries can in fact eliminate large trade deficits. The good news is that the trade deficit can be eliminated quite rapidly. The bad news is that it almost always requires a major, and prolonged, recession. Given the size of the U.S. trade deficit, it is unlikely that we will have a mere recession—a depression is more likely.

However deep, or prolonged, the economic downturn is going to be, it is impossible to imagine that the United States will continue to attract in excess of $400 billion worth of foreign capital every year. And when the foreigners stop sending their saving to America so that we can finance our consumption habits, the dollar will decline.

THE EURO

I do not particularly like the euro, as it is the ultimate fiat currency, but it does offer the world an alternative reserve currency to the dollar. If it weren't for the fact that dollars are being created at the rate of about 600 billion a year, I probably wouldn't have given the euro a second thought.

But the inflation of the dollar, the debunking of the U.S. economic miracle, the arrogance of U.S. foreign policy and, perhaps most important, the detrimental impact that the War on Terrorism is bound to have on U.S. liberty—not to mention the misallocation of capital and increase in debt that go hand-in-hand with war—are all virtual guarantees that the dollar is going to lose some of its superhero status.

There were two reasons why the dollar became the reserve currency of the world. One, it was convertible into gold—which is no longer true. Two, the dollar was in demand to settle international transactions as the United States became the world's largest economy and trading nation.

The introduction of the euro has created a viable alternative to the dollar. Neither currency is backed by gold, so the one is just as bad as the other, and the aggregate economy of the European Union is similar in size to the United States'. But Europe has one big advantage over the United States: It has a trade surplus. We still have to work off our trade deficit, and we know that is going to hurt.

The euro is also likely to get a booster shot from U.S. foreign policy. Backlash at American imperialism has already caused several countries to convert massive amounts of dollar reserves to euro reserves.

The real clincher will be the expansion of the European Union, though. As more and more countries join the Union, the demand for euros will increase, and the need for dollars will decrease.

GOLD, THE SAVIOR OF CAPITAL

Most people would expect a monetary crisis to cause the gold price to increase, especially one that rocks the globe like the South East Asian Crisis. Some believe that gold failed to protect capital during that crisis, but here are the facts.

The gold price did not increase in U.S. dollars—but the United States was not in crisis. The gold price in Japanese yen, however, increased by 34 percent between 1995 and 1996. The next year the gold price jumped more than 40 percent in both Philippine pesos and Malaysian ringgit, and 67 percent in Korean won. Indonesia suffered the most during the South East Asian Crisis and the gold price, accordingly, increased more than 400 percent in rupiah.

The next currency crisis may well be the almighty dollar. Gold will once again fulfill its role as a store of wealth and protector of capital. The question is just whether you own any.

The dollar is likely to fall approximately 50 percent from its current level. That would free the dollar-denominated gold price to find its way back toward its true value of $699 an ounce (as of 2002). Given the mounting pressure on the dollar, there is virtually no chance that it will not collapse.

CONCLUSION

Our model demonstrates beyond any doubt that the gold price is ultimately defined by the inflation of the dollar relative to the inflation of gold. Any deviation from this theoretical gold price can be adequately explained and is temporary.

What is important for us in 2003 is that the gold price is either going to increase to $700 an ounce or more, or the U.S. money supply has to decrease by 50 percent. This is not the same as saying that the inflation rate has to decline by 50 percent—this is saying that we need a 50 percent decrease in the amount of dollars outstanding, which is a practical impossibility. Therefore, the only conclusion is that the gold price is going up.

Buying gold now is the lowest risk investment you can make. And the upside is a once-in-a-lifetime opportunity. If you do not already have gold or gold-related investments in your portfolio, I suggest you call one of the following people and rectify the situation immediately.

Gold and War

War is unpredictable and destructive. It has the effect of unnerving financial markets, increasing volatility, and strangling the economy by misallocating capital.

Whether the gold price increases or decreases as the war progresses, it should not deter you from owning gold. The weak U.S. economy, exacerbated by new misallocations of capital, will weigh heavily on the U.S. dollar. Volatility introduced by war can be endured if you have both patience and fortitude.

The increase in the gold price earlier this year was due to uncertainty surrounding the Middle East. The subsequent decrease in the gold price was neither unexpected nor unwelcome. This is a very, very good time to increase your ownership in gold and related investments.

A FEW LAST THOUGHTS

You may have noticed that we modified the gold price between 1979 and 1982 to ignore the effect of the Iranian Hostage Crisis. If we compare the modified gold price, as shown in Figure 22.1, to the theoretical gold price, the two differ by only 17.5 percent, on average, from 1971 to 2002. That means our model predicted the actual (modified) gold price with 82 percent accuracy, on average, from 1971 to the present. Given the simplicity of the model and the accuracy of the results, I have no doubt that we will see $700 an ounce before long.

Nixon decided to keep the Treasury's gold and decline the revered dollar in 1971. Similarly, Thailand asked its citizenry for physical gold to save the baht during the South East Asian Crisis. In the final analysis, the world seems to always turn to gold.

Alan Greenspan said the following on May 20, 1999: "Gold still represents the ultimate form of payment in the world . . . Gold is always accepted." The Federal Reserve Chairman offered this remark as one of the reasons why the United States should not sell its gold reserves. So has gold lost its value as monetary asset?

During a "true" Gold Standard, gold is money, and as such most of the gold is in the hands of the public, not held by governments. We would again be in a situation where the public owns most of the gold in the word.

Gold is money by evolution of choice, not decree. In this regard governments have always been forced, ultimately, to follow the will of the people, not the other way around.

This is not the first time that governments have experimented with fiat currencies. All previous experiments, bar none, ended in disaster. Our current experiment with a monetary system based entirely on fiat currencies is unlikely to end any differently.

CHAPTER 23

BECOMING A TWENTY-FIRST-CENTURY GOLD GUERRILLA

Kenneth W. Royce
Aka Boston T. Party

"The budget should be balanced, the Treasury should be refilled, public debt should be reduced, the arrogance of officialdom should be tempered and controlled, and the assistance to foreign lands should be curtailed lest Rome become bankrupt. People must again learn to work . . . "

—Marcus Cicero, Roman statesman (106–43 BCE)

Kenneth W. Royce—aka Boston T. Party, and founder of www .freestatewyoming.org—is a shooting instructor, speaker, and the author of 12 books on guns, history, law, politics, privacy, and government, selling well over 100,000 copies.

Ken's contribution below contains a tremendous amount of practical information into why and how someone should hold physical gold, especially gold coins. His preferred gold coins to own are U.S. Eagles or Krugerrands, one good reason being because "you need a copy of

World Coins *to identify many of the funky foreign (gold bullion) coins." But the contribution addresses many issues of gold ownership including: "Gold versus Silver Coins," "Bullion versus Numismatic Coins," "Where and How to Buy," "How to Transport," and many more topics I'd only occasionally thought about.*

By my reckoning, his piece is the perfect bookend to Jon Nadler's opening piece, which gave a very personal history of why and how someone should own gold. Ken not only tells you how to own it, he tells you how to keep it.

Folks, gold has finally closed over $1,000/oz. for the first time, and for many successive days. This likely indicates the formation of a long-expected >$1,000 floor. That established, the unsuppressed "buoyancy" of spot price will shoot gold up very quickly. I don't expect any lengthy return to <$1,000 price. If you haven't any gold, start buying NOW. Forget all about how you could have bought earlier/cheaper. Gold is cheap at any price.

Precious metals are a rare example of investment assets that aren't concurrently a creditor's claim. To be clear, I'm not describing gold stocks, or even numismatics kept in trust for your IRA. These have been very capably covered by other authors herein. What I mean, however, is this: gold coins held . . . in . . . your . . . own . . . hand. Totally private and portable wealth. No reporting. No tracking. Not all of your gold and silver should (or even could) be stored in such a fashion—but *some* of it *must* be. I'm speaking of crisis wealth that you can quickly, universally, and discreetly convert to other assets or cash within an unsophisticated market.

PLATINUM VERSUS GOLD

The platinum bullion market is a much more specialized one than gold, and selling platinum (especially to unsophisticated buyers who never see the stuff) is assuredly more difficult. (Most of them will mistakenly believe platinum to be some kind of silver trick!)

GOLD VERSUS SILVER COINS

Since most of the idea here is *portable* wealth, gold is the natural choice being (depending on the respective markets) 20 to 100 times more valuable by weight. Currently, the gold:silver spot price ratio is about 60:1. (For today's spot prices, go to: www.kitconet.com/images/ sp_en_6.gif) It makes rather more sense to have a handful of gold versus 100 lbs of silver.

While you should have some silver in your bullion portfolio (mainly for its fantastic relative upside *vis-a-vis* gold), I would place that silver (except for a bag of 90 percent junk dimes, for trading) in secure long-term storage.

1,000-ounce silver bars: There's a reason for their adequate supply and low premium. Silver buyers do not want them! Eight pounds of bulk, expensive, and hard to trade. I'd rather have 16 ounce gold coins for the same cost.

BULLION VERSUS NUMISMATIC COINS

The higher a coin's premium, the more difficult it is to unload at top dollar. The buy/sell spread is too wide, and professional coin brokers are usually required. While very rare and pricy numismatics have their place in some portfolios (or in discreet international wealth transfers), they are not the kind of easily liquidated gold discussed here. Your $8,500 MS65 St. Gaudens has a market only with coin collectors and dealers. To the uninitiated and pedestrian buyer on the street (where you may be forced to sell some day) it's just a "really purty" coin with 0.9675 ounces of gold.

A bullion/numi "hybrid" is the so-called "semi-numismatic" that sells for a premium less than 15 percent (thus, according to some coin brokers, legally avoiding certain arcane/rarely enforced reporting requirements). If you could just as easily *recoup* semi-numi premiums when you sell, great—but you can't. You'll get close to spot, instead. So, again, stick with bullion for your portable gold.

U.S. EAGLES VERSUS FOREIGN GOLD BULLION

A prime advantage of the U.S. Eagle is its dollar face value. An ounce coin has a face value of $50. A tenth-ounce coin shows $5 on its little face. This can be used to your advantage in two obvious ways: in payment to reduce the titular dollar amount of the transaction, and in leaving the U.S. border regarding its mandatory reporting requirement of all cash (and cash-like) amounts in excess of $10,000.

The reverse edge of this double-edged sword is that the U.S. government could confiscate (i.e., steal) your Eagle coins and "reimburse" you for merely their face value. Exactly this occurred in 1933 with FDR's "anti-hoarding" Executive Order 6102:

> Section 2. All persons are hereby required to deliver on or before May 1, 1933, to a Federal Reserve bank or a branch or agency thereof or to any member bank of the Federal Reserve System **all gold coin, gold bullion, and gold certificates** now owned by them or coming into their ownership on or before April 28, 1933 . . . Section 4. Upon receipt of gold coin, gold bullion, or gold certificates delivered to it in accordance with Section 2 or 3, the Federal reserve bank or member bank **will pay thereof an equivalent amount of any other form of coin or currency coined or issued under the laws of the Unites States**.

Immediately thereafter, the dollar was devalued in terms of gold from $20 to $35/oz. The reason why there are still pre-1933 gold coins at all today is that many people were wise enough not to fall for the trap.

So, if the spot price: face value disparity of Eagles is of no advantage to you—or you fear "compensatory confiscation" at a thieverous 1:1 ratio—then own other gold bullion instead. I prefer coins of 22k (.917) fineness, such as the Krugerrand. (The Britannia is also .917, but uncommon.) The Canadian Maple Leaf and Australian Kangaroo are beautiful coins, but without any copper alloy, resulting in a very soft and easily damaged coin. They bend at a harsh word, and that compromises marketability. Many coin dealers don't want them, because their customers don't want them. I had a dinged Maple, and all I was offered was 95 percent of spot—a $50 loss had I accepted it

The bastard weight (i.e., other than troy ounce-based) coins of Europe are .900 fine (many of them modern Official Government

Restrikes), and thus durable, but less attractive to the general gold public. (You need a copy of *World Coins* to identify many of these funky coins—carrying this dictionary-sized reference work about is quite the hassle.) Keep it simple and easy with Krugerrands and Eagles, because that's what the market prefers, especially during a period of having to educate buyers.

OUNCE OF FRACTIONAL WEIGHT?

The smaller the coin, the more divisible your gold wealth, and thus the higher the premium. Krugerrands and Eagles are minted in ounce, half-ounce, quarter-ounce, and tenth-ounce. I would skip the half- and quarter-ounce coins altogether. If you want divisibility, go all the way with tenths. The ratio between ounce and tenth-ounce coins is your preference, but I would recommend 10 to 20 percent of your gold bullion be in tenths, and the remaining 80 to 90 percent in ounce coins.

Granted, a tenth-ounce gold coin today (October 2009) buys about $120 Federal Reserve Notes, which is not small enough for daily commerce. For that, use silver bullion or local cash. Where a tenth-ounce coin really has its place is in facilitating international travel. Gold is gold—worldwide—and every venal border guard requiring a bribe for passage will instantly know the value of such a coin.

There are even smaller gold coins that may work just as well at borders, such as the bargain souvenir Maxmillian:

> All Maximillian's coins show a denomination. The tiny "Maximillians" don't. They are essentially "jetons," that is non-monetary tokens, essentially souvenirs. Modern souvenir Maximillian gold tokens, as usually seen, are about half the size of a U.S. dime and dated between 1864–1867 though they were really made in the 20th century. Most of the ones that I've seen are 10K gold.
>
> —www.coinsite.com/content/cdanswers/cdarchive59.asp

WHERE AND HOW TO BUY

Buy with cash. Not check; not credit card—*cash*. Buy anonymously and securely, meaning in person and not by mail. Buy in a state that does not charge sales tax on bullion (or at least not on the amount you plan to spend). Coin shops, coin shows, antique stores, and gun shows are the best sources. No ID is generally required (but this could change overnight by decree).

Know in advance exactly what you are doing. Before you walk in the door, you should have priced your desired bullion coins on the Internet and be very familiar with current buy/sell spreads. Know how much you wish to spend, and if that amount triggers any Cash Transaction Report. Beware the *malum prohibitum* crime of "structuring." Whether you ask for a receipt is your call, as there are pros and cons to that. (You might scan/encrypt your receipts, then burn them.)

Using some simple privacy tactics is recommended, such as not parking at the coin shop, but a few blocks away. Why have your license plate on the store's cameras? I describe such at length in my 2009 book *One Nation, Under Surveillance—Privacy from the Watchful Eye* available through www.javelinpress.com.

WHERE AND HOW TO STORE OR CACHE YOUR COINS

Before you simply hide your coins among your socks, think through who you're hiding your coins *from*:

- Family/friends with routine household access
- A burglar with lots of time on his hands
- Some government agency with unlimited time and access

Also ask yourself how *quickly* you envision needing to retrieve your coins. Less than a minute? A half-hour? Much of the afternoon? Can such be done without drawing attention from others in the house, or the neighbors? (i.e., rethink burying your coins in the backyard.)

Have more than one hiding place; have several or many. Store only enough bullion at home to get you down the road or out of the country. The rest should be hidden "off-campus." (A country retreat, perhaps.) If buried, be very careful that the location is not vulnerable to geological or developmental changes. (Encrypt the GPS coordinates and directions.)

Bullion is metal, so try to hide them among metal objects *naturally* about. (Sprinkling your yard with buried nuts and bolts is just silly.) This tactic will not defeat a good metal detector, but it can help. Use your imagination here.

Finally, never tell or hint to anyone about this. Instead, archive the location and description of bullion into an encrypted PGP text file (using the IDEA algorithm for a single key), burn that file onto CD, and secure with a trusted person. Another trusted person gets the pass-phrase (at least of 12 characters, mixing upper/lower/numerals/ASCII characters). Then, if you ever need your gold retrieved *for* you, put the two trusted people together when necessary. Meanwhile, your secret is safe.

HOW TO TRANSPORT YOUR COINS

On your person, secure in clothing and not in bags, cases, or parcels. A coin belt is unobtrusive and wears well.

Within a car, your bullion is easily hidden, and it would take a full vehicle search to discover it. Again, use your imagination.

By commercial flight, you take a real risk going through airport security with any substantial wealth in bullion (even though such is not currently illegal, although it someday will be). Since nearly all checked bags are now X-rayed (and away from your supervision), you will have to carry the coins with you. A handful of coins randomly dumped in your carry-on bag or purse will look like pocket change (especially if they are tenth-ounce coins). Don't go overboard with this technique, as too many coins will look suspicious. One idea is to coat the bullion with a dull copper-colored paint. This disguise would pass most cursory inspections, assuming the paint hadn't chipped. If TSA wants to riffle through your bag, insist that it be done within your eyesight. An "SSSS" on your boarding card and baggage claims means that you will be shunted through secondary security. It is quite thorough (i.e., intrusive). This may alter your tactics if carrying a large—though lawful—quantity of bullion.

A final way to transport gold is through a *respectable* digital gold-currency provider with a totally foreign situs (legal and computer server). The only two that come to my mind are www.goldmoney.com and www.pecunix.com. (I would definitely avoid egold. It rolled over to the feds, *twice*.) All DGC providers have registration requirements, and they do keep records, so your transactions haven't the privacy of cash.

HOW TO TRADE YOUR GOLD BULLION

This is easy between savvy people. I've seen gold traded for vehicles, guns, and even land. If U.S. Eagles are used, you can (if it matters) get a receipt based on face value.

Gold coins work. Its inherent allure and six millennia of trading history have proven gold.

WHERE AND HOW TO SELL

The lower the premium of your coin, the less to lose when you sell. (This assumes that spot price has remained constant in the meantime. If it's risen dramatically, then that capital gain will more than cover any premium.) Since you bought with cash, insist on cash when you sell. Gold buyers are inherently more knowledgeable than the general public, so you must either educate your public or sell to a coin dealer. Insist on cash. Only if you absolutely must, take a coin dealer's check that is immediately cashable at his bank. Some amounts will trigger formal or informal reporting requirements. Know Before Ye Go.

WHAT ABOUT POSSIBLE CONFISCATION MEASURES IN THE FUTURE?

It takes two to confiscate: one to confiscate and the other to *allow* it. Gold and silver are ultimately protected by that other precious metal: *lead*. I believe that peaceable folks owning gold and silver have committed no moral crime and pose no threat. They have a right to protect their honestly earned wealth, even if stored in bullion.

CONCLUSION

INDIAN PEASANTS

"Few men have virtue to withstand the highest bidder."

—George Washington, Commander-in-Chief of
American revolutionary forces, First President
of the United States (1732–1799)

Like most Americans, as well as many citizens of other Western democracies, before you read this book you were probably only marginally familiar with the idea of gold as an investment, let alone as its primary role—"wealth insurance." You might have seen television ads touting gold coins and bullion but rarely did you hear Wall Street analysts or brokers talking about gold. Maybe occasionally an analyst would comment when the price of gold reached another high, but never was gold discussed in the context of it being a permanent part of an investor's portfolio. More important, you probably had no clue whether you could rely on the advice you were being given— rely on the "who."

There are some individuals and cultures where gold's primary function has been recognized for centuries, however. In much of the developing world, where poverty and destitution are still common every day occurrences that can destroy the economic futures of whole families and communities, and where governments have proven less adept at managing their country's paper currency, gold's more traditional role as a monetary store of value not only still thrives, it's on the rise. In fact, approximately 10 percent of the world's known global stock of gold, about 15,000 tonnes, is owned by the private citizens of India, the majority of which is held in rural areas, presumably by farmers.

Make no mistake, even though much of this gold is in the physical form of gold jewelry, the reason the Indian citizenry purchases gold jewelry is not vanity. And it's not because they know that gold has appreciated in value by an average compounded annual rate of over 19 percent against the U.S. dollar when measured over the last eight years through November 2009. It's because they don't trust Indian banks or the Indian financial system. And for good reason!

Hundreds of millions of Indians intuitively realize that all the paper money or fiat currency that has ever been issued by literally hundreds of governments through the ages has eventually become worthless. Since the Federal Reserve was established in 1913, the U.S. dollar has lost 96 percent of its purchasing power; the dollar is now worth 4 cents of what it was worth then! Gold is the only money that has kept its value through the centuries.

GOLD AND TRUST

Gold has been on my investment radar screen ever since I graduated from college and became a commercial banker in Alaska in the late 1970s right up through my MBA education and brief Wall Street career in the 1980s, through my subscribing to the *International Speculator* in the 1990s, to meeting Doug Casey and attending my first Eris conference in 2000, and finally making my first investments in gold soon afterward. In my professional career, I've been aware of the importance of trust and how important "who" is in business ever since having to approve those first loans I made as a bank branch manager in my twenties to choosing the right business partners and building a bed-and-breakfast country inn at 30 to raising $5 million to start a company to farm geoduck clams for export to China in my forties, to trying to help my friends and family members weather the worst economic crisis since the Great Depression in my fifties.

Alaska was where I first became interested in gold. It was there while panning for gold for a whole day and finding one small flake, in a stream supposedly rich with placer gold, where I gained an appreciation for gold's rarity. The Chilkoot Trail, made famous by the prospectors going to the Yukon gold fields during the Klondike Gold Rush, is billed as one of the toughest hikes in America. Climbing that trail with my wife, Mary, in 1978, knowing that each and every prospector had to bring/carry a thousand pounds of supplies with him into the Yukon Territory, gave me additional first-hand experience about the efforts men will put themselves through to acquire gold. Having a bank customer invite me into the bank vault in Skagway, Alaska, so I could try on his $250,000 gold nugget watch fob gave me a true appreciation for the value of gold. Visiting Chicken, Alaska, just down river from Dawson in the Yukon Territory just after a shootout between rival miners in 1978 gave me an appreciation for the lengths men still go to keep gold.

A few years back Rick Rule and I were discussing the analogy of the United States being in a similar stage as the Roman Empire at the beginning of its 400-year decline. Rick said that he had a similar discussion with Murray Rothbard, author of *The Ethics of Liberty,* who had made the point that there was a lot of wealth in this United States, implying that any collapse would take a long time. However, Wall Street's fascination with esoteric financial products, many of them financial derivatives, has been growing geometrically for years. Warren Buffett succinctly summed up his views on these new products in saying that, ". . . derivatives are financial weapons of mass destruction." The country's exploding debt has resulted in a proliferation of questionable investment products, the most infamous of which has to be subprime mortgages. As 2008 and 2009 has shown with the mass destruction of $50 trillion dollars in paper wealth worldwide, economic catastrophe may be lot closer then we all realize.

It makes sense to have some kind of "wealth insurance" in place. Gold has a long history of providing just such a role.

SAGE INVESTORS, *ÉTHIKAI ARETAI*

No book on gold would be complete without a look at the importance of trust. As you now hopefully realize, gold is also all about trust. Trust in your money. But just as important is the trust of your advisors that you will rely on to purchase gold. The "who" in your decision-making process.

For the last seven years, I've been sending out a letter to all my friends and family members that I call my "Annual Investment Summary." In it I reviewed my investment performance to date as well as made recommendations regarding the resources I rely on to make my decisions. That advice included the investment advisors I relied on for my investment advice.

There were three reasons I wrote and sent out this letter. The first reason was that I wanted to share my investment thinking, particularly as it pertains to gold, so that my friends and family members might stand a chance of duplicating my efforts so that they, also, could earn similar outstanding investment returns. Secondly, and more important, with the economy worsening these past few years, with some friends and family members losing their jobs and bankruptcy even looming for a few, helping loved ones survive this economic downturn I had become almost maniacal in my belief that they should purchase gold in some form as a kind of "wealth insurance." More recently, my annual letter had become my shout to "Own gold!"

My third reason for writing the letter was to refer the names of the sage investors that I'd come to know and value with my friends and family members. Initially, I referred Doug Casey, Rick Rule, and Bill Bonner, but more recently, I'd also begun listening and learning from the other sage investors found in this book.

Aristotle, the Greek philosopher, tells us that there are two different kinds of human excellences, excellences of thought and excellences of character. His phrase for excellences of character—*êthikai aretai*—is usually translated as moral virtue or moral excellence. Although I firmly believe that the information written by the sage investors in this book could not be timelier or more valuable, what really should put an exclamation point after our message that "who investors rely on for advice to purchase gold being as important as the decision to own gold" is their êthikai aretai.

AUTHOR'S NOTE

LEADING EXPERTS ON GOLD

Is there someone you believe is a leading expert on gold that you think could have been included in this book? If so, I'd like to hear from you.

As you probably realize now, there are two primary qualifications. First, this person has to demonstrate knowledge about the subject matter. I'd be more interested in someone who has been a long-time advocate of holding gold in an investment portfolio as a form of "wealth insurance" rather than someone who has recently become aware of gold's price rise and has begun recommending gold as an investment. Second, he or she should be a person of character. If your advisor is someone you trust, a "customer's man," tell me how that came about.

Email me at thegoldenrulebook@gmail.com.

SAGE INVESTORS

I'm sure there are sage investment advisors who own gold, but don't talk about it as much as some of their other recommendations. Maybe they limit their advice to the energy markets, or to foreign equities, or they are now focused on China. They view their gold holdings as permanent and more like insurance while growing their investment portfolio through other types of investments.

Again, it's not just a good track record that I'm interested in. I'd like to specifically hear about why you think your advisor might be a sage investor. Additionally, give me a general idea of what types of investments he or she focuses on and why you think your advisor is using safe strategies to both keep and generate wealth.

Email me at sageinvestors1@gmail.com.

Or just contact me at Jim Gibbons, 2101 4th Avenue E., Suite 201, Olympia, WA 98506.

ABOUT THE AUTHOR

Jim Gibbons lives on Puget Sound with his wife, Mary, and their three children, Katie, Lucas, and Ian. He has been studying and learning from sage investors regarding gold's role in the world economy for over 30 years. For the last 12 years he's also been raising geoduck clams for export to China. Prior to becoming a shellfish farmer he built and developed his own country inn (The Heron in La Conner), wrote screenplays for 10 years, and worked for the National Bank of Alaska, IBM, Merrill Lynch and Control Data.

ABOUT THE
CONTRIBUTORS

Pamela and Mary Anne Aden. Pam and Mary Anne Aden are close friends of Rick and Bonnie Rule, which is how I first heard about them. After that, I began reading their commentaries and listening to their talks as much as I could. It's no surprise why other sages included in this book follow their work. Someday I hope to visit them in Costa Rica.

Contact Information
Pamela and Mary Anne Aden
The Aden Forecast
Dept. SJO 874
P.O. Box 025216
Miami, FL 33102-5216
1-305-395-6141
www.adenforecast.com

Bill Bonner. With six children, several homes on multiple continents, and a supportive and independent thinking wife of 30 years, Bill seems to have plenty of family stories and lessons he seamlessly blends into his writings. Although I've only met one of his children, in reading the *Daily Reckoning* for the last ten years, I feel like I've gotten to watch them all grow up. While his investment advice and economic analysis has been first rate, I believe it's his personal stories and his wit that have made his letter if not the most successful, surely one of the top five in the business.

Contact Information

Bill Bonner
Agora Financial
808 St. Paul Street
Baltimore, MD 21202
1-800-708-1020
www.agorafinancial.com

Doug Casey. In an issue of *International Speculator* written in early 2000, Doug wrote about a recent trip of his to Shanghai as well as recommending the works of a well-known science fiction writer. I wrote Doug and explained that I was four years and $4 million into a startup operation to grow luxury seafood, geoduck clams, for export to China and wondered if he had any contacts. I also managed to name drop and say that not only was the science fiction writer a good friend of mine, he was the very first investor in my company, Seattle Shellfish. It turns out the author was one of Doug's favorite authors and an invitation for both of us to attend that summer's Eris Conference quickly followed. It was one of the more important occurrences in my life.

Contact Information

Doug Casey
Casey Research
166 South Main Street, Suite 2
Stowe, VT 05672
1-888-512-2739
www.caseyresearch.com

Michael Checkan. Michael was one of the very first people I met through Eris. Since then I see him at all the other conferences I attend and continue to enjoy his talks when he gives them and the occasional shared beers or meal when we can find the time. To learn more about how the Perth Mint Certificate Program can help you find a safe haven for some of your assets in an increasingly troubled world, please contact his company, Asset Strategies International.

Contact Information
Michael Checkan
Asset Strategies International, Inc.
1700 Rockville Pike, Suite 400
Rockville, Maryland 20852-1631
1-800-831-0007
www.assetsi@assetstrategies.com

Brent Cook. Legendary gold mining stock analyst, Robert Bishop, summed up Brent's skills best when he said, "after years of visiting mining projects with Brent, and liberally picking his brain when not in the field, I have gained the utmost respect for Brent's views on rocks. Market psychology, promotion, capital structure, people, and many other factors dictate whether a stock will rise or fall, but in the final analysis, the rocks always prevail. Brent Cook knows rocks."

Contact Information
Brent Cook
Exploration Insights
www.explorationinsights.com

Adrian Day. With a track record like that found in Adrian Day's Global Analyst, it's not surprising that Adrian is an honors graduate of the London School of Economics and an author of two books on the subject of global investing: *International Investment Opportunities: How and Where to Invest Overseas Successfully* and *Investing Without Borders.* Adrian tells me that he is also now hard at work on another book.

Contact Information
Adrian Day
Adrian Day Asset Management
801 Compass Way, Suite 207
P.O. Box 6643
Annapolis, MD 21401
1-410-224-2037
www.adriandayassetmanagement.com

David Galland. I like David a lot. He's about my age, has children my age, holds similar values, and thinks a lot like I do. I recently questioned him about his views on cryogenics, which I support. In *Casey's Daily Dispatch* on August 19, 2009, David wrote, "Jim is an old friend who I know has done a lot of research on the topic, so I included the company name (www.alcor.org) for those of you who are interested. And he is right, so far I have just talked the talk. . . ." Like David, I have an almost innate curiosity about the future. In the event that my "trip" is successful, I still hope to convince David to sign up for Alcor, so I can have such an engaging friend as company. David is yet another fellow Erisian I met at Doug's annual conference. Like me, he also enjoys a good micro beer while enjoying a game of pool.

Contact Information
David Galland
Casey Research
166 South Main Street, Suite 2
Stowe, VT 05672
1-888-512-2739
www.caseyresearch.com

Louis James. David Galland once said that Louis James was one of the most intellectually honest people he knew. Knowing Louis as I do, I might word it a little differently. "Louis is the kind of guy you'd like at your side during a knife fight in a dark alley." I don't know a thing about Louis's self-defense skills; what I'm referring to is his integrity in defending the things he values. Much of what Louis values revolve around increasing individual freedom and decreasing the scope of government. They are goals I share.

Contact Information
Louis James, Editor
Casey Research
166 South Main Street, Suite 2
Stowe, VT 05672
1-888-512-2739
www.caseyresearch.com

Richard Maybury. Richard describes himself as a geopolitical invest-ment analyst, although I like to think of him as a philosopher. He wrote the Uncle Eric series of books for older children and young adults as a means to help explain free market economics, law, and his-tory. I bought a set for my children and consider them to be some of the finest books I've read. Richard bases much of his work in com-mon law and writes extensively about two basic laws: (1) Do all you have agreed to do. (2) Do not encroach on other persons or their property. It's hard not to argue that the world wouldn't be a better place if everyone just followed those laws.

Contact Information
Richard Maybury
Henry Madison Research
P.O. Box 84908
Phoenix, AZ 84908
1-800-509-5400
www.richardmaybury.com

Jon Nadler. I have heard Jon speak on many occasions and have always been impressed. In fact, when I first heard pieces of Jon's life history I knew his story would be perfect for the book. It's a story that everyone should not only read or hear, but adopt as if it were their own. The best way to stay in touch with Jon's thinking is via his market commentaries at Kitco.

Contact Information
Jon Nadler
Kitco Precious Metals
620 Cathcart, Suite 900
Montreal, Quebec H3B 1M1
1-866-925-4826
www.kitco.com

Congressman Ron Paul. I first met Congressman Ron Paul at the 2002 Eris Conference and then again at the 2005 conference. I've also heard him speak publicly at the 2008 Freedom Fest Conference.

Like most, if not all, the other sages in this book, Ron Paul adheres deeply to Austrian school economics, displaying pictures of economists Friedrich Hayek, Murray Rothbard, and Ludwig von Mises on his office wall. Ron Paul wears many hats. Wearing a hat as the founder of *The Foundation of Rational Economics and Education*, a site dedicated to liberty that publishes his *Freedom Report*, is one of his favorite that he wears.

Contact Information
The Office of U.S. Rep. Ron Paul
203 Cannon HOB
Washington, D.C. 20515
1-202-225-2831
www.free-nefl.com
www.campaignforliberty.com
www.ronpaul.org

Morgan Poliquin. Seven or eight years ago I began attending the Cambridge House Resource Investment Conferences to help further my education into gold and precious metals mining. It was here that I first met Morgan Poliquin and his father, Duane, two of my favorite miners. Of course, I'd read and heard about them many times via many of the contributors in this book, one of whom has said, "These are the people who consistently go where the big deposits, and the big money, are."

Contact Information
Morgan Poliquin
Almaden Minerals
750 West Pender Street, Suite 1103
Vancouver, B.C. V6C 2T8
1-604-689-7644
www.almadenminerals.com

John Pugsley. I first met Jack at the 2000 Eris Conference and found the talk he gave on the evolution of human social behavior to be one of the more interesting. It was during his talk that I first heard about The Bio-Rational Institute (www.biorationalinstitute.com), an organization he founded that is dedicated to "fostering personal fulfillment and social progress through an understanding of the evolutionary roots of human behavior." Like me and every other contributor in this book, Jack is a staunch believer in individual liberty and free markets.

Contact Information
John Puglsey
The Stealth Investor
6965 El Camino Real
Suite 105, #580
Carlsbad, CA 92009
1-760-672-1711
www.stealthinvestor.com

Robert Quartermain. Robert Quartermain's entrepreneurial successes rival many of those found in Silicon Valley. In fact, Robert's silver company is one of the most well known and successful in the world. Interestingly, Rick Rule has described the very beginnings and founding of Bob's company as having occurred on Rick's living room floor.

Contact Information
Robert Quartermain
Silver Standard Resources Inc.
999 West Hastings Street
Suite 1180
Vancouver, BC V6C 2W2
Canada
Phone: 1-604-689-3846
www.silver-standard.com

Ken Royce (aka Boston T. Party). I first met Ken while attending my first Eris conference in 2000 when Ken was the conference chair who put the program together. Since that time I've gotten to know Ken quite well. His *Boston's Gun Bible* is a classic within the shooting and 2nd Amendment community, and his novel *Molôn Labé!* has inspired a recent relocation wave to Wyoming. I've read both books as well as many of his other books. He is also a shooting instructor, and sometime in the near future I hope to enroll my whole family in one of his Wyoming-based classes.

Contact Information
Ken Royce
www.javelinpress.com

Rick Rule. It was at Doug Casey's Eris Society Conferences where I first got to know Rick. Not only does Rick have an appreciation for the economic benefits that nature provides, being lovers of nature, he and his wife Bonnie are avid hikers. We managed to share several hikes in the mountains of Colorado and have since shared some walks along the shores of Stanley Park, near Rick and Bonnie's home in Vancouver, British Columbia.

Contact Information
Rick Rule
Global Resource Investments Ltd.
7770 El Camion Real
Carlsbad, CA 92009
1-800-477-7853
www.gril.net

Dana Samuelson and Dr. Bill Musgrave. How could you not be impressed by a duo that must be nearing the half-billion-dollar mark in terms of value of the rare coins and bullion that they've traded? Several of the leading gold experts in this book always recommend Dana and Bill's services when asked, myself included.

Contact Information
Dana Samuelson and Dr. Bill Musgrave
American Gold Exchange, Inc.
P.O. Box 9426
Austin, TX 78766-9426
1-800-613-9323
www.amergold.com

Franklin Sanders. Richard Maybury first steered me to Franklin, and in reading Franklin's contribution, it's easy to see why. Whether you agree or not with his point of view, and I happen to wholeheartedly agree with it, Franklin's willingness to stand by his convictions is what impresses me the most about him. Additionally, Franklin's knowledge in coins and bullions is second to none.

Contact Information

Franklin Sanders
The Moneychanger
P.O. Box 178
Westpoint, TN 38486
1-888-218-9226
www.the-moneychanger.com

Peter Schiff. Whether it's via his books, his weekly columns, or in his speeches, Peter is always presenting original and thought-provoking considerations that every investor should keep in mind. One report that I would like to particularly call your attention to is "The Collapsing Dollar: The Powerful Case for Investing in Foreign Equities," which can easily be downloaded from the Euro Pacific Capital website.

It's now official: Peter is running for the U.S. Senate. When asked about his apparent lack of political experience, he correctly pointed out that his inexperience was his "greatest attribute — the fact that I haven't had experience ruining the country, that I haven't brought the banking system to its knees, and helped destroy the health care system." I couldn't agree more. While at Freedom Fest, I wished Peter good luck in his coming Senate campaign. I do so again here.

Contact Information

Peter Schiff
Euro Pacific Capital, Inc.
88 Post Road West, 3rd Floor
Westport, CT 06880
1-203-662-9700
1-800-727-7922
www.europac.net

Van Simmons. When I began investigating the rare coin and bullion coin market, several different sage investors mentioned here steered me toward Van, President of David Hall Rare Coins. Now that I've met him, it's easy to see why. He is without a doubt one of the more personable people I've met. More important, when it comes to gold coins and bullion, Van is one of the most knowledgeable folks in the numismatics business.

Contact Information
Van Simmons
David Hall Rare Coins
P.O. Box 6220
Newport Beach, CA 92658
1-800-754-7575
www.davidhall.com

Eric Sprott. I once invested in a "shell company," a company with virtually no assets, which then got purchased by Sprott Resources, a company run by Eric. I promptly doubled my money. I can't think of a better character reference that the fact that everyone in the know tries to get in early on Eric's projects. Eric personifies both the excellence of thought as well as excellence of character that Aristotle speaks of.

Contact Information
Eric Sprott, Sprott Asset Management
Royal Bank Plaza
South Tower
200 Bay Street
Suite 2700, P.O. Box 27
Toronto, Ontario M5J2J1
1-888-362-7172
www.sprott.com

James Turk. I once asked James whom he would recommend a close relative use for advice on purchasing gold if James were on his deathbed. Without hesitation he said, "given the circumstances you describe,

I would name just one, my oldest son Geoffrey." The ability to pass your character and values on to the next generation says a lot about a person. Fortunately, for you, his son is CEO of GoldMoney.com.

Contact Information
James Turk
Net Transactions Limited
1st Floor; 32 Commercial Street
St. Helier, Jersey
JE2 3RU
British Channel Islands (UK)
Tel: 011-44-1534-511-977
www.goldmoney.com

Paul van Eeden. As a regular guest on radio and television shows throughout the world, Paul's analysis and understanding on the price of gold is without peer. In large measure, just so I can hear him speak, I make it a point of going to the Cambridge House Resource Investment Conferences and Agora's Wealth Symposium where Paul is often a speaker. As a result of hearing Paul's lectures, I realized almost a hundred thousand dollars in profits on just one stock he kept mentioning. I was so pleased by the results, and some others based on talks Paul's given, that I can't help but thank him every time we see each other.

Contact Information
Paul van Eeden
www.paulvaneeden.com

Addison Wiggin. I will always remember my first meeting with Addison. It was just after he'd introduced the morning's first speaker at an Agora Financial Investment Symposium I was attending. He apologized for the brevity of our conversation, explaining that he'd been awake all night with some friends so they could watch the sun rise over Vancouver and needed to take a quick nap. I think that experience captures the Addison Wiggin I've come to know. He's the kind of person who in his younger years would have stayed up many nights to watch the sunrise with some good friends and a bottle of wine. Now in middle age, Addison still knows what matters in life.

Contact Information
Addison Wiggin
Agora Financial
808 St. Paul Street
Baltimore, MD 21202
1-800-708-1020
www.agorafinancial.com

INDEX